ACCESS TO JUSTICE IN MAGISTRATES' COURTS

This book examines access to justice in summary criminal proceedings by considering the ability of defendants to play an active and effective role in the process.

'Access to justice' refers to the ability of defendants to understand and effectively participate in summary criminal proceedings, because it is a vital principle of justice that 'justice should not only be done, but should manifestly and undoubtedly be seen to be done' by all participants in the process (*R v Sussex Justices, ex parte McCarthy* [1924] 1 KB 256).

The book is based on socio-legal research. The study is ethnographic, based on observation conducted in four magistrates' courts in South East England and interviews with both defence lawyers and Crown prosecutors.

Setting out an argument that defendants have always been marginalised through particular features of magistrates' court proceedings (such as courtroom layout and patterns of behaviour among the professional workgroups in court), the political climate in relation to defendants and access to justice that has persisted since 2010 has further undermined the ability of defendants to play an active role in the process.

Ultimately, this book argues that governments have come to see lawyers as potential drivers of efficiency rather than potential champions of access to justice. That understanding has significant implications for how access to justice in criminal cases in constructed.

Access to Justice in Magistrates' Courts

A Study of Defendant Marginalisation

Lucy Welsh

•HART•

OXFORD • LONDON • NEW YORK • NEW DELHI • SYDNEY

HART PUBLISHING

Bloomsbury Publishing Plc

Kemp House, Chawley Park, Cumnor Hill, Oxford, OX2 9PH, UK

1385 Broadway, New York, NY 10018, USA

29 Earlsfort Terrace, Dublin 2, Ireland

HART PUBLISHING, the Hart/Stag logo, BLOOMSBURY and the Diana logo are
trademarks of Bloomsbury Publishing Plc

First published in Great Britain 2022

A catalogue record for this book is available from the British Library.

A catalogue record for this book is available from the Library of Congress.

ISBN: HB: 978-1-50993-783-7
       ePDF: 978-1-50993-785-1
       ePub: 978-1-50993-784-4

Typeset by Compuscript Ltd, Shannon

To find out more about our authors and books visit www.hartpublishing.co.uk.
Here you will find extracts, author information, details of forthcoming events
and the option to sign up for our newsletters.

Preface

THIS BOOK IS about the ability of defendants to effectively participate in summary criminal court proceedings. It was initially inspired by my own experiences as a practitioner, which led me to undertake research for my PhD in socio-legal studies. But, rather than start with my own story of what I saw in magistrates' courts as a practitioner, I'm going to explain what an outsider to the proceedings – my late father – observed when he accompanied me to court to watch cases one day. By way of background, Paul Welsh was a highly educated, intelligent, middle class, white man. He had been a chemical physicist, then a (head)teacher, before completing his own PhD and becoming a Research Fellow in the field of education policy.

Given his own inquiring mind, dad had come to court to watch interesting cases a few times. On one occasion, while I was part-way through my PhD research, he attended a magistrates' court. I asked him what he thought of it and, while I was going back over observation notes to write this book, I rediscovered the note that I had made of that conversation. It reads:

> The biggest problem was a lack of understanding the process. It was very hard to follow what was happening, so dad found it very hard to take notes (unlike my own ability to complete my notes rapidly). Noting that a problem of that nature might be alleviated by representation. The difficulty understanding the process was compounded by specialist language and unfamiliar social conventions (bowing to the judge etc.). He only realised part way through the morning that people are supposed to stand when addressing the judge. Professionals were publicly showing deference by calling the judges 'sir' and using phrases like 'if it pleases you'. The different court clerks behaved very differently; the one sitting with magistrates was much more active and willing to cut across what the prosecutor or magistrates were saying. The whole process was very quick and there seemed to be a lot of agreement between the parties about how cases were to proceed. It seemed more like a management, as opposed to a legal, process. Dad was surprised that defendants are not always required to be present. The structure of the process was unfamiliar and, within that, the legal issues were unfamiliar plus the acoustics were very bad. Some defendants seemed familiar with the process and others seemed like they were not bothered by it. In the case of defendants who needed interpreters, the District Judge seemed careful to ensure that the defendant understood, but there was slightly less willingness to show the same care by the court clerks and magistrates. There was very little attempt to engage with defendants; they were just there to be processed. Legal professionals seemed to agree a lot and to co-operate. There was very little input from defendants. Defendants tended to appear passive.

So, here we have a highly educated man unable to follow proceedings due to their complexity and the unfamiliar behaviour of courtroom professionals. It was also striking, when I rediscovered these notes years later, that it was clear to him that the process of summary justice was – in this court at least – more driven by managerial principles than by legal ones, and that the defendant appeared to be there to be given justice rather than to participate in the process of justice.

As we shall see, these themes recurred again and again in both my practitioner experience and during the course of the research that was conducted for this book. The behaviour of the workgroup, the structure of the courtroom and demands for efficient case progression have all hindered the ability of defendants to effectively participate in cases against them. If we are to take defendant participation seriously, we need to reconsider how courtrooms are structured and the way in which cases are progressed by the professional workgroup. It is likely that a cultural change can only be facilitated if lawyers are properly funded. We must make sure that all courtroom professionals are properly empowered to facilitate as much effective voluntary defendant participation as possible. The legitimacy of the system is dependent upon it.

Lucy Welsh
Sussex
June 2021

Acknowledgements

THIS BOOK IS based on doctoral research conducted at the University of Kent, between 2011 and 2016. The work was supported financially by a Kent Law School Studentship. Naturally, this work could never have even begun to take shape without the support of my supervisors, Rosemary Hunter and Helen Carr, in addition to the support of the student and staff community at Kent Law School. My supervisors challenged my assumptions in ways that allowed me to grow intellectually, and provided invaluable expertise and advice throughout the process. I'm also grateful to have studied alongside a cohort of PGR students who produce research that challenges assumptions and norms, many of whom I am glad to also be able to call friends. I also owe my LLM supervisor, Steve Uglow, a debt of gratitude for encouraging me to take my studies further and helping me begin the PhD process despite his retirement. My examiners, Andrew Sanders and Dermot Walsh, not only made my viva a pleasant experience, but also provided valuable feedback that I have carried forward into future work.

Andrew is also to be thanked, alongside Amir Paz-Fuchs, Abenaa Owusu-Bempah and Dan Newman, for reading drafts of these chapters and providing me with insightful and constructive feedback. I know that this book has improved for their input, and I admire them all greatly. Thanks also to the anonymous reviewers for their constructive suggestions when I proposed writing this book. My friends and colleagues at Sussex Law School also deserve to be thanked for fostering an environment where it is possible to engage with research critically and creatively as part of its commitment to equality and social justice.

The other person who suffered the trials and tribulations of writing this book but nevertheless agreed to read the near final draft for me is my partner Vivek Seth. His unwavering support, carefully considered opinion and boundless kindness are invaluable in too many ways to mention.

I also thank the commissioning and editorial team at Hart – especially Kate Whetter – who made this process run smoothly while also giving me the freedom to work in a way that was most productive for me. Additionally, I am grateful to the *Journal of Law and Society* (Wiley), to *Social and Legal Studies* and *Common Law World Review* (Sage), and to the British Society of Criminology for allowing me to reuse material from previously published articles.[1]

---

[1] L Welsh 'The effects of changes to legal aid on lawyers' professional identity and behaviour in summary criminal cases: A case study' (2017) 44(4) *Journal of Law and Society* 559–85; L Welsh 'Are magistrates' courts really a 'law free zone'? Participant observation and specialist use of language' (2013) 13 *Papers from the British Criminology Conference* 3–16; L Welsh and M Howard

My parents and the friends who I think of as family are owed a debt of gratitude for providing both practical and emotional support, and for keeping me as sane as is possible throughout all of these processes. I'm so glad that I got to share my PhD graduation ceremony with both of my parents, who – in so many ways – set the scene for me to be able to do this work in the first place.

Last, but certainly not least, I thank the legal professionals without whom I could not have conducted this research. This includes the members of magistrates' courts who I observed, and the participants who agreed to be interviewed. It also extends beyond that group of participants. There are the legal professionals who I worked alongside over the course of a decade, and my former colleagues who put up with me working part time while I pursued various academic activities and have continued to support and show interest in what I do since leaving practice. Ultimately, I believe we are all working towards a common goal – a criminal justice system that functions fairly for all parties.

'Standardization and the Production of Justice in Summary Criminal Courts: A Post-Human Analysis' (2019) 28(6) *Social and Legal Studies* 774–93; D Newman and L Welsh 'The practice of modern defence lawyers: Alienation and its implications for access to justice' (2019) 48(1-2) *Common Law World Review*. 64–89.

Contents

1

Introduction

Accessing Justice
in Magistrates' Courts

THIS BOOK EXAMINES the (in)ability of defendants to meaningfully participate in criminal cases that are dealt with in magistrates' courts. It is based on (auto)ethnographic research conducted in an area of South East England as I made the transition from practising criminal defence solicitor to socio-legal academic researching the process of summary criminal justice as it is administered in magistrates' courts. One significant event, which has gone some way to develop my understanding of the (in)ability of defendants to meaningfully participate in summary justice, occurred while I was conducting observations of the magistrates' court workgroup.

In the particular case, I was sat in the public gallery at the back of the court, with observation schedule and pen in hand. During one administrative hearing, the magistrates had retired to consider their decision in the case. The defendant was in the dock, which had wooden panels from the floor to about three feet in height, then Plexiglas panels with gaps of a few inches between them from three feet high to ceiling. No one was in the dock with the defendant, it not being a custodial remand case. The defendant was represented by a solicitor who I knew to be diligent and very experienced. That solicitor was one who had a reputation among colleagues for being concerned about clients' rights and needs. Once the magistrates had retired, the defence solicitor stood and started chatting informally to the prosecutor about matters unrelated to the case, as was very common practice and something which I – as a practitioner with over 10 years' experience working in criminal defence services – did not regard as problematic of itself. But what made this interaction stand out as problematic here was that the solicitor stood up, and leaned on the dock with their back to their client, the defendant, while they spoke with the prosecutor. The defendant sat in the dock resting his head in his hands, and was not spoken to for the duration of the magistrates' retirement. Although I have no doubt that all the professional parties concerned did the job that they were supposed to do, and everyone was perfectly courteous in their interactions with the defendant, the process of summary justice was very much done *to* the defendant, rather than with the defendant – or, as Owusu-Bempah puts it, the defendant was 'treated as an object on which the criminal law is imposed'.[1] I can also only guess that, if the dynamic had been pointed out to that solicitor, they would have been as surprised as I then was to realise the power relations that were being played out. While this book is not a treatise on poor lawyer/client relationships, the image of the lawyer literally turning their back on this isolated individual while they chatted informally with the professional workgroup has stayed with me several years later, and become symbolic of the defendant's overall position in summary criminal courts. This fuelled my own interest in the myriad ways that summary justice operates to either assist or undermine the process of defendant participation.

I. THE GENESIS AND AIMS OF THE BOOK

Throughout my years in criminal defence practice I saw numerous changes to summary criminal procedure which appeared to undermine traditional adversarial principles. However, I also saw little meaningful resistance to such changes. Instead, advocates tended to adapt their working routines to accommodate change. As a lawyer, the changes troubled me, but there appeared to be little ability to resist change while maintaining a service for clients. As an academic, I sought to consider possible explanations for these changes and their impact on (the debates surrounding) access to justice.

Despite the fact that all criminal cases begin in the magistrates' courts and the vast majority of cases also conclude there, as a result of 'the fascination that most lawyers have for jury trials',[2] magistrates' courts have been comparatively neglected in academic research. While recent works have considered the way in which neoliberal demands for regulation and efficiency have resulted in greater marginalisation and penalisation of those who come into contact with the agencies of criminal justice,[3] few studies consider the interaction of structural changes brought about by neoliberalism with the cultural factors surrounding the agency of the magistrates' courtroom workgroup.[4] This book therefore

---

[1] A Owusu-Bempah 'Understanding the Barriers to Defendant Participation in Criminal Proceedings in England and Wales' (2020) 40(4) Legal Studies 609–62; 610.

[2] B Bell and C Dadomo 'Magistrates' Courts and the 2003 Reforms of the Criminal Justice System' (2006) 14(4) *European Journal of Crime, Criminal Law and Criminal Justice* 339; 341.

[3] See generally E Bell, *Criminal Justice and Neoliberalism* (Palgrave Macmillan, 2011); P Squires and J Lea, 'Introduction: Reading Loïc Wacquant – Opening Questions and Overview' in P Squires and J Lea (eds), *Criminalisation and Advanced Marginality. Critically Exploring the Work of Loïc Wacquant* (The Policy Press, 2012); Bell and Dadomo (n 2).

[4] Two exceptions are the work detailed in J Ward, *Transforming Summary Justice* (Routledge, 2017) and D Newman, *Lawyers, Legal Aid and the Quest for Justice* (Hart Publishing, 2013). The former concentrates on processes in magistrates' courts, while the latter concentrates on the lawyer/client relationship. This book seeks to marry those two separate aspects of summary criminal justice into a coherent whole.

investigates that structural/cultural intersection by considering the impact of neoliberal-styled policies on the culture of magistrates' court proceedings. It takes that investigation further by examining how this intersection affects defendants' marginalisation through their inability to meaningfully participate in proceedings. The majority of significant studies of summary criminal justice were conducted in the 1970s and early 1980s,[5] which meant that it was timely to re-examine magistrates' court activities in light of more recent political trajectories that moved through various iterations of neoliberal ideology and austere times following the 2008 financial crisis.[6]

Alongside, and related to, fluctuations in political trajectory, there have been significant changes to the provision of legally aided representation in summary criminal proceedings (chapter two). Academic interest in criminal legal aid generally has increased rapidly in the last few years,[7] and political interest in criminal legal aid is a live issue as I write this book against the background of two ongoing inquiries: the Independent Criminal Legal Aid Review,[8] and a Justice Committee inquiry entitled *The Future of Legal Aid*.[9] With a couple of exceptions,[10] as Kemp has observed, there has not been much empirical investigation[11] into the operation of legal aid in the context of the working culture of magistrates' courts and the policies which affect that culture. This work therefore aims to partially address the deficit in academic research relating to access to justice in magistrates' courts in particular.

---

[5] See, for example, P Carlen, *Magistrates' Justice* (Martin Robertson, 1976), D McBarnet, *Conviction: Law, the State and the Construction of Justice* (Macmillan, 1981) and A Bottoms and J McClean, *Defendants in the Criminal Process* (Routledge, 1976).

[6] For discussion about that crisis, see generally R Aliber and G Zoega (eds), *The 2008 Global Financial Crisis in Retrospect* (Palgrave Macmillan, 2019); A Tooze, *Crashed. How a Decade of Financial Crises Changed the World* (Penguin Books, 2018).

[7] See generally D Newman, 'Are lawyers alienated workers?' (2016) 22(3), *European Journal of Current Legal Issues*; R Dehaghani and D Newman, '"We're vulnerable too": an (alternative) analysis of vulnerability within English criminal legal aid and police custody' (2017) 7(6) *Oñati Socio-Legal Series* 1199–1228; D Newman and L Welsh, 'The practices of modern criminal defence lawyers: alienation and its implications for access to justice' (2019) 48(1–2) *Common Law World Review* 64–89; R Dehaghani and D Newman, 'Criminal legal aid and access to justice: an empirical account of a reduction in resilience' (2021) *International Journal of the Legal Profession* online first; L Welsh, 'The effects of changes to legal aid on lawyers' professional identity and behaviour in summary criminal cases: a case study' (2017) 44(4) *Journal of Law and Society* 559–585; J Thornton, 'Is Publicly Funded Criminal Defence Sustainable? Legal Aid Cuts, Morale, Recruitment and Retention in the English Criminal Law Professions' (2020) 40(2) *Legal Studies* 230; J Thornton, 'The Way in Which Fee Reductions Influence Legal Aid Criminal Defence Lawyer Work: Insights from a Qualitative Study (2019) 46(4) *Journal of Law and Society* 559; R Vogler, L Welsh, A Clarke, S Wiedlitzka and L McDonnell, *Criminal Cases Review Commission: Legal Aid and Legal Representatives. Final Report* (Brighton, University of Sussex, 2021).

[8] See www.gov.uk/government/groups/independent-review-of-criminal-legal-aid.

[9] See committees.parliament.uk/work/531/the-future-of-legal-aid/.

[10] Ward (n 4) and Newman (n 4).

[11] V Kemp, *Transforming Legal Aid: Access to Criminal Defence Services* (Legal Services Commission, 2010) www.justice.gov.uk/downloads/publications/research-and-analysis/lsrc/TransformingCrimDefenceServices_29092010.pdf.

In doing so, this book focuses on three separate, yet interconnected, issues that have an impact on the ability of a defendant to play a meaningful, effective, and active, role in cases that are brought against them in magistrates' courts: cuts to legal aid, the behaviour of defence lawyers and ever-increasing demands for efficiency (including digitalised practices). A book of this sort necessarily takes a narrow focus, and should be read in conjunction with works on other issues pertaining to the meaning of effective participation[12] and other legal provisions, such as the Criminal Procedure Rules (Cr.PR) (which includes facilitating participation of all parties as part of its overriding objective). A close examination of cuts to legal aid and demands for efficiency reveals a trajectory of political ideology in relation to defendants that can be applied elsewhere, allows us to re-examine the state of the lawyer-client relationship, and highlights practices in a much neglected area of study – summary criminal courts. The central thesis of this work is that defence lawyers are important to aid participation, but there is a need for all members of the magistrates' court workgroup to go further to facilitate participation if defendants are to experience their role in a more meaningful way.

Clearly this work is predicated on a particular understanding of access to justice in the magistrates' courts, which are themselves caught in political manoeuvres through the decisions of policy-makers. However, access to justice is an extremely broad and ambiguous concept,[13] as is neoliberalism. The concept of neoliberalism is discussed further below, but we will first turn to a consideration of the meaning of access to justice, defendant participation and the role of legal aid.

II. DEFENDANT PARTICIPATION, ACCESS TO JUSTICE AND LEGAL AID

The ability of defendants to participate in the criminal process is a multi-faceted issue, consisting of issues that include, but are not limited to, rules of evidence that effectively force defendant participation while undermining their right to be presumed innocent;[14] the ability of vulnerable defendants to be afforded the same protections as vulnerable witnesses,[15] or in other parts of the criminal

---

[12] See generally Owusu-Bempah (n 1), J Jacobson and P Cooper (eds) *Participation in courts and tribunals: concepts, realities and aspirations.* (Bristol University Press, 2020).

[13] A Adams-Prassl and J Adams-Prassl, 'Systemic Unfairness, Access to Justice and Futility: A Framework' (2020) 40(3) *Oxford Journal of Legal Studies* 561–90.

[14] H Quirk, *The Rise and Fall of the Right to Silence* (Routledge, 2016); A Owusu-Bempah, *Defendant Participation in the Criminal Process* (Routledge, 2017).

[15] See especially S Fairclough, 'The consequences of unenthusiastic criminal justice reform: A special measures case study' (2021) 21(2) *Criminology & Criminal Justice* 151–68.

process;[16] issues that arise in the police station;[17] the architecture of the court-room itself;[18] and the Cr.PR which reshape the role that defendants and their lawyers play in the system.[19] Even though there is broad agreement among practitioners and commentators that 'participation is essential to the delivery of justice',[20] 'the extent to which defendants can be said to participate in the proceedings is often limited',[21] but the idea of what amounts to '"effective participation" has received little scrutiny' in recent years.[22]

Nonetheless, there has been judicial recognition that mere presence in proceedings is insufficient to ensure effective participation, as 'presence is a passive form of participation'.[23] While presence might facilitate effective participation, it does not guarantee that a defendant will be treated with respect to their needs as an autonomous individual. Judicial reasoning indicates that effective participation requires that a defendant can hear, understand and follow proceedings.[24] As Owusu-Bempah points out, the courts require that the defendant can 'maintain a level of general understanding and active engagement throughout the trial. They do not need perfect engagement.'[25] Even though many practitioners strive to actively facilitate participation in the justice system through respectful and sympathetic treatment,[26] the assumption in case law that defendants can effectively participate through their lawyers acts 'to exclude the defendant from proceedings and undermines their role as a participant' in their own right.[27] This is especially the case when set in the context of efficient working practices demanded of magistrates' court practitioners and the organisational culture adopted by the workgroup. Where these procedural aspects of summary justice silence defendants they (further) disempower people

---

[16] H Howard, 'Effective Participation of Mentally Vulnerable Defendants in the Magistrates' Courts in England and Wales – The "Front Line" from a Legal Perspective' (2021) 85(1) *Journal of Criminal Law* 3–16.

[17] See generally L Skinns, A Sorsby and L Rice, '"Treat them as a human being": dignity in police detention and its implications for "good" police custody' (2020) *British Journal of Criminology*; A Pivaty, *Criminal defence at police stations: a comparative and empirical study* (Routledge, 2019); R Dehaghani, 'Interrogating vulnerability: reframing the vulnerable suspect in police custody' (2021) 30(2) *Social and Legal Studies* 251–71.

[18] See especially L Mulcahy, *Legal Architecture. Justice, Due Process and the Place of Law* (Routledge, 2011) and L Mulcahy and E Rowden, *The democratic courthouse: A modern history of design, due process and dignity* (Routledge, 2019).

[19] See generally Owusu-Bempah (n 14); E Johnston, 'The adversarial defence lawyer: Myths, disclosure and efficiency – A contemporary analysis of the role in the era of the Criminal Procedure Rules' (2020) 24(1) *International Journal of Evidence and Proof* 35–58.

[20] J Jacobson, 'Introduction' in Jacobson and Cooper (n 12) 1.

[21] A Owusu-Bempah, 'The Interpretation and Application of the Right to Effective Participation' (2018) 22(4) *International Journal of Evidence and Proof* 321–41; 321.

[22] Ibid, 322. This is subject to the notable exception of Jacobson and Cooper (n 12).

[23] Owusu-Bempah (n 1) 611.

[24] *Lee Kin* [1916] 1KB 337; *Stanford v UK* (ECHR, 23 Feb 1994); *SC v UK* (2005) 40 EHRR 10.

[25] Owusu-Bempah (n 21) 325.

[26] Jacobson and Cooper (n 12).

[27] Owusu-Bempah (n 21).

from the already marginalised sections of society from which many defendants are drawn.[28] As Hunter reported, 'consistently, data on offenders backgrounds suggest high levels of vulnerability',[29] which is likely exacerbated by barriers to participation.

Turning to the relationship between defendant participation and access to justice, we will similarly find numerous interpretations of the latter phrase. Lack of consensus about the term 'access to justice' led the Fabian Society to strongly recommend that a new statutory right to justice should be created,[30] though that recommendation is yet to find favour with government. The concept of access to justice itself emerged as a social right in the 1970s,[31] and interrogating the meaning of this social right is important to avoid the 'tendency to conflate access to justice with legal aid'.[32] Adams-Prassl and Adams-Prassl,[33] for example, highlight that short time limits, lack of legal representation when cases consist of complex evidence, complicated application forms, and the absence of opportunities to make 'meaningful representations' can each have a different impact on the ability of a person to access justice.[34] As we will see throughout this book, each of those factors is present in magistrates' court proceedings.

Paz-Fuchs et al consider two aspects of access to justice; the procedural element of 'access' and the substantive element of 'justice'. Combining the two, we find a concept which requires that people have the opportunity to pursue a case that furthers justice in some way.[35] Cornford also sets out two aspects of access to justice: one descriptive and one normative. The descriptive aspect of access to justice, according to Cornford, refers to 'the extent to which citizens are able to gain access to legal services necessary to protect and vindicate their rights'.[36] The normative aspect of access to justice is more contested, though Cornford suggests that it is 'normatively central … that every citizen should equally be able to protect her legal rights. We might call this the ideal of equal access.'[37] Cornford goes on to break this normative aspect of access to justice down through its relationship with the doctrines of rule of law and citizenship.

---

[28] See generally Owusu-Bempah (n 1); J Campbell, *Entanglements of Life with the Law: Precarity and Justice in London's Magistrates Courts*. (Cambridge Scholars Publishing, 2020).

[29] G Hunter, 'Policy and Practice Supporting Lay Participation' in Jacobson, J and Cooper, P (eds) *Participation in Courts and Tribunals* (Bristol University Press, 2020).

[30] The Fabian Society, 'The Right to Justice: The final report of the Bach Commission' (London, Fabian Society, 2017).

[31] M Cappelletti, B Garth and N Trocker, 'Access To Justice: Comparative General Report.' (1976) 40(3/4) *The Rabel Journal of Comparative and International Private Law* 669–717.

[32] J Robins and D Newman, *Justice in a Time of Austerity* (Bristol University Press, 2021) 1.

[33] Adams-Prassl and Adams-Prassl (n 13).

[34] Adams-Prassl and Adams-Prassl (n 13) 576.

[35] A Paz-Fuchs, J Kinghan and L Yeatman, *Clinical Legal Education: Theory and Practice* (Oxford University Press, forthcoming).

[36] T Cornford, 'The Meaning of Access to Justice' in E Palmer, T Cornford, A Guinchard and Y Marique (eds), *Access to Justice: Beyond the Policies and Politics of Austerity* (Hart Publishing, 2016) 28.

[37] Ibid, 28.

It is clear then that access to justice is neither a fixed nor universally understood concept. Alternative approaches consider overlapping ways that vindicate the rights of diverse groups, the range of technologies through which inequity can be equalised, and outcome-based equality of arms.[38] Inequality of arms has long been recognised as a potential breach of the right to a fair trial under Article 6 ECHR.[39] While no issue is taken with these diverse approaches, the analysis of findings in this book goes beyond outcomes and vindication of rights, and considers a defendant's ability to fully understand and participate in the process of summary justice as a key part of access to justice that enhances the legitimacy of criminal proceedings. Tyler's extensive work has demonstrated the importance of defendant perceptions of legitimacy in the criminal process for defendants, victims and society at large. Thus, the simple provision of legally aided advice is certainly important, and the research presented in this book was grounded in an assumption that the presence of defence lawyers can help defendants understand, and therefore participate, in the criminal process. This, in turn, aids defendant access to justice.[40] Much about the original assumption stands, but this work goes further and refutes Posner's suggestion that access to justice can be operationalised simply by providing bare minimum legal counsel for indigent defendants.[41]

As well as being symbolic places of justice, courts are workplaces for the many professionals that keep the criminal process moving forward. This infuses them with a very particular culture (chapter three), which is almost impenetrable to many defendants. The presence of a defence lawyer in court helps level the playing field for those who are not privy to the verbal and non-verbal cues that exist in any workplace. Most significantly, defence lawyers tend to be able to quickly assimilate and interpret information that is provided by the prosecutor, the judge or magistrates and other courtroom professionals including the probation service, clerks and the ushers. Yet the way in which defence lawyers facilitate defendant participation can (and needs to) be interrogated to enhance understanding of the role of the defence lawyer in magistrates' courts, and identify where change might be facilitated. It is only through both access to properly funded legal advice and defendant understanding of proceedings that a defendant is offered a meaningful choice about participation in the process against their state-funded and supported adversary. Ultimately, as Owusu-Bempah says, 'the defendant is intrinsically worthy of dialogue and the criminal trial should attempt to engage them as such'.[42] Through this book, it is clear that defence

---

[38] Ibid.

[39] Paz-Fuchs et al (n 35).

[40] This is what Owusu-Bempah describes as 'effective participation by proxy': Owusu-Bempah (n 21) 332.

[41] R Posner, *The Problematics of Moral and Legal Theory* (Harvard University Press, 1999).

[42] Owusu-Bempah (n 1) 613.

lawyers want – among other things – to aid participation, but the realities of the criminal justice system do not always enable that ideal to be realised. If defence lawyers are to be able to truly improve effective participation, the conditions in which they operate need to be favourable to that aim. In this way, the problem of access to justice in summary criminal cases is not only about a lack of adequate access to lawyers (through legal aid cuts), but also 'some idea of, say, fairness, desert, need, participation or equality' – that is, the 'justice elements of access to justice'.[43] In effect, 'understanding and engagement by legal representatives should not be treated as a substitute for that of the defendant'.[44]

It follows that this book adopts an approach to access to justice that consists of two elements. First, it advocates meaningful operation of the right to legal assistance, which could be considered the descriptive aspect of access to justice. Second, it considers access to justice as the ability to participate effectively, which could be interpreted as the normative aspect of access to justice. The stance thus adopted in this book is that the descriptive aspect of access to justice is vitally important, but that it is only truly constructive if it operates in conjunction with the normative aspect (which goes beyond the mere provision of publicly funded legal assistance). My own normative understanding of access to justice overlaps with Cornford's approach to demands for equality, in that both interpretations situate access to justice within disparate power relationships and imbalances within the justice system.

III. THE NATURE AND STRUCTURE OF SUMMARY JUSTICE

Magistrates' courts process summary-only charges[45] and either-way offences[46] if magistrates' sentencing powers are deemed sufficient,[47] and they send indictable-only cases[48] to be dealt with at the Crown Court. Magistrates also commit either-way offences to the Crown Court when their sentencing powers are considered insufficient. Given that all criminal defendants make their first appearance in the magistrates' court, it is here that bail decisions are made for all those accused of crimes, save for defendants who have been charged with murder, in

---

[43] Paz-Fuchs et al (n 35).

[44] Owusu-Bempah (n 1) 618.

[45] Offences which carry a maximum penalty on conviction of six months' imprisonment.

[46] Offences which can be dealt with in either a Crown Court or magistrates' court.

[47] Magistrates can impose a maximum penalty of six months' imprisonment for any number of summary offences, and one either-way offence. Their sentencing powers increase to a maximum of 12 months' imprisonment if a person is convicted of two or more either-way offences. Either-way offences are those that can be dealt with in either a magistrates' or a Crown Court because they carry a maximum potential sentence of more than six months' imprisonment. For example, theft carries a maximum sentence of seven years' imprisonment, but many low-level theft offences do not warrant a sentence of more than a maximum six months' imprisonment.

[48] Offences which are considered too serious to be dealt with in the summary court.

which case the magistrates have no powers except to send the proceedings directly to the Crown Court.[49] Compared to the Crown Court, magistrates' courts hear more trials, convict 30 per cent more defendants following trial and imprison more people than Crown Court judges.[50] Research indicates that magistrates often require defendants to prove their innocence, contrary to the legal burden of proof,[51] and despite specific training about the importance of the burden and standard of proof that requires the prosecutor to prove all elements of the case beyond a reasonable doubt.[52]

Perhaps as a result of magistrates' court conviction rates, defence advocates view magistrates as 'pro-prosecution'.[53] Sanders noted that magistrates 'regard defence solicitors as representing a particular viewpoint, but see the Crown Prosecution Service (CPS) as neutral … In reality, the CPS represents the police side of the adversarial system as enthusiastically as most defence solicitors do their clients.'[54] Darbyshire also notes that 'magistrates too readily believe police witnesses. Research and commentaries on this point all substantiate this defence lawyers' claim.'[55]

Nonetheless, magistrates' court processes operate within limits set by law which are designed to prevent both unfair treatment and wrongful conviction. As McBarnet noted,

> the criminal justice process is the most explicit coercive apparatus of the state and the idea that police and courts can interfere with the liberties of citizens only under known law and by means of due process of law is thus a crucial element in the ideology of the democratic state.[56]

Several commentators have suggested models of the criminal process[57] which are useful to provide descriptions of overarching issues in summary criminal justice.

---

[49] Ss 114 and 115 Coroners and Justice Act 2009, SI 2010/145 (c18).

[50] A Sanders, 'Core Values, the Magistracy, and the Auld Report' (2002) 29(2) *Journal of Law and Society* 324; 328.

[51] Ibid. See also P Darbyshire, 'For the New Lord Chancellor – Some Causes for Concern About Magistrates' (1997) (Dec) *Criminal Law Review* 861 and A Sanders, *Community Justice. Modernising the Magistracy in England and Wales* (Institute of Public Policy Research, 2000).

[52] T Grove, *The Magistrate's Tale* (Bloomsbury Publishing, 2003).

[53] A Mulcahy, 'The Justifications of "Justice": Legal Practitioners' Accounts of Negotiated Case Settlements in Magistrates' Courts' (1994) 34(4) *British Journal of Criminology* 411; 420. In 2016, magistrates' court conviction rates sat at around 15% higher than Crown Court conviction rates (Crown Prosecution Service, *Key Measures 2017–2018*, www.cps.gov.uk/key-measures).

[54] Sanders (n 50) 33.

[55] Darbyshire (n 51) 871.

[56] McBarnet (n 5) 8.

[57] See especially, H Packer, *The Limits of Criminal Sanction* (Stanford University Press, 1968). In addition to those offered by Packer, King suggested a further six models of the criminal justice system (M King, *The Framework of Criminal Justice* (Croom Helm, 1981)). Two of those models – the justice model and the punishment model – have features which resonate with Packer's due process and crime control models. The third model is one of rehabilitation which relies on the expertise of professionals who will consider appropriate methods of diagnosis and treatment. The fourth model is the bureaucratic model, which is concerned with the management of crime and of criminals. The

For example, the fact that magistrates' courts process high volumes of cases at speed resonates with Packer's crime control model of criminal justice, in which the efficient disposal of cases is the system's paramount concern. The model anticipates high numbers of guilty pleas that can be concluded swiftly. The criminal justice system is regarded as inherently able to process a large number of early guilty pleas because preliminary controls can be trusted to adequately discard weak or inappropriate prosecutions.[58]

In contrast, the due process model[59] concerns itself with the power of the state versus the power of the individual, and is concerned with 'quality control'.[60] Quality control demands ensuring strict compliance with the rule of law, the burden and standard of proof and the defendant's rights. The model promotes the use of defence advocates, even if such advocates infrequently raise due process issues.[61] Atiyah observed that the due process model establishes an adversarial obstacle course which the prosecution must take time to complete in order to maintain a just system.[62] Due process models of (summary) justice promote procedural fairness as a key element of substantive justice (that is, a fair result). Due process adherents would thus argue that unfair processes are unable to produce fair outcomes. While neither substantive nor procedural fairness specifically require complete understanding and participation on the part of defendants, the likelihood of proceedings being (perceived as) fair (in satisfaction of due process values) increases the more that understanding and participation are enabled. As such, while due process concerns itself with over- all fair procedures, the ability of defendants to understand and participate in summary justice are equally important in themselves, as well as lending support to overall due process ideology.

Despite this rhetoric, McBarnet noted that magistrates' courts operate 'as courts freed from the due process of the common law'.[63] Galligan also observed that due process considerations do not appear to be supported in magistrates' courts by firm legal rules.[64] These issues are explored in depth in chapters three, four and five.

Packer[65] rightly acknowledged that any criminal justice system is likely to display features of more than one model at any point in time. The fact that it is hard to identify a single dominant model indicates that relationships between

---

fifth model focuses on the necessity to degrade the criminal and is called the status passage model. Finally, the power model concerns itself with the maintenance of class domination.

[58] K Roach, 'Four Models of the Criminal Process' (1999) 89 *Journal of Criminal Law and Criminology* 671.

[59] Packer (n 57).

[60] Roach (n 58) 3.

[61] A Ashworth and M Redmayne, *The Criminal Process,* 3rd edn (Oxford University Press, 2005).

[62] P Atiyah, *Law and Modern Society* (Oxford University Press, 1995) 226.

[63] D McBarnet (n 5) 143.

[64] D Galligan, 'Regulating Pre-Trial Decisions' in Lacey, N (ed) *A Reader on Criminal Justice* (Oxford University Press, 1994).

[65] Packer (n 57).

criminal law, criminal justice and procedure are not clear-cut. Broad themes can however be identified, which are likely to reflect politicised approaches to criminal justice. This notion was recognised by Carlen when she stated 'a magistrates' court is an institution rhetorically functioning to perpetuate the notion of possible justice in a society whose total organisation is directed at the maintenance of the capitalist exploitation of labour, production and control.'[66] As such, the rhetoric of summary justice differs from its practice in that, so far as magistrates' courts are concerned,

> the legal process allows the trial to fulfil simultaneously two functions: the ideological function of displaying the rhetoric of justice in action by being tipped (visibly) in favour of due process and the accused, (and) the pragmatic function of crime control by being tipped (invisibly) but decisively in favour of conviction.[67]

These observations demonstrated that summary justice has long been viewed as performed by institutions in which little regard was given to defendants' rights. Unfortunately, much about McBarnet's analysis stands.

IV. AN INTRODUCTION TO THE MAGISTRATES' COURT WORKGROUP

There are a number of actors in the magistrates' courtroom workgroup, the most prominent of which are magistrates, court officers (also known as clerks or legal advisers, depending on their position in the institution), prosecutors and defence advocates. However, before considering how these actors affect the operation of summary justice, it is important to acknowledge the local nature of magistrates' court proceedings. The level of familiarity among members of the courtroom workgroup will affect its stability[68] and the extent to which advocates are prepared to risk damaging relationships which, in turn, affects the advocate's negotiating power. As Eisenstein and Jacob noted, in a courtroom workgroup which had low levels of familiarity among members, there was a greater number of contested cases and less emphasis on negotiation than in courtroom workgroups which they regarded as stable and familiar.[69] The effect of the magistrates' court workgroup on the ability of defendants to effectively participate in proceedings is discussed in detail in chapter three.

---

[66] Carlen (n 5) 98.

[67] McBarnet (n 5) 100.

[68] R Young, 'Exploring the Boundaries of Criminal Courtroom Workgroup' (2013) 42 *Common Law World Review* 203.

[69] J Eisenstein and H Jacob, *Felony Justice: An Organisational Analysis of Criminal Courts* (Little Brown, 1977). Tepperman similarly noted that the courtroom typically contains 'networks of friendship that moderate conflicts' that may arise (L Tepperman, 'The Effect of Court Size on Organisation and Procedure' (1973) 10(4) *The Canadian Review of Sociology and Anthropology* 346; 364).

Although familiarity is thus a significant feature of magistrates' court workgroup culture, and Young notes that the local context can vary 'enough to make a discernible difference to court outcomes',[70] previous socio-legal scholars have identified some features of courtroom culture that appear to be of general relevance when considering how magistrates' courts operate. In order to understand the way that summary justice operates (before the in-depth analysis in chapters three, four and five), each of these subgroups is considered in turn alongside an examination of models of summary criminal justice.

The most obvious members of the magistrates' court workgroup are the magistrates themselves. While it was historically desirable for magistrates to be legally qualified,[71] professional legal qualification is no longer necessary.[72] This led Bottoms and McClean to note that magistrates are seen by advocates as 'amateurs without training who could not be expected to do a decent job'.[73] The costs of training for magistrates had reduced, by 2015, to one-third of its 2008/9 cost,[74] but would-be magistrates also undergo a period of mentorship with a magistrate after undertaking formal training. This enables magistrates to develop understanding about a courtroom which operates via rituals executed on a daily basis by the professionals who work therein.[75] It is via such procedures that the cultural practice of law evolves in criminal courts, and such practices affect the way that defendants experience the proceedings. This is not to suggest that 'overt collusion to manipulate justice exists; what does exist are the shared understandings of habitués'[76] which 'may become so routine and commonplace that the habitué forgets that the outsider finds them strange.'[77]

Magistrates are frequently criticised for failing to represent various socio-cultural groups,[78] in that 'the lay magistracy is overwhelmingly drawn from managerial and professional occupations',[79] and disproportionately represents those who are retired.[80] Clements asserted that, because they are not socially representative, magistrates have an 'inability (and sometimes indifference) to see the injustice that confronts the defendants in their daily lives and … lack … life experience of what it is like to be socially excluded by poverty.'[81] There thus exist

[70] Young (n 68) 204.
[71] M Davies, 'A New Training Initiative for the Lay Magistracy in England and Wales – A Further Step Towards Professionalisation?' (2005) 12(1) *International Journal of the Legal Profession* 93.
[72] Ibid.
[73] Bottoms and McClean (n 5) 89.
[74] The Secret Barrister, *Stories of the Law and How it's Broken* (Palgrave Macmillan, 2018).
[75] Bottoms and McClean (n 5).
[76] Ibid 55.
[77] Ibid 55.
[78] R Morgan, 'Magistrates: The Future According to Auld' (2002) 29(2) *Journal of Law and Society* 308; Darbyshire (n 51); The Secret Barrister (n 74).
[79] Davies (n 71).
[80] Morgan (n 78) Darbyshire (n 51).
[81] L Clements, 'Little Justice – Judicial Reform and the Magistrates' in Thomas, P (ed), *Discriminating Lawyers* (Cavendish, 2000) 207. As Carlen noted in 1976, magistrates' interpretation

different socio-cultural expectations between those who often constitute the Bench and 'the overwhelmingly socio-economically disadvantaged defendants appearing before them'.[82] This means that defendants are likely to be viewed by the Bench as a different category of citizen to its members and the professional workgroup that operates in court (chapters three and four).

While lay magistrates deal with 91 per cent of all cases in the magistrates' courts,[83] legally qualified District Judges (formerly known as stipendiary magistrates) also sit in summary criminal proceedings. Morgan and Russell, and Sanders, are of the view that District Judges (DJs) are more efficient[84] than lay justices[85] and apply legal rules more fairly.[86] DJs make greater use of custody than magistrates do, but this may be a result of the fact that they tend to hear the most serious cases that are dealt with in magistrates' courts.[87] Dennis found that 'professional court users have significantly greater levels of confidence in stipendiaries … they regard stipendiaries as quicker than lay justices, more efficient and consistent in their decision-making.'[88] As a result, defence lawyers prepare cases more thoroughly and do not make unrealistic submissions to DJs that they might attempt when addressing lay magistrates.[89] These now quite old findings are supported by the discussion in chapter four.

Whether a DJ or a lay Bench is sitting, the court is assisted by a clerk or legal adviser who provides advice to unqualified (or lay) magistrates,[90] and assumes a more administrative role when a DJ is hearing cases. Darbyshire has raised concerns about the consistency of clerks' behaviour, stating in the late 1990s that 'Court clerks' practices are, in my observation, just as varied and sometimes perverse as they were in the 1970s.'[91] This is also supported by my findings, as discussed in chapter four.

---

of legal and social rules is bound up in 'pre-existent regulative elements of a capitalist social formation' (Carlen (n 5) 100).

[82] A Sanders, *Community Justice. Modernising the Magistracy in England and Wales* (Institute of Public Policy Research, 2000) 11.

[83] Sanders (n 51).

[84] Sanders (n 50).

[85] Zander stated that magistrates 'slow down the system and cost a fortune' (M Zander *Cases and Materials on the English Legal System* (Oxford University Press, 2007) 21) while Morgan and Russell note that District Judges deal with 22% more cases than lay Benches in a standard court session, and this is not at the expense of inquisition and challenge, and there are fewer adjournments before District Judges. (R Morgan and N Russell, 'The Judiciary in the Magistrates' Courts' (2000), library. npia.police.uk/docs/homisc/occ-judiciary.pdf. By 2002, Morgan had increased this estimate from 22% to 30% (Morgan (n 55)).

[86] Sanders (n 50).

[87] I Dennis 'Judging Magistrates' (2001)(Feb) *Criminal Law Review* 71.

[88] Ibid 71. See also Morgan (n 78) and P Darbyshire, *Sitting in Judgment: The Working Lives of Judges* (Hart Publishing, 2011). My findings support this claim.

[89] Morgan (n 78) 311.

[90] Davies (n 71).

[91] Darbyshire (n 51) 873.

Sanders also noted that magistrates' clerks play a highly influential role in decision-making processes.[92] In this context, the clerk's responsibility is 'for managing the court organisation and most magistrates' courts operate under a considerable amount of pressure ... The clerk in court has to achieve a balancing of competing interests.'[93] Astor further noted that clerks tended to place greater importance on compliance with rules than on ensuring that defendants understood the process.[94] As such, defendants remained bystanders in the proceedings because 'explanations would have taken time in a busy list.'[95]

The court clerk plays an important role in Bottoms and McClean's liberal bureaucratic model of summary criminal justice, which is a hybrid of the crime control and due process models.[96] In this model, the 'humane and enlightened clerks to the justices'[97] agree that there is a need for formal procedures which ensure justice is seen to be done, but also require restricted protections so that the system does not become over-burdened and collapse.[98] The role of the court clerk is discussed further in chapter four, but it is worth noting here the system of a reduction in sentence in exchange for entering an early guilty plea.[99] This provides an example of the liberal bureaucratic model in operation[100] because it offers an *inducement* to plead guilty without removing the defendant's *right* to plead not guilty.[101] Such systems encourage swift case progression, which, as we will see in chapters two and three in particular, has become increasingly important to governments since 1979.

V. NEOLIBERALISM AND CRIMINAL JUSTICE

Since earlier studies of summary criminal justice took place, successive governments have espoused a broadly neoliberal ideology in relation to the pursuit of an 'open-ended and contradictory process of politically assisted market rule'.[102] Ward notes that there is not a wealth of academic work which connects

---

[92] Sanders (n 50).

[93] H Astor, 'The Unrepresented Defendant Revisited: A Consideration of the Role of the Clerk in Magistrates' Courts' (1986) 13(2) *Journal of Law and Society* 225, 228.

[94] Ibid.

[95] Ibid: 233.

[96] Bottoms and McClean (n 5).

[97] Bottoms and McClean (n 5) 228. Darbyshire would probably disagree with this statement given her comments about court clerks/legal advisers below (P Darbyshire, 'A Comment on the Powers of Magistrates' Clerks' (1999)(May) *Criminal Law Review* 377).

[98] Bottoms and McClean (n 5).

[99] See s 73 Sentencing Act 2020.

[100] Atiyah (n 62).

[101] Other examples exist, such as the potential for adverse inferences to be drawn from exercising the right to remain silent during police investigations. See especially Quirk (n 14).

[102] J Peck, *Constructions of Neoliberal Reason* (Oxford University Press, 2010) xii. See especially D Harvey, *A brief history of neoliberalism* (Oxford University Press, 2005).

alterations to criminal justice procedure within the courts to neoliberalism.[103] One explanation for this ontological gap might be the dynamic nature of neoliberal ideology as it has been mediated by right- or left-leaning, or centrist, British political movements as they have come and gone since the late 1970s. Neoliberalism is consequently used as a broad term for a complex and often contradictory set of political practices that tend to substitute economic market rationalities for welfare rationalities,[104] often through processes of privatisation, outsourcing and re-regulation of elements of the Keynesian welfare state.[105] Through recognition that the market is not a naturally occurring phenomenon, but instead requires constant protection and advancement, 'neoliberalism leads to more rather than less state involvement and intervention'.[106]

In line with Mirowski's analysis of the neoliberal project aim to marketise government functions,[107] regulation of the criminal justice system has steadily increased since the early 1980s. There has been a welter of legislation which has created new offences, amended sentencing provisions, or dictated how proceedings ought to be conducted.[108] As the financial crisis of 2008 took hold, and austerity politics became the prevailing governmental narrative well in to the 2010s, public services were dominated by discourse surrounding budgetary cuts and more urgent demands for efficiency savings. Nonetheless, much of the broadly neoliberal narrative adopted in the UK since the late 1970s remained influential throughout Conservative, New Labour, Coalition and the return to Conservative government over the last three decades, as the following discussion illustrates. Ward argued that neoliberalism has resulted in transformations to criminal justice that can be celebrated for modernisation and efficiency but can also be criticised for drastically altering the delivery of criminal justice and reducing it to its bare bones.[109]

The incoming Conservative government of 1979 was able to capitalise on three factors to justify increasingly intrusive regulation of criminal proceedings. The first was the apparent failure of welfarist approaches that prevailed after World War II to reduce crime.[110] Margaret Thatcher drew on the issue of

---

[103] J Ward, 'Transforming "Summary Justice" Through Police-led Prosecution and "Virtual Courts"' (2015) 55 *British Journal of Criminology* 341.

[104] J Peck, 'Zombie neoliberalism and the ambidextrous state' (2010) 14 *Theoretical Criminology* 104.

[105] P Mirowski, 'Postface: Defining Neoliberalism' in *The Road from Mont Pèlerin* (Harvard University Press, 2009).

[106] A Whitworth, 'Neoliberal paternalism and paradoxical subjects: Confusion and contradiction in UK activation policy.' (2016) 36(3) *Critical Social Policy* 412–31, 414.

[107] Mirowski (n 105) 436.

[108] See especially J Chalmers and F Leverick, 'Quantifying criminalisation' in RA Duff et al (eds), *Criminalization: The Aims and Limits of the Criminal Law* (Oxford University Press, 2014) 54–79; F Leverick and J Chalmers, 'Criminal law in the shadows: creating offences in delegated legislation' (2018) 38(2) *Legal Studies* 221–41. The first iteration of the Criminal Procedural Rules came into force in 2005.

[109] Ward (n 103).

[110] R Lowe, *The Welfare State in Britain Since 1945* (Macmillan, 1999).

rising crime rates as part of the Conservative Party manifesto of 1979,[111] though crime rates continued to rise into New Labour's 1997–2010 term, prompting former Prime Minister Tony Blair's 'Tough on Crime, Tough on the Causes of Crime' mantra.[112] The second was an ideological favouring of processes of individualism, responsibilisation and consumerism,[113] which created divisions in society meaning that those who do not participate in the market in accordance with a neoliberal agenda are pushed further towards the margins of society.[114] As Brown explains, responsibilisation 'tasks the worker, student, consumer or indigent person with discerning and undertaking the correct strategies of self-investment and entrepreneurship for thriving and surviving; it is in this regard a manifestation of human capitalisation'.[115] Those groups who 'fail' to discern and undertake the 'correct' strategies to thrive in society are labelled as undeserving of all but the most basic forms of state assistance. This 'othering' process occurs as a by-product to neoliberal dogma, through what Whitworth describes as the creation of the entrepreneurial subject who is expected to react with '[p]roactive "agility" rather than passive "docility"' to predict and react to (potential) risks that threaten an individual's power in the market-place.[116] The third issue of significance is the desire to reduce state expenditure, based in the assumption that the market will always manage information more effectively and efficiently than the state.[117] Reductions in state expenditure were regarded as achievable via measures to improve the efficiency of working practices in public institutions though corporate management techniques, also referred to as New Public Management (NPM).[118] Through NPM, privatisation, de- and re-regulation, neoliberalism became 'a peculiar form of reason that configures all aspects of existence in economic terms',[119] including the criminal justice

---

[111] The Conservative Party, '1979 Conservative Party General Election Manifesto', www.conservative-party.net/manifestos/1979/1979-conservative-manifesto.shtml.

[112] B Loveday, 'Tough on crime or tough on the causes of crime? an evaluation of Labour's crime and disorder legislation' (1999) 1(2) *Crime Prevention and Community Safety* 7–24.

[113] J Dean, *Democracy and Other Neoliberal Fantasies* (Duke University Press, 2009); J Oksala, *Foucault, Politics and Violence* (Northwestern University Press, 2012).

[114] D Faulkner, 'Policy and Practice in Modern Britain: Influences, Outcomes and Civil Society' in P Green and A Rutherford (eds), *Criminal Policy in Transition* (Hart Publishing, 2000); D Garland, *The Culture of Control: Crime and Social Order in Contemporary Society* (University of Chicago Press, 2002); Bell (n 3).

[115] W Brown, *Undoing the Demos: Neoliberalism's Stealth Revolution* (MIT Press, 2015) 132–33.

[116] Whitworth (n 106) 419.

[117] Mirowski (n 105).

[118] H Sommerlad, 'The implementation of quality initiatives and the new public management in the legal aid sector in England and Wales: bureaucratisation, stratification and surveillance' (1999) 6 *International Journal of the Legal Profession* 311; H Sommerlad, 'Reflections on the reconfiguration of access to justice' (2008) 15:3 *International Journal of the Legal Profession* 179–93; K Stenson and A Edwards, 'Policy Transfer in Local Crime Control: Beyond naïve emulation' in T Newburn and R Sparks (eds), *Criminal Justice and Political Cultures* (Willan Publishing, 2004); Sanders (n 61).

[119] Brown (n 115) 17.

process. These approaches enabled governments to justify removing or under-mining rights afforded to defendants via the adversarial system (see especially chapters two and five). Those standpoints also justify demanding ever more speedy case progression at reduced cost (chapters three and four). Growing concerns about expenditure in relation to state funded agencies have increased governments' desire for efficiency and the withdrawal of state supported assis-tance to those agencies involved in criminal case progression. This procedurally punitive turn[120] is also reflected in austerity measures via restrictions on the availability of publicly funded representation.

In order to examine the impact of neoliberalism on access to justice, this book considers how neoliberalism's rise to political popularity affected govern-ments' approaches to summary criminal justice; how magistrates' courts, and the professionals working within them, operate; how political influences interact with the magistrates' court workgroup culture and how the result-ing practices affect the ability of defendants to participate in the proceedings. The argument of this book in relation to neoliberalism is that its preference for market inspired techniques of managerialism encouraged greater regulation of summary criminal justice in order to promote further efficiency. The culture of summary criminal courts has always tended to marginalise defendants from active participation in the process but demands for efficiency (and cost cutting) alongside reduced access to legal advice, have exacerbated those processes of marginalisation. However, such processes of marginalisation are less likely to be regarded as ethically problematic to a political agenda that encourages indi-vidual responsibility, in which the criminal is accountable for their own fate and, consequently, is not entitled to more than minimal state support.

Further, and as a result of the strong workgroup culture that operates in magistrates' courts (chapter three), there has been little resistance to the imple-mentation of neoliberal policies. The solidarity that exists among members of the court workgroup means that they tend to cooperate rather than act in antagonistic ways, despite the adversarial nature of the proceedings. This coop-eration coincides with lawyers' business interests on the basis that it enables advocates to maintain good working relationships and a good reputation with court personnel. The fact that lawyers operate (and have been trained) in a system permeated with liberal bureaucratic principles which favour speedy case progression and high rates of early guilty pleas[121] enables managerial demands for efficiency, accelerated by austerity, to be implemented with relative ease. These principles encourage procedures that facilitate volume processing over individualised treatment.

---

[120] On the neoliberal punitive turn, see especially L Wacquant, *Punishing the Poor. The Neoliberal Government of Social Insecurity* (Duke University Press, 2009); Bell (n 3); Garland (n 114).
[121] Bottoms and McClean (n 5).

A paradox exists in the tensions between lawyers' business needs, their relationships with government (upon which they depend for funding) and their relationships with their clients.[122] As demonstrated in chapter five, to ensure their continued existence lawyers must follow procedures imposed by government whilst also being aware that those procedures might undermine their clients' rights. Lawyers are also reliant on good relationships with their clients to ensure that their businesses are prosperous. Defence solicitors are therefore placed in a position which requires them to manage the needs of their clients, the needs of government, and of the courts, who are likely to have opposing views about how cases should be dealt with. As relative latecomers to feature in summary criminal proceedings (chapters two and four), defence lawyers appear to take the view that co-operation, as opposed to resistance, will be in their long-term business and, by default, client interests. Furthermore, the competitive nature of the structure of criminal defence services discourages firms from working together to collectively resist policies which challenge their work.[123] In essence, it seems that firms themselves have been co-opted into market-based understandings of their services through contracting schemes (chapter two), even though they provide what is ultimately a state-funded, and state-led, process.

Through the application of a broadly neoliberal ideology in magistrates' courts, it seems a preference for managerialism has combined with a strong and stable workgroup culture to exacerbate the inability of defendants to properly play a role in the process of summary criminal justice. Alongside increased individualism and responsibilisation – also espoused by predominantly neoliberal advocates – there is little motivation to assist defendants by improving their ability to participate, or to assist the community of defence lawyers who are simply expected to adjust their work to comply with greater managerial demands. Neoliberal ideologists expect both defendants and their lawyers to manage their own participation in the criminal process and in wider society, and view failure to successfully do so as a consequence of making 'incorrect' choices.

VI. THE PROCESS OF INVESTIGATING SUMMARY JUSTICE

Against the theoretical background set out in the preceding sections, my empirical research took the form of a case study of magistrates' courts in an urban[124] local justice area of South East England.[125] Generally, the more urban

---

[122] L Welsh, 'The effects of changes to legal aid on lawyers' professional identity and behaviour in summary criminal cases: a case study' (2017) 44 (4) *Journal of Law and Society* 559–85.

[123] D Newman and L Welsh, 'The practice of modern defence lawyers: Alienation and its implications for access to justice.' (2019) 48(1–2) *Common Law World Review* 64–89.

[124] Ministry of Justice, *Transforming Legal Aid: Delivering a More Credible and Efficient System* (Ministry of Justice CP14/2013, 2013).

[125] There are 42 criminal justice areas across England and Wales (Ministry of Justice, *Transforming legal aid: delivering a more credible and efficient system* (Ministry of Justice CP14/2013, 2013)) which are further divided into 144 local justice areas (www.openjustice.gov.uk/courts/criminal-cases/).

the area, the greater the level of fragmentation in the criminal legal aid provider market. At the time of conducting the research, the top eight legal aid providers in the area conducted between 20 and 30 per cent of the market share of work[126] and there were 11 firms which provided legally aided criminal defence representation in the area. One CPS office served all the courts in the locale. An analysis of population statistics[127] and police recorded crime[128] suggested that the area had quite a high per capita crime rate, particularly for violent crime and criminal damage/arson. However, one particularly socio-economically deprived part of the area disproportionately accounted for the crime rates, contributing to 28 per cent of the recorded crime rate and having the highest level of recorded crime of all of the area's districts.

The case study method entails a focus on a specific organisation or community and 'is concerned with the complexity and particular nature of the case in question'.[129] Case studies aim to 'generate an intensive examination of a single case',[130] while the depth of the data gained could provide insights that may be more broadly applicable. Through case studies we can understand the implications of change, challenge assumptions about how the law operates and provide new insights into legal problems.[131] While it is important to acknowledge that local practices and procedures may result in behavioural variation, many of the trends previously noted in other case studies, such as those conducted by Young,[132] Newman[133] and Carlen,[134] demonstrate that common themes exist. We can therefore surmise that the study paints a picture that is close to the reality of modern summary justice.

The empirical research consisted of the equivalent of four weeks of observation conducted between October 2012 and February 2013, followed by 19 semi-structured interviews (seven prosecutors[135] and 12 defence solicitors)

---

[126] KPMG LLP, *Ministry of Justice Procurement of Criminal Legal Aid Services: Financial Modelling* (London, 2014).

[127] Office for National Statistics, '2011 Census, Population Estimates by Single Year of Age and Sex for Local Authorities in the United Kingdom' (2013), www.ons.gov.uk/ons/rel/census/2011-census/population-estimates-by-single-year-of-age-and-sex-for-local-authorities-in-the-united-kingdom/index.html.

[128] Office for National Statistics, 'Police Recorded Crime by Offence Group and Force Area, English Regions and Wales, Number of Offences, Year to December 2014', www.ons.gov.uk/ons/publications/re-reference-tables.html?edition=tcmpercent3A77-373433.

[129] A Bryman, *Social Research Methods* (Oxford University Press, 2012) 66.

[130] Ibid 71.

[131] D Allen and A Blackham, 'Using empirical research to advance workplace equality law scholarship: benefits, pitfalls and challenges' (2018) 27:3 *Griffith Law Review* 337–65.

[132] Young (n 68).

[133] Newman (n 4).

[134] Carlen (n 5).

[135] Two of the prosecutors interviewed had moved from defence to prosecution work several years before this research was conducted. Moving from defending to prosecuting, in light of the better salaries and benefits on offer, is in my experience a longstanding trend in criminal justice work. This issue has been raised in evidence to the Justice Committee. See Justice Committee, *Oral evidence:*

over the summer of 2013. The purpose of the observation and interviews was to become 'immersed in a social setting for some time … with a view to gaining an appreciation of the culture of a social group'[136] beyond my own experience as a defence advocate. Generally, observations expose that the social order of the magistrates' court is 'an outcome of agreed-upon patterns of action that were themselves products of negotiations between the different parties involved,[137] as expanded upon in chapter three. This understanding allows us to appreciate the importance of workgroup culture to defendants' experience of the proceedings.

Baldwin noted that the substantial advantage of observing criminal courts is that they are open to the public and so no difficulties arise in obtaining access for research.[138] As demonstrated by studies conducted by, among others, Carlen,[139] McBarnet,[140] and Newman,[141] observation of court processes can assist in uncovering the nature of relationships between court personnel and patterns of workgroup behaviour.[142] While Baldwin notes that courtroom observers may feel a sense of 'exclusion, estrangement, and alienation'[143] from the proceedings (akin to defendants), my experience working in these courts allowed me to understand the nuances of court personnel behaviour. Conducting observations also allowed me to step back from my ordinary involvement in summary criminal procedures to make a preliminary assessment of the behaviour of advocates and defendants in court.

During observation I watched the daily practices of the five magistrates' courts in the area from the public galleries, and made notes of the proceedings using an observation template. There was a risk that, by my presence, the usual rhythm of working life would be affected and that the participants may have altered their behaviour. However, the fact that I was effectively a participating observer did, I think, minimise that risk. As a familiar and trusted face – someone who was already a member of the workgroup and could consider the workgroup's interests – I was able to 'participate freely

---

(a) *Court capacity,* HC 284; (b) *The future of legal aid* (HC 289, House of Commons, Tuesday 9 February 2021), https://committees.parliament.uk/oralevidence/1718/pdf/, and through informal conversations with the same inquiry.

[136] Bryman (n 129) 369.

[137] Ibid 19.

[138] J Baldwin, 'Research on the Criminal Courts' in R King and E Wincup (eds), *Doing Research on Crime and Justice* (Oxford University Press, 2000).

[139] Carlen (n 5).

[140] McBarnet (n 5).

[141] Newman (n 4).

[142] Baldwin (n 138).

[143] Ibid 245.

without drawing attention' to myself or arousing suspicion.[144] Participants commented that they did not feel a need to be on their best behaviour when they saw me conducting observations in court, which they acknowledged they would have felt if a stranger was present. I had a similar experience to Flood, who observed:

> Being active in the field as participant can mean that others identify one as belonging to a particular group ... My being so categorised meant that my situation was perceived as harmless and enabled me to observe things that I might not have been able to see if my position was different.[145]

Further, while the presence of a participant observer can result in reactive effects, several advocates (both prosecuting and defending) commented that, although my presence as observer was unusual, they paid little attention to me because I was already an 'insider' or 'on their team'. This meant that, as well as benefiting from my own knowledge of how courts work, I was able to observe usual, as opposed to moderated, courtroom behaviour. This point does, however, have to be balanced against the risk of over-identification with the research subjects. It is therefore important for researchers in my position to retain reflexivity about their role and recognise potential bias that the role entails.

Despite those potential pitfalls, some of my findings have been generated specifically as a result of my familiarity with the proceedings, particularly in chapter four. My position in the field meant that I was familiar with particular uses of language and procedures, which meant that I could recognise issues in the empirical data that may not be recognised by non-participant observers. This became most apparent as I was researching the ways that law is applied and adapted for use in magistrates' courts, where the hermeneutic tradition of entering into and understanding the culture, shared values and shared language became most obvious.[146]

I observed a total of 183 cases across the magistrates' courts that I visited. Guilty pleas were entered in 41 per cent of cases observed. Not guilty pleas were entered in 27 per cent of cases. No pleas were entered in 31 per cent of cases because, for example, the defendant did not attend, the case was listed for a pretrial administrative or procedural hearing, or because the hearing considered the seizure of property. In the remaining cases, mixed pleas were entered (different

---

[144] T Brannick and D Coghlan, 'In Defense of Being "Native": The Case for Insider Academic Research' (2007) 10(1) *Organizational Research Methods* 59–74, 69.

[145] J Flood, 'Socio-Legal Ethnography' in R Banakar and M Travers (eds), *Theory and Method in Socio-Legal Research* (Hart Publishing, 2005) 43.

[146] Brannick and Coghlan (n 144). I came across a similar issue in a later study, where it was decided with colleagues that I would interview more senior practitioners because my non-lawyer colleagues struggled to share the epistemic community and were concerned that they were not able to get the same depth of understanding and nuance that I could reach (Vogler et al (n 7)).

pleas were entered to separate charges on the same charge sheet or summons). The types of hearings observed were as follows:

Hearing type	Percentage of cases observed
Sentencing	37
Adjournments[147]	14
Case management	14
Trials	2
Defendant fails to attend; warrant issued	8
Breach of bail	3
Property seizure	2
Other[148]	20

As well as generating data in its own right, observation allowed the 19 interview responses to be contextualised within the interviewee's usual working environment. By combining observation and interviews, I was able to notice things which the interviewee may take for granted.

While this book is about access to justice through defendant participation in magistrates' courts, I decided not to interview defendants themselves, but rather to interview advocates who had experience of procedural change. I also drew inferences about the effects for defendants from the observation data. The reason for not interviewing defendants, aside from the fact that such interviews would have been both practically and ethically more difficult to manage, was that practitioners are able to make comparisons before and after reform and can identify the particular effects of specific interventions. Defendants, by contrast, are unlikely to be able to compare any experience that they might have had pre- and post-reform, particularly in relation to demands for efficiency. Nevertheless defendants' opinions would have the potential to add another dimension to our understanding of summary criminal justice.

To somewhat compensate for the lack of defendant voice, both prosecutors and defence lawyers were interviewed. Not only was it important to empirically explore the effects of those procedures as viewed by advocates on both sides of the adversarial process, but adding the voices of prosecutors introduced some perspectives that could either support or challenge the views of defence lawyers, thereby enabling a fuller picture of the process of summary justice to be

---

[147] The number of simple adjournments did not give the appearance of being particularly frequent despite the relatively high percentage of adjournments recorded. Adjournments tended to occur when the Probation Service required more time to prepare a Pre-Sentence Report because particular assessments needed to be made, such as suitability for accredited courses.

[148] This can include hearings regarding applications for further evidence or to move the trial and applications to vary bail.

obtained. As Kemp suggests, it is valuable to understand 'interactions between different legal agencies, particularly between prosecutors and defence solicitors, when they seek to deal with cases more efficiently and effectively in court'[149] so that the impact of a range of influences can be considered. Here, my role as practitioner appeared to offer a significant advantage. I do not doubt that the willingness of prosecutors to be interviewed resulted at least partly from my familiarity with the courts I was examining. Brannick and Coghlan, and Ross, recognise access as a significant benefit involved in insider research.[150]

While insider researchers do have to be wary of only seeking 'out informants who are most like them',[151] interviewing prosecutors went some way to counter that potential issue as I had (and have) never practised as a prosecutor. This meant that I was able to examine the issues from both adversarial perspectives rather than only my own professional standpoint. As Kemp notes, it is important that the effects of policy are understood, especially at a local level and on a 'whole system' basis.[152] Furthermore, I sampled every practising defence solicitor[153] and every prosecutor in the relevant area, hoping to achieve a broad range of opinion across the case study and avoid the pitfall of assuming that answers or perspectives were already known to me. The use of an identical semi-structured interview schedule for all interviews also allowed me to not only obtain comparable data, but to resist temptation to only follow up narratives that aligned with my own. The semi-structured nature of the interviews additionally retained the freedom to discuss each topic in broader terms. In order to avoid imposing my own views and experiences on interviewees, a degree of openness in question formulation was necessary to avoid 'pigeon-holing' participants' responses, and to limit interviewer bias while also encouraging me to address the same points with all participants.

I interviewed all of the prosecuting and defending advocates who responded positively to my enquiry. Due to the voluntary nature of participation, the data had the potential to be affected by self-selection bias. For example, the participants could have been drawn from a particularly politically motivated sub-section of the profession. Triangulating the interview data with courtroom observations, alongside interviewing both prosecutors and defence lawyers, minimised this risk. It is also noteworthy that most interviewees were candid

---

[149] Kemp (n 11) 15

[150] Brannick and Coghlan (n 144); L Ross, 'An account from the inside: Examining the emotional impact of qualitative research through the lens of "insider" research' (2017) 4(3) *Qualitative Psychology* 326–37.

[151] Brannick and Coghlan (n 144) 69.

[152] Kemp (n 11).

[153] I did, however, decide that I would not interview solicitors from my own firm as I felt that I was too familiar with the firm's procedures and client matters to be able to conduct an impartial interview. I also did not want to upset or encroach on designated hierarchical patterns in my office. In essence, I was too close to the material, and risked upsetting work roles too much, to be able to conduct an appropriate analysis of the data that would have been produced.

about the areas in which their businesses and practices were struggling, and how – for defence lawyers – that might negatively affect their clients.

Given that, as with most ethnographic case studies, I adopted a qualitative approach, I conducted a thematic analysis of the data[154] via 'recurring motifs in the text'.[155] One of the key benefits of interview research is its ability to provide insight into participants' perceptions, which may then feed into behaviour. However, it must also be remembered 'that all accounts from interview can only be understood in the context of the interview and any information given cannot be taken to mean the "truth"'[156] because they reflect self-reported post-incident behaviour, which may or may not match actual behaviour.[157] Again, that limitation is mitigated by combining the interview data with observation of actual behaviour, alongside analysis of studies (conducted by non-participant observers) which uncovered comparable data and reached similar conclusions. Where interviewees' accounts were consistent with other data, and with each other, we can infer that they paint a picture that nears authenticity.

As I had previously practised alongside all of the legal professionals that I interviewed, I shared some of the class and educational (though not necessarily gender or racialised) privileges that this status afforded me. On these points it is important to acknowledge my own role as practitioner-researcher/participant-observer. In some ways, this study was semi-autoethnographic. To me, the research on which this book is based sits at the intersection of insider research and autoethnography, but it would be disingenuous to avoid examining the part that my own practitioner role has played in shaping the work.

Ethnography involves researchers observing and participating in the community that is the subject of the research. Researchers are guided in their findings by iterative and interpretivist processes and often later connect their findings to other studies in the field.[158] As an insider approaching the field, it would be a fallacy to suggest that I was not informed by own experiences and beliefs. On some occasions, those beliefs were challenged by the research process, and on others the beliefs were affirmed. The example of the solicitor turning their back on their client in the dock described above was perhaps my first – but not only – experience of disconcert that I experienced during the research process. These experiences perhaps reflected my own process of moving from insider to outsider during the course of this work. This process was 'a journey

[154] B Lange, 'Researching Discourse and Behaviour as Elements of Law in Action' in R Banakar and M Travers (eds), *Theory and Method in Socio-Legal Research* (Hart Publishing, 2005) 194.

[155] Bryman (n 129) 554.

[156] S Bano, '"Standpoint", "Difference" and Feminist Research' in R Banakar and M Travers (eds), *Theory and Method in Socio-Legal Research* (Hart Publishing, 2005) 103.

[157] H Sommerlad, 'The implementation of quality initiatives and the new public management in the legal aid sector in England and Wales: bureaucratisation, stratification and surveillance' (1999) 6 *International Journal of the Legal Profession* 311.

[158] Brannick and Coghlan (n 144).

from nearness to distance'[159] though not back, as I then exited the profession, illustrating that my position as an insider was not static.[160]

Taking ethnography a step further, autoethnography 'uses personal experience ("auto") to describe and interpret ("graphy") cultural texts, experiences, beliefs, and practices ("ethno")'.[161] Autoethnographic research methods require clear reflexivity in their understanding of the ways in which 'personal experience is infused with political/cultural norms and expectations'.[162] Elements of this work, were, therefore, autoethnographic: I was a defence solicitor researching the magistrates' court workgroup in the geographical area where I was also professionally practising. My interpretation of the experiences and practices of the workgroup that I was analysing are likely to have influenced the research access, design and analysis. However, this work is not what has, rather pejoratively, been termed 'mesearch'.[163] While autoethnography places the researcher towards the centre of the research endeavour, to 'offer accounts of personal experience to complement, or fill gaps in, existing research',[164] The aim of this work was to ensure that my own experiences were not used to fill in gaps but to enrich understanding of the material analysed and to merely provide additional support for patterns identified. In this way, this book is not about my story, but my own story can add further insight in places. When working with the data, I was keen to avoid autobiographical elements in light of the risk of introducing too much bias. This was achieved by interviewing those on the opposite side to the adversarial process to myself (ie prosecutors) and by using the same semi structured interview schedule when speaking with all participants. As part of the process of deeper reflexivity required during writing, I introduced elements of the findings where I experienced dissonance with my own previous role, as well as areas that resonated with my own experience. So, while autoethnographic work requires 'working at the intersections of *auto*biography and *ethnography*',[165] the aim of this work is skewed more towards the role of an insider ethnographer, than an autoethnographer.

While '[t]raditionalists view the inclusion of a subjective, personal view as a contaminant, spoiling an otherwise pure piece of research',[166] both insider ethnography and autoethnography are required to illustrate how researcher perspective informs and develops research processes, rather than trying to

---

[159] Brannick and Coghlan (n 144) 66.

[160] Ross (n 150).

[161] T Adams, C Ellis and S Holman Jones, 'Autoethnography' in J Matthes, C Davis and R Potter (eds), *The International Encyclopaedia of Communication Research Methods* (John Wiley and Sons, 2017) 1.

[162] Ibid.

[163] E Campbell, '"Apparently Being a Self-Obsessed C**t Is Now Academically Lauded": Experiencing Twitter Trolling of Autoethnographers' (2017) 18(3) *Qualitative Social Research* 16.

[164] Adams et al (n 161) 3.

[165] Adams et al (n 161) 2.

[166] Campbell (n 163) 10.

perpetuate a narrative that suggests true objectivity is possible.[167] As such, this work adopts a subjectivist view that 'denies the possibility of theory-neutral language'.[168] All research – and particularly qualitative research – occurs within prescribed social, economic and political considerations. It is through those conditions that thick narrative develops, from which narratives which are not fixed nor only understood in isolation develop. Recognising these aspects of (insider) research has the power to make it less remote and more relatable through depth of understanding and insight that outside researchers might not be privy to.[169] As Brannick and Coghlan say, '[c]omplete memberships have an opportunity to acquire understanding in use rather than reconstituted understanding'.[170] This illustrates that, while insider knowledge cannot be taken to be 'more truthful or more accurate' than outsider knowledge,[171] it can produce a rich story with detailed depth and nuance.

As an established member of the magistrates' court workgroup that I was later researching, I did see myself as a complete member of the organisational system and community about which I was conducting research, yet I was becoming outside through the planned and formalised nature of the research process, as well as through my own employment transition from practitioner to academic.[172] While that perspective distinguishes this work from others – including Ward,[173] Newman,[174] and Carlen[175] – who have conducted research on court processes by temporarily joining 'the organisation for the purposes and duration of the research',[176] it also requires honesty about the assumptions that I made. Undoubtedly I hoped to find advocates acting with the utmost integrity to defend their clients and uphold both the law and due process provisions. This was the most obvious type of role conflict that I encountered when I found myself 'caught between loyalty tugs, behavioural claims, and identification dilemmas'.[177] That conflict required me to activate reflexivity through deep engagement with other studies in the field and trace patterns that I could identify. I was also acutely aware of the ways that defence advocates feel that professional decision-making has been constrained by rules of criminal procedure that have been introduced in the early twenty-first century. No doubt I felt somewhat protective towards my colleagues, who, in fairness, acknowledged that

---

[167] Adams et al (n 161).
[168] Brannick and Coghlan (n 144) 62.
[169] Campbell (n 163).
[170] Brannick and Coghlan (n 144) 66.
[171] Adams et al (n 161) 3.
[172] See generally Brannick and Coghlan (n 144); P Adler and P Adler, *Membership roles in field research* (Sage, 1987).
[173] Ward (n 4).
[174] Newman (n 4).
[175] Carlen (n 5).
[176] Brannick and Coghlan (n 144) 59.
[177] Brannick and Coghlan (n 144) 70.

patterns of behaviour sometimes operate to the detriment of their clients' best interests. This depth of understanding allowed me to authentically 'articulate tacit knowledge that has become deeply segmented because of socialisation in an organisational system and reframe it as theoretical knowledge'.[178] The process was both intellectually exciting and motivated me to continue the endeavour of seeking to influence the field.

Some of the comments made during the interviews, such as 'You're obviously aware of the system we have here' (defence solicitor C), betrayed the fact that I was seen as someone who would be able to understand whatever concerns were raised because I understood what occupied participants' minds. While I found this position awkward on occasions, I also appreciated the participant's apparent views that I was someone who would share genuine concerns about the system through my own experiences rather than as a passive but interested third party. Although the research involved matters of professional perception rather than personal experience, legal aid lawyers do share what Cooke refers to as a shared orientation which includes a sense of personal satisfaction derived from their work.[179] Consequently, expressions of empathy were expedient to build rapport,[180] especially in the context of public media vilification of criminal defence lawyers as 'fat cats'.[181] As a result, my insider role allowed me to obtain rich and detailed data with relative speed and ease.

VII. STRUCTURE OF THE BOOK

Each of the chapters in this book seeks to develop the normative framework (about defendant participation) around which the empirical research (the case study) was conducted. To this end, we continue, in chapter two, with a detailed examination of the political context in which summary criminal justice operates through a particular focus on changes to publicly funded criminal defence services. The early development of criminal legal aid is charted before considering how neoliberal approaches to legal aid have demanded ever-greater efficiency at reduced cost. A flawed belief in the value of market-based approaches has led to a system of publicly funded representation which is fragile, reduces the number of people able to access legally aided representation and has had a

---

[178] Ibid 60.

[179] E Cooke, 'The Changing Occupational Terrain of the Legal Aid Lawyer in Times of Precariousness' (.PhD thesis, University of Kent, 2019).

[180] Ross (n 150).

[181] See J Slack and J Doyle, 'Legal aid payouts to fat cat lawyers will be slashed by a third, says Justice Secretary' *The Daily Mail* (London, 10 April 2013); D Wooding, 'Fat-cat lawyers raking in £3 million per trial for defending suspects in rape, terror murder and fraud cases' *The Sun* (London, 1 January 2017). More recently, see J Ames, 'Tony Blair was wrong to brand lawyers fat cats, says ally' *The Times* (London, 3 June 2019).

detrimental effect on the quality of representation that defendants are able to access. Consequently, the meaning of defendant participation has been lost in political concerns around cost and efficiency.

Having set out some of the political issues that permeate criminal justice and the way it is experienced by the parties, chapter three examines the cultural practices of magistrates' courts within the literature and as demonstrated through my research. In this chapter, the findings of studies that demonstrate how defendants were marginalised at a time when only a small number of defendants were legally represented are considered, then compared to more recent studies which consider the nature of the courtroom workgroup culture, particularly given the increasingly professionalised nature of magistrates' court proceedings. Practices which marginalised defendants in the 1970s persist today, and there are two factors which exacerbate such marginalisation; the court's desire to conduct cases at speed and the strength of the professional networks that operate in magistrates' courts. These factors operate to increase the defendant's inability to play an active role in the proceedings. At this point, the strength of the organisational culture becomes apparent, and we can begin to reflect on how those issues affect upon the level of marginalisation generally experienced by defendants. High degrees of co-operation exhibited by members of the workgroup allowed efficiency drives to become ingrained in the culture of the workgroup and these processes have exacerbated the inability of defendants to participate while maintaining the relative stability of the local workgroup.

Once the politicised and cultural aspects of summary justice have been examined, we turn, in chapter four, to considering the role of law in magistrates' courts. It has previously been suggested that magistrates' courts operate without much resort to legal provisions.[182] Instead, I found that the law permeates summary criminal proceedings but is used in routinised ways and referred to in implicit terms so that the frequent references to law made by court personnel would be difficult for a non-participant to identify. Neoliberal-styled policies and legislation designed to improve efficiency at reduced cost have increased the legalisation of proceedings while the courtroom workgroup culture has adapted to such provisions and made them part of the routine business of summary criminal proceedings. As such, both factors have a role in intensifying the inability of defendants to effectively participate in the proceedings.

Chapter five examines the effect of changes to legal aid provision on the construction of relationships in magistrates' courts. Restrictions in the availability of legally aided representation and the bureaucratic nature of the application process have strained relationships between court workgroup personnel and defendants. That strain results from solicitors being more prone to risk-taking behaviour in terms of whether or not they will be paid for work conducted,

---

[182] Darbyshire (n 88).

which affects the level and quality of representation that defendants receive. Further, solicitors appear to feel somewhat aggrieved that low remuneration rates combined with the court's desire to act efficiently may mean that they are forced into decision making at what they consider to be a premature stage in the proceedings. The bureaucratic nature of the legal aid application process both causes delay and excludes defendants from participation in the proceedings at an early stage.

On the basis of the above analysis, the conclusion posits that the inability of defendants to effectively participate in summary criminal proceedings has intensified as neoliberal styled techniques of governance became politically popular. As governments have, in recent decades, made ever more urgent demands for greater efficiency in the criminal justice system, the culture of summary justice has adapted to political intervention in such a way that defendants are further marginalised from the proceedings. Workgroup culture has always had the effect of casting defendants as dummy players,[183] but managerial demands for efficiency, the increased legalisation of proceedings and changes to criminal legal aid introduced by governments that have adopted broad tenets of neoliberal ideology have all intensified that marginalisation. Initiatives to save money and increase efficiency have been absorbed into the day-to-day practices of summary criminal proceedings.

If we are to improve the process of participation in summary justice to increase its legitimacy, there is a need for greater recognition and understanding of the role that defendants play in summary criminal courts. That need will not be fulfilled by increasing the availability and funding of legal aid alone. A shift in the working practices and culture of summary justice *and* greater access to properly funded defence services is necessary to improve access to justice through defendant participation.

---

[183] In 1976, Carlen described defendants as 'dummy players' in summary criminal courts to highlight the way in which defendants are unable to leave the 'game' which is the court process but, at the same time, are unable to actively exercise a role in procedures because they lack the skills necessary to fully engage with the nuances of the proceedings (Carlen (n 5)).

2

Politics, Legal Aid and Access to Justice

I. INTRODUCTION

THIS CHAPTER FOCUSES on one aspect of access to justice by examining the provision of publicly funded representation in summary criminal cases. It also looks at how this form of access to justice has changed as governmental strategies towards criminal justice altered – particularly since the early 1980s. The chapter aims to conduct a detailed interrogation of the effects of shifts in government strategy on criminal justice through the analysis of the expansions and contractions in legal aid policy.[1]

Many states recognise that access to a lawyer in criminal cases is part of the right to a fair trial, and lawyers should be provided at state expense where a suspect or defendant is unable to pay for one themselves. For signatory Member States – including the UK – that right is enshrined in Article 6(3)(c) of the European Convention on Human Rights (ECHR). This is significant because the UK was not only involved in drafting the ECHR but was also one of the first signatories to it in 1951. Consequently, although the UK did not recognise direct access to the European Court of Human Rights until 1998,[2] the English and Welsh legal system has long recognised and acknowledged the importance of access to legal advice in criminal cases (subject to a means and merits test). Yet, as we shall see, governments took an inconsistent approach to enabling people to activate their right to legal advice, culminating in reduced numbers of people being able to seek the legal advice they are entitled to receive.[3]

Tracking and interrogating the provision of publicly funded representation can highlight contradictions between the rhetoric and practice of different forms

---

[1] The concepts of 'state' and 'governance' are complex and contested, but this chapter analyses governments' approaches to legal aid policy in criminal proceedings according to broadly prevailing political ideas at particular times. As such, the term 'state' is used interchangeably with the term 'governance' when discussing the policy directions taken by governments at various times. See generally B Jessop, *The State: Past, Present, Future* (Polity, 2015).

[2] Direct access to the ECtHR was enabled following the enactment of the Human Rights Act 1998.

[3] The Law Society. 'Fix the broken system' (2019) www.lawsociety.org.uk/campaigns/criminal-justice.

of governance (including through rights) in relation to criminal justice. Indeed, Sokhi-Bulley highlights how rights have become technologies of governance that are privileges 'afforded only to those who are visible within our societies because they are responsible', deserving citizens.[4] Wacquant[5] and Garland[6] have both highlighted the increased demonisation of defendants, through which they have been categorised as undeserving of state assistance. As such, their right to a fair trial and due process of law are devalued. That prevailing ideology makes it publicly and politically difficult to contest policies that undermine defendants' rights to (free) representation. As such, a close examination of legal aid policy is a vehicle for identifying broader trends in criminal justice policy and access to justice for defendants.

The chapter begins by setting out the dominant political values that appear to have influenced policymakers in the development of legal aid in criminal cases. The modern liberal origins of legal aid and its development during different political phases are then examined to set the scene for future discussion. The pace of change seems to have accelerated since the 1970s, as different governments – who have each emphasised different aspects of neoliberal philosophy – became more distrustful of lawyers' behaviour. At the same time, those governments have required lawyers' assistance to ensure that the process of summary criminal justice is efficient. The drive for efficiency, which began with the 1979 Conservative government, and continued with the New Labour government of 1997–2010, was later also mobilised as another element of austerity measures by Coalition and Conservative governments of the 2010s. The measures introduced have been designed to regulate advocates' behaviour and control cost but have resulted in a fragile system of publicly funded representation that is unlikely to withstand rapid reform. These issues highlight the discord between political values and principles of adversarial justice and reflect a chronological shift (further) away from due process to crime control models of criminal procedure (chapter one). As that shift intensifies, the ability of defendants to actively participate in the process diminishes.

Before we begin tracking fluctuations in provisions relating to criminal legal aid, it is important first to understand the key principles of the criminal legal aid system in magistrates' courts. While I do not specifically address legal aid in relation to Crown and higher court cases, some general principles may be transferable.

---

[4] B Sokhi-Bulley. *Governing (Through) Rights* (Hart Publishing, 2016), 4.

[5] L Wacquant, *Punishing the Poor. The Neoliberal Government of Social Insecurity* (Duke University Press, 2009).

[6] D Garland, *The Culture of Control: Crime and Social Order in Contemporary Society* (University of Chicago Press, 2002).

II. THE MECHANICS OF LEGAL AID

The scope of legal aid availability, the procedures for granting and later claiming payment for legally aided work, and payment rates all are managed by the Ministry of Justice's Legal Aid Agency (LAA). This means that the legal aid system provides a prime example of how influential government policy can be in relation to determinations about access to justice. Before moving onto the analysis that follows, it is important to know how the funding system in magistrates' courts operates.

Broadly speaking, there are two types of legally aided representation available to defendants in magistrates' courts; advice, assistance and advocacy under a Representation Order granted by the LAA and one-off representation under the Duty Solicitor at Court scheme. The Duty Solicitor is available to anyone who has been held in police custody to appear in court or defendants charged with an imprisonable offence but only for a single hearing (excluding trials). In all cases, applications for legal aid are submitted electronically to LAA administration centres, which is a branch of the Ministry of Justice. The application must be submitted along with numerous documents (wage slips, records of previous convictions, charge sheets, bank statements and, for self-employed applicants, full tax returns and accounts).

Applicants must pass both a merits test and a means test to obtain legally aided representation. The merits test considers the interests of justice, and the criteria are broadly based either on the risk of loss of liberty or livelihood, case complexity or the inability of defendants to follow the proceedings properly.[7] The administration of the test shifted first from court legal advisers to non-legally qualified court support staff, then from court administration staff to administrators at the LAA amid the executive's concerns that court legal advisers were too often persuaded to grant legal aid so that they would be relieved of some of their duties towards unrepresented defendants.[8] The removal of legal adviser discretion in granting legal aid was only one of a number of measures designed to reduce legal aid expenditure, which are discussed further throughout this chapter.

---

[7] The full criteria, found in s17 LASPO are: whether the individual, if convicted, would be likely to lose their liberty or livelihood, or suffer serious damage to their reputation; whether consideration of a substantial question of law is involved; whether the individual may be unable to understand the proceedings or to state their own case; whether the proceedings may involve the tracing, interviewing or expert cross-examination of witnesses on behalf of the individual; and whether it is in the interests of another person that the individual be represented.
Under s 17(3), the Lord Chancellor is empowered to add or vary a criterion. These criteria have been developed from the tests recommended by the Widgery Committee in 1966 (Home Office, *Report of the Departmental Committee on Legal aid in Criminal Proceedings* (Cmnd 2934, 1966)).
[8] R Young, 'Will Widgery Do? Court Clerks, Discretion and the Determination of Legal Aid Applications' in R Young and D Wall (eds), *Access to Criminal Justice: Legal Aid, Lawyers and the Defence of Liberty* (Blackstone Press, 1996).

To qualify for legally aided representation in the magistrates' court under the means test, a defendant must not have an annual disposable income in excess of £3,398. The threshold eligibility for the means test has not been reviewed in line with inflation since 2010, although a review was ongoing at the time of writing in early 2021.[9] By that time, the lack of review meant that 'the means testing of legal aid is set at a level that can require people on low incomes it make contributions to legal costs that they could not afford while maintaining a socially acceptable standard of living'.[10] In at *least* 20 per cent of magistrates' court cases observed by Campbell, 'the defendant was impoverished, if not destitute'.[11]

When legal aid is granted, lawyers are paid a standard fee for their services by the government. The fees are paid on a per case basis according to specific case categories. Broadly, category one fees cover guilty pleas, uncontested breaches of probation orders and discontinued cases. Category two fees cover trials, cases that are fully prepared to trial but either the defendant pleads guilty or the case is discontinued, contested breaches of probation orders and cases in which mixed pleas (ie a guilty plea to one charge and a not guilty plea to another) are entered. Category three fees deal with committals to the Crown Court that are discontinued. The categories are further subdivided into lower, higher and non-standard fee claims based on the amount of work done. A non-standard 'escape' fee (when lawyers are paid on an hourly basis) is available if the time spent on case preparation crosses a fee threshold.[12]

III. WHICH POLITICAL VALUES SHAPE ACCESS TO CRIMINAL JUSTICE?

The existence of publicly funded representation is an important component of an adversarial system. Such representation exists to ensure equality of arms, to ensure that the presence of defence lawyers protects both the accused and the system from (the appearance of) state abuse of power and to legitimate punishment.[13] In other words, and important in the context of this book, the provision of legally aided representation is designed to allow for 'a parity of

---

[9] The Law Society 'Legal Aid Means Test Review Restarted' (19 October 2020), www.lawsociety.org.uk/en/topics/legal-aid/legal-aid-means-test-review-re-started.

[10] D Hirsch, 'Report on the Affordability of Legal Proceedings for Those who are Excluded from Eligibility for Criminal Legal Aid under the Means Regulations, and for Those Required to Pay a Contribution Towards their Legal Costs' (Loughborough University, 2018).

[11] J Campbell, *Entanglements of Life with the Law: Precarity and Justice in London's Magistrates Courts* (Cambridge Scholars Publishing, 2020) 7.

[12] See also L Welsh, 'The Effects of Changes to Legal Aid on Lawyers' Professional Identity and Behaviour in Summary Criminal Cases: A Case Study' (2017) 44(4) *Journal of Law and Society* 559–85.

[13] F Regan, 'Criminal Legal Aid: Does Defending Liberty Undermine Citizenship?' in R Young and D Wall (eds), *Access to Criminal Justice: Legal Aid, Lawyers and the Defence of Liberty* (Blackstone Press 1996).

participation', even if that participation is by proxy.[14] As such, a state which values the due process and access to justice principles discussed in chapter one should support access to representation in order to provide at least some legitimacy to state instigated (and funded) processes of prosecution because the adversarial nature of the process assumes that the two sides will have access to approximately equal resources to conduct their cases.[15] If defendants are marginalised from participation in the process because they do not understand the proceedings, the defendant appears to be unjustly treated by state authorities and the legitimacy of state-imposed punishment becomes questionable. As Tyler noted, defendants themselves are more likely to comply with sanctions imposed by criminal courts if they consider the procedure to be fair in principle.[16]

The provision of legally aided representation to those who would otherwise be unable to participate in the proceedings meaningfully is, therefore, an important part of state provision of services in a society which values civil liberties. Policymakers who favour due process principles would also favour the provision of legal representatives to maintain procedural safeguards in an attempt to ensure that justice is achieved. Analysing whether the realities of criminal justice allow justice to be achieved enhances our understanding of how rules of procedure are 'functional to criminal law's role as a system of regulation'.[17]

The post-World War II British state was characterised by a welfarist ideology that capitalised on sentiments of collective social responsibility promoted during the war.[18] Under the welfarist approach to post-war government, social rights were delivered through agencies of the state, such as the National Health Service and state-funded education. There was some recognition that social structural forces might fail some individuals rather than failure being a product of individual inadequacy because, Rose argued, other approaches had failed to cure the social problems caused by industrialisation, such as class division and uncertainty over social responsibilities.[19] Historically, the UK has a 'tradition of managing marginalised populations and the use of the welfare state and welfare

---

[14] H Sommerlad, 'Some Reflections on the Relationship between Citizenship, Access to Justice, and the Reform of Legal Aid' (2004) 31(3) *Journal of Law and Society* 345, 348.

[15] R Young and D Wall, 'Criminal Justice, Legal Aid and the Defence of Liberty' in R Young and D Wall (eds), *Access to Criminal Justice: Legal Aid, Lawyers and the Defence of Liberty* (Blackstone Press 1996).

[16] See especially T Tyler 'What is Procedural Justice? Criteria Used by Citizens to Assess the Fairness of Legal Procedures' (1988) 22(1) *Law and Society Review* 103; T Tyler, 'Procedural Justice, Legitimacy, and the Effective Rule of Law' (2003) 30 *Crime and Justice* 283–357. Hunter et al have identified four key elements of procedural justice as: allowing opportunities for parties to participate or express views; transparent, principled decisions; treating people with dignity; and trust generated by listening and explaining (R Hunter et al 'Judging in lower courts: Conventional, procedural, therapeutic and feminist approaches' (2016) 12(3) *International Journal of Law in Context* 337–360)'.

[17] N Lacey, *In Search of Criminal Responsibility* (Oxford University Press 2016) 14.

[18] R Lowe, *The Welfare State in Britain Since 1945* (Macmillan, 1999).

[19] N Rose, 'Governing "Advanced" Liberal Democracies' in A Barry, T Osborne and N Rose (eds), *Foucault and Political Reason. Liberalism, Neo-liberalism and Rationalities of Government* (UCL Press, 1996).

sanctions to reform the behaviour of problematised populations',[20] including those deemed criminals.[21] However, the economist Keynes believed the role of the welfare state 'was not only a moral duty but an economic remedy',[22] which would ensure that everyone had an equal opportunity to participate in the market and thereby promote overall economic growth.

The Keynesian economic theory took hold in the post-war British state, and its legacy remains influential in society today. The basic rationale was that by improving life chances via structural intervention such as improved access to education and healthcare, more people would be able to contribute usefully to society, and, consequently, the well-being of society as a whole would improve.[23] Under welfarist techniques of governance, social security could be enhanced and the risk of deviant behaviour could be reduced via state intervention in social domains such as education, health and employment. Governments operating under this model tended to view specialist professionals favourably because it was assumed that expert knowledge could assist in structural reform and social stability, as well as protect individuals from institutionalism.[24] These approaches were not universally accepted as advocates of minimal state intervention – often from the (neo)liberal school of thought – were concerned that the welfare state would stifle both economic freedom and economic efficiency.[25]

Although there was debate about the exact form that welfare states should take, post-war governments generally considered it appropriate for state agencies to provide at least minimum levels of support for those who needed assistance in their socio-economic lives. That approach was bolstered by the growing recognition that social problems 'were not necessarily the fault of the individual who experienced them'.[26] Legal aid developed as part of those principles via the Legal Aid and Advice Act 1949. As part of the post-war consensus that dominated British politics for several years from 1945, Rutherford argued that the path of the British criminal process indicated broad agreement among the main political parties, which meant that criminal justice issues tended to be politically non-contentious.[27]

---

[20] J Flint and C Hunter 'Governing by civil order: towards new frameworks of support, coercion and sanction?' in H Quirk, T Seddon and G Smith, *Regulation and Criminal Justice* (Cambridge University Press, 2011) 192.

[21] For further discussion, see L Welsh, L Skinns and A Sanders, *Criminal Justice* 5th edn (Oxford University Press 2021), ch 10.

[22] J Donzelot, 'Pleasure in Work' in Graham Burchell, Colin Gordon and Peter Miller (eds), *The Foucault Effect: Studies in Governmentality* (Harvester Wheatsheaf, 1991) 261.

[23] J Dean, *Democracy and Other Neoliberal Fantasies* (Duke University Press, 2009).

[24] T Marshall, *Social Policy in the Twentieth Century* (Hutchinson and Co, 1975). This view of professionals was not unanimously agreed (below).

[25] See, eg, N Barry, 'Conservative Thought and the Welfare State' (1997) 45 *Political Studies* 331–45.

[26] J Stewart 'The Mixed Economy of Welfare in Historical Context' in Martin Powell (ed), *Understanding the Mixed Economy of Welfare* (Policy Press, 2007), 31.

[27] A Rutherford, *Transforming Criminal Policy* (Waterside Press, 1996).

However, as high crime rates became 'a normal social fact' in the 1970s, the structural rehabilitative stance taken by leftist politics was seen as failing to prevent crime.[28] This, coupled with rising unemployment resulting from the financial crisis and intra-party political discord, led to greater polarisation of viewpoints among party members.[29] At this time, a political shift in favour of crime control policies, which have tended to be outcome and efficiency-focused, can be seen. This paved the way, from the 1980s, for both major political parties to seek public popularity via ideas of increasing punitive populism.[30] There have been two significant consequences for criminal cases in England and Wales that are inextricably linked and run almost parallel to each other in terms of development. There are, however, particular moments of interfusion, which are highlighted below.

First, the Thatcher government of the 1980s promoted a market-based ethos of individualisation and responsibilisation. Deregulation (ie rolling back state intervention in public services) is one key feature of neoliberal ideology, which, despite receiving some support before the 1970s, had not really taken hold in the UK until Margaret Thatcher was elected.[31] These policies justified reductions in welfare provision and restrictions on state assistance for 'undeserving' citizens (including suspects and defendants), a group sometimes referred to as 'the precariat'.[32] The precariat

> consists of a multitude of insecure people, living bits-and-pieces lives, in and out of short term jobs without a narrative of occupational development ... they have a more restricted range of social, cultural, political and economic rights than citizens around them.[33]

Racialised and gendered policies and practices also exacerbate problems experienced by insecure and socio-economically disadvantaged populations.[34] Precariat groups, despite suffering unstable incomes and lost citizenship rights,[35] were no longer seen 'as fellow "welfare citizens" with legitimate needs',[36] which made it easier to implement policies that undermined the rights of insecure groups.

---

[28] Garland (n 6) 348.

[29] See generally K Morgan, 'Britain in the Seventies – Our Unfinest Hour?' (2017) *Revue Française de Civilisation Britannique XXII- Hors série*; B Jessop, *The Future of the Capitalist State* (Wiley, 2002).

[30] G Hughes, E McLaughlin and J Muncie, *Crime Prevention and Community Safety. New Directions* (Sage, 2002).

[31] See generally S Clarke, *Social Work and Community Development* (Ashgate, 2017).

[32] Wacquant (n 5).

[33] G Standing, 'The Precariat – The New Dangerous Class' (Policy Network Essay, 2011) eprints. soas.ac.uk/15711/1/Policy%20Network%20article,%2024.5.11.pdf 3. See especially G Standing, *The Precariat: The New Dangerous Class* (Bloomsbury, 2011). See also M Johnson (ed), *Precariat: Labour, Work and Politics* (Routledge, 2016).

[34] Welsh et al (n 21).

[35] Campbell (n 11).

[36] J Lea and S Hallsworth, 'Bringing the State Back In: Understanding Neoliberal Security' in P Squires and J Lea (eds), *Criminalisation and Advanced Marginality. Critically Exploring the Work of Loïc Wacquant* (Policy Press, 2012) 21.

When New Labour was elected in 1997, its governmental approach – the 'Third Way' – was influenced by developments in globalisation, a continuation of the view that post-war social democracy was no longer viable and the idea that people must accept their responsibilities as members of a community.[37]

Second, Thatcher's government promoted discourse that presented publicly funded services as costly and ineffective.[38] Aspects of the Third Way continued themes developed by the more radically neoliberal preceding Conservative governments, particularly in seeking alternatives to state provisions of services. The Thatcherite view that there is no alternative to the market continued (and continues) in many aspects of public services, despite the fact that many aspects of the welfare state remain publicly funded. As if to mitigate the contradiction, the policies adopted by New Labour infused public services with business principles. This was achieved through re-regulating areas of socio-economic life that remained under state control (chapter one). Broadly, New Labour developed a culture of audit in criminal justice policy which placed the demands of efficiency and case management above the needs of defendants.[39] This move prioritised economy and efficiency over traditional adversarial principles so that debates about the meaning of access to justice have been lost in concerns about efficiency and – later – in austerity measures initiated by more recent governmental policies. Sommerlad demonstrated that governments' preference for decentralisation, privatisation, performance contracts in public services and output measurements[40] have led to the exclusion of marginalised welfare citizens from debates about citizenship. At the same time, demands for efficiency, value for money and quality have neglected to consider the complex issues surrounding access to justice.[41] As such, the principles underlying the question of access to justice are obscured and converted into issues revolving around concerns about cost and efficiency.[42] A detailed examination of legal aid funding can, therefore, demonstrate some of the tensions at the heart of modern politics in relation to criminal justice; how can policies that favour market-based, competitive practices also promote legitimacy through the delivery of publicly funded services to which people are entitled?

---

[37] S Driver and L Martell, 'Left, Right and the Third Way' (2000) 28(2) *Policy & Politics* 147–61.

[38] M Drakeford, 'Private Welfare' in Martin Powell (ed), *Understanding the Mixed Economy of Welfare* (Policy Press 2007).

[39] See generally H Sommerlad, 'Criminal Legal Aid Reforms and the Restructuring of Legal Professionalism' in R Young and D Wall (eds), *Access to Criminal Legal Aid: Legal Aid, Lawyers and the Defence of Liberty* (Blackstone Press, 1996); E Cape, 'Rebalancing the Criminal Justice Process: Ethical Challenges for Criminal Defence Lawyers' (2006) 9(1) *Legal Ethics* 56. The nature and impact of these efficiency drives are discussed more fully in ch 3.

[40] These are features of an ideology often referred to as New Public Management, though the exact features of this ideology have often been debated. See generally C Hood, 'A Public Management for all Seasons?' (1991) 69(1) *Public Administration* 3–19; C Pollitt and G Bouckaert, *Public Management Reform: A Comparative Analysis* (Oxford University Press 2000).

[41] H Sommerlad 'Reflections on the Reconfiguration of Access to Justice' (2008) 15(3) *International Journal of the Legal Profession* 179–93.

[42] Ibid.

In order to properly contextualise these trends, it is necessary to analyse the origins of legal aid and political reactions throughout its development. When analysed in this way, the examination of legal aid policy is useful to help us identify policy trajectories in relation to criminal justice policy more generally and their impact on the position of defendants in proceedings. The analysis begins by considering the origins of legally aided representation from the early twentieth century.

IV. THE DEVELOPMENT OF LEGAL AID POLICY

During the nineteenth century, as the UK slowly became a more democratic political culture, the criminal justice system faced problems achieving legitimacy.[43] At the same time, and as criminal trials became increasingly professionalised (chapter four) in light of urbanisation, lawyers and campaign groups began to argue 'that unrepresented defendants damaged the image of English justice'.[44] As a result of campaigns, the Poor Prisoners' Advice Act 1903 made provisions for the first paid legal aid scheme. Although opposition to the Bill would have been difficult to sustain in principle, the government 'worried that more representation would encourage defendants to contest trials ... trials would become longer and more expensive'[45] and so access to free legal advice was conditional upon accused people indicating the nature of their defence. In this way, defendants have always had to prove, in some way, that they are deserving of access to free legal advice. Suggestions that magistrates should advise defendants about the availability of legal aid resulted in protest, even among the Bill's supporters.[46] This reaction illustrates the tension that continues to exist in terms of the state's desire to both present the criminal justice process as legitimate and its desire to control expenditure. Arguably, as a result of that tension, and despite protest by campaign groups, the government took a 'highly complacent'[47] approach to the provision of legally aided representation in criminal cases.

A campaign led by the Howard League for Penal Reform resulted in the reluctant passing of the Poor Prisoners' Defence Act 1930.[48] The availability of legal aid was expanded via the introduction of an early 'interests of justice' test, which allowed magistrates discretion in determining whether an

---

[43] Lacey (n 17).
[44] T Goriely, 'The Development of Criminal Legal Aid in England and Wales' in R Young and D Wall (eds), *Access to Criminal Justice: Legal Aid, Lawyers and the Defence of Liberty* (Blackstone Press 1996) 34.
[45] Ibid, 35.
[46] Ibid.
[47] Ibid, 38.
[48] Ibid.

individual should, in exceptional circumstances, be represented at local public expense in magistrates' court cases.[49] The government failed to monitor or coordinate how the scheme operated, and magistrates often remained reluctant to grant legal aid.[50] Hynes and Robins noted that only 327 of the 19,079 people that magistrates sent to prison in 1938 had benefited from legally aided representation.[51] Goriely described government attitudes to legal aid at this time as 'at best begrudging, and sometimes overtly hostile'.[52]

Legal aid development slowed until the late 1940s when the Report of the Committee on Legal Aid and Legal Advice in England and Wales (1945) (the Report) was published. The suggestions contained in the Report were supported by welfarist approaches to government that prioritised social inclusion over cost in the belief that social cohesion would assist long-term economic and social stability.[53] Its objectives included that legal aid should be available to people of small or moderate means, that contributions should be payable and a merits test should be applied and judged by legal practitioners, who should receive adequate remuneration for conducting legally aided work.[54] Legal aid was, however, a low priority in comparison to other welfare reforms (such as the NHS) and the Legal Aid and Advice Act (which implemented many of the Report's recommendations) was not passed until 1949. At this time, as Sommerlad noted, 'the establishment of legal aid represented the beginning of a new stage in the relationship between law and society and was thus fundamental to the development of an inclusionary form of citizenship',[55] designed to enable greater levels of participation in the justice system.

So far as criminal legal aid was concerned, the Report proposed that the exceptional circumstances provisions imposed under previous legislation should be removed in order to encourage magistrates to grant legal aid where the interests of justice so required and that any doubt should be exercised in favour of the defendant. The recommendations also included that fixed payment fees should be abolished and costs should be borne nationally rather than by local councils,[56] advocating the development of a 'judicare model' through which private firms are contracted to provide services by the state.[57] Several of the

[49] Department for Constitutional Affairs, *A Fairer Deal for Legal Aid* (Cm 6591, 2005).
[50] Goriely (n 44).
[51] S Hynes and J Robins, *The Justice Gap. Whatever Happened to Legal Aid?* (Legal Action Group, 2009).
[52] Goriely (n 44) 41.
[53] R Smith, 'Proposals for the Reform of Legal Aid in England and Wales. Response' (JUSTICE, February 2011).
[54] Legal Action Group, 'A Strategy for Justice: Publicly Funded Legal Services in the 1990s' (Legal Action Group, 1992).
[55] Sommerlad (n 14) 348.
[56] Goriely (n 44).
[57] See also T Smith and E Johnston, 'Marketisation and Competition in Criminal Legal Aid: Implications for Access to Justice' in K Albertson, M Corcoran and J Phillips (eds), *Marketisation and Privatisation in Criminal Justice* (Policy Press, 2020).

Report's recommendations were very gradually adopted by parliament in subsequent years. However, by 1950 there remained 'no acceptance … that lawyers were needed in summary courts, where the number of certificates was only 0.3 per cent of all those dealt with'[58] and, until the 1960s, defence advocates were paid by way of a fixed fee drawn from local taxes.

During this period, 'the courts and government were agreed that legal aid was a dangerous innovation which was bound to lead to more contested cases'.[59] As such, despite various parliamentary reports suggesting legal aid expansion, governments remained concerned about relaxing the criteria which must be met to obtain publicly funded representation. Thus, the tension between cost and efficiency as against due process and defendant rights remained evident, even during periods in which welfarist political philosophy prevailed. This highlights tensions between crime control-oriented political policy (cost and efficiency) and principles of due process adversarial justice systems (representation and opportunity to participate).

V. EXPANDING THE PROVISION OF LEGALLY AIDED REPRESENTATION

In 1959, the remit of legally aided representation in criminal cases was expanded to include allowance for freestanding advice and assistance, rather than only representation at court proceedings.[60] In 1963, the 'exceptional circumstances' requirement in summary proceedings was removed.[61] In 1966, a committee chaired by Lord Widgery produced a report on legal aid in criminal proceedings ('the Widgery report') with the aim of reviewing the entirety of legal aid provision in criminal cases. While the Widgery report concluded that the legal aid system worked adequately, it also provided guidance to magistrates about when the interests of justice test would be satisfied. Those criteria have been most recently repeated, with minor amendment, in section 17 Legal Aid, Sentencing and Punishment of Offenders Act 2012 (LASPO).[62] These developments provide an example of a phase during which the criminal justice process was becoming increasingly aligned with 'welfarist aspirations'.[63] The Widgery report sought to persuade the government to take a broad approach to publicly funded representation, but, six months after its publication, the government had failed to give any indication of how it proposed to deal with its recommendations.[64]

---

[58] Ibid, 43.
[59] Young and Wall (n 15) 4.
[60] Goriely (n 44).
[61] Ibid.
[62] See n 7.
[63] Lacey (n 17) 117.
[64] M Zander, 'Departmental Committee Report: Legal Aid in Criminal Proceedings' (1966) 29(6) *Modern Law Review* 639.

Therefore, although this period saw significant changes to the structure of legal aid, the government appeared to remain somewhat resistant to further expansion of funding. Assisting those that the state suspects to have behaved criminally has never, it seems, been a popular idea despite the provisions of the ECHR.

By the early 1970s, an alternative form of welfarism was prevailing, which supported the extension of legal aid in principle. That phase of governance was influenced by increased interest in equality and individuals' rights, in light of concerns about the 'patriarchal, able-bodied, and race-blind ideology',[65] which had informed the development of the welfare state. This shift was fuelled by several factors, including active radical lawyers demanding improvement and academic and campaign group interests in principles of access to justice,[66] including JUSTICE and the Legal Action Group.[67] The first Law Centre in the UK opened in North Kensington in 1970, intending to provide good quality, systematic change in legal services.[68] In 1973, as if to provide evidence of this shift, the Law Society introduced the 'green form' scheme, which allowed solicitors to perform a simplified means test in order to assess initial eligibility for publicly funded advice in relation to any matter of English law.[69] Furthermore, section 37, Criminal Justice Act 1972, forbade magistrates from sending first-time offenders to prison if they were not legally represented. These provisions indicate that governments were prepared to facilitate increased access to publicly funded representation at a time when the importance of individual rights was being promoted, including the right to participate in the criminal justice process through legal representation.

VI. STATE CRISIS AND LEGAL AID

The expansion of eligibility for publicly funded representation in magistrates' courts, combined with a rise in the number of people prosecuted, meant that by 1986/87, spending on summary criminal legal aid accounted for a quarter of all legal aid costs and four-fifths of defendants appearing on criminal charges in magistrates' courts were now represented.[70] By this time, more than half of all green form claims related to matters of criminal, family or personal injury law.[71]

---

[65] Sommerlad (n 14) 355.

[66] Mauro Cappelletti significantly influenced debates around access to justice in the 1970s. See especially M Cappelletti, B Garth and N Trocker, 'Access to Justice: Comparative General Report' (1976) 40(3/4) *The Rabel Journal of Comparative and International Private Law* 669–717.

[67] Goriely (n 44).

[68] See generally J Robins and D Newman, *Justice in a Time of Austerity* (Bristol University Press, 2021).

[69] Legal Action Group (n 54).

[70] Ibid.

[71] The Fabian Society, 'The Right to Justice: The Final Report of the Bach Commission' (Fabian Society, 2017).

Expansion of legally aided representation during this period is somewhat incongruent with conventional accounts of the rollback of state-funded services as Conservative neoliberal policies became dominant after Thatcher became Prime Minister in 1979. However, several factors may provide at least partial explanations for the expansion of legal aid at this time.

First, rising crime rates (which were partly a reflection of social discontent and increasing levels of unemployment) had contributed to the crisis of the welfare state.[72] As the criminal process can never legitimately be completely removed from state control (given the functions of the legislature, policing and institutions of punishment[73]), rising crime rates meant that a different, more aggressive form of re-regulation was justified. Second, the adequacy of state-led prosecutions was under public scrutiny in the face of several infamous miscarriages of justice that occurred as a result of police malpractice, such as *R v Lattimore et al*[74] and cases that uncovered the extent of improper police behaviour in the wake of insurgency in Northern Ireland.[75] These factors contributed to the creation of the independent Crown Prosecution Service in 1986,[76] which bolstered demands for defence representation to provide equality of arms. Furthermore, lawyers could play a role in holding state-led forces to account in the wake of tough police action in relation to inner-city riots and industrial action that occurred during this time,[77] thereby legitimising the institutional power of the criminal process. These crises seemingly interrupted, or at least delayed, the wholesale rollback of state-funded representation in criminal cases.

Furthermore, Young and Wall observed that these changes happened because 'once it was recognised that defence lawyers actually facilitated speedier court proceedings … grants of legal aid were made much more freely'.[78] Lawyers enable efficiency because they often form mutually convenient, cooperative

---

[72] A James and J Raine, *The New Politics of Criminal Justice* (Longmans, 1998).

[73] There have, however, been significant attempts to marketise and privatise prisons and probation services, with limited success from a political perspective. See generally K Albertson, M Corcoran and J Phillips (eds), *Marketisation and Privatisation in Criminal Justice* (Policy Press, 2020). Some sectors of policing have also been vulnerable to marketisation and privatisation, including forensic services. See generally A White, 'What is the Privatization of Policing?' (2020) 14(3) *Policing* 766–77 and discussion in L Skinns et al, 'Police Custody Delivery in the Twenty-First Century in England and Wales: Current Arrangements and their Implications for Patterns of Policing' (2017) 4(3) *European Journal of Policing Studies* 325–48.

[74] [1976] 62 Cr App R 53. Also known as the Confait case, in which three vulnerable people were wrongfully convicted of a murder which they could not have committed.

[75] Including the well-known cases of the Birmingham Six and Guildford Four, and media response to those cases. See generally C Walker and K Starmer, *Miscarriages of Justice: A Review of Justice in Error* (Oxford University Press); G McKee and R Franey, *Time Bomb: The Guildford Four* (Bloomsbury, 1988); C Mullin, *Error of Judgement* (Poolbeg, 1990).

[76] The CPS was created via the Prosecution of Offences Act 1985.

[77] See, eg, the case of the Tottenham Three – *R v Silcott, Braithwaite and Raghip* (1991) *The Times*, 6 December 1991. In relation to industrial action at the time, see R Vogler, *Reading the Riot Act: The Magistracy, the Police and the Army in Civil Disorder* (Open University Press, 1991).

[78] Young and Wall (n 15) 4.

networks to ensure swift case progression (chapter three).[79] Greater levels of defence representation facilitate the routinisation of courtroom procedures as advocates tend to standardise practices as workloads and pressure increases.[80] As Smith and Cape observed, the criminal justice process came to adopt procedures that depended on the presence of specialist defence lawyers to ensure their smooth operation.[81] This phase of legal aid development, which Goriely described as 'a fivefold increase in real terms',[82] is, therefore, significant in its complexity. Agencies of the state had faced a number of public setbacks to its appearance of fairness and legitimacy, and lawyers had the potential to redress any perceived imbalance while also increasing the efficiency of court proceedings through re-regulation strategies. Lawyers, therefore, fulfilled important functions for the government even though contemporary neoliberal Conservative politics was becoming increasingly sceptical about the behaviour of public service professionals.[83]

As some of these complexities demonstrated, it seemed that the fears of the Home Office in the early 1900s had been unfounded – the presence of lawyers actually assisted the smooth administration of the proceedings.[84] Legally aided criminal defence services burgeoned in the 1960s and early 1970s when experts emphasised the ethical, service-led, and altruistic nature of professional work.[85] This context may have informed the development of a habitus in which lawyers traditionally identify with symbolic (individualised, procedurally rigorous) approaches to justice. However, by the mid-1980s, 'the growth in the numbers prosecuted ... levelled off, yet the numbers receiving legally aided representation continued to rise'.[86] This growth led the government to introduce various initiatives and reviews to reduce legal aid expenditure, driven by preferences for market-based performance management techniques, concerns about efficiency

---

[79] See generally D Newman, *Legal Aid, Lawyers and the Quest for Justice* (Hart Publishing, 2013); R Young, 'Exploring the Boundaries of the Criminal Courtroom Workgroup' (2013) 42(3) *Common Law World Review* 203–39.

[80] D Wall, 'Keyholders to Criminal Justice? Solicitors and Applications for Criminal Legal Aid' in R Young and D Wall (eds) *Access to Criminal Justice: Legal Aid, Lawyers and the Defence of Liberty* (Oxford, Blackstone Press 1996); L Welsh and M Howard, 'Standardization and the Production of Justice in Summary Criminal Courts: A Post-Human Analysis' (2019) 28(6) *Social & Legal Studies* 774–93. See further ch 3.

[81] T Smith and E Cape, 'The Rise and Decline of Criminal Legal Aid in England and Wales' in A Flynn and J Hodgson (eds), *Access to Justice and Legal Aid: Comparative Perspectives on Unmet Legal Need* (Hart Publishing, 2017).

[82] Goriely (n 44) 45.

[83] J Le Grand, 'Knights, Knaves or Pawns? Human Behaviour and Social Policy' (1997) 26(2) *Journal of Social Policy* 149; Sommerlad (n 41).

[84] Goriely (n 44).

[85] However, the concept of professionalism, especially among legal aid lawyers, has never been unquestioningly accepted. See E Cooke, '*The Changing Occupational Terrain of the Legal Aid Lawyer in Times of Precariousness*' (Doctoral thesis (PhD), University of Kent 2019).

[86] L Bridges, 'The Reform of Criminal Legal Aid' in R Young and D Wall (eds), *Access to Criminal Justice: Legal Aid, Lawyers and the Defence of Liberty* (Blackstone Press 1996) 480.

and distrust of professional behaviour. Le Grand notes how, against a desire to increase efficiency in public services, professionals have increasingly come to be seen as self-serving and obstructive.[87] Lacey offers a further, perhaps related, reason for governments' persistent reluctance to develop a relationship of trust with defence lawyers. She points to the historically circumspect view of defence lawyers' professional credentials stemming from the criminal justice system's traditional reliance on lay involvement in case determination through the use of magistrates and juries. The discourse which advocated distrust of public sector professionals has been particularly obvious in relation to publicly funded lawyers – who have been depicted as 'fat cats' by politicians and the media[88] – and Sommerlad has gone so far as to say that anti-lawyer discourse has played a 'central role' in governmental approaches to legal aid.[89] This attitude recast the delivery of 'justice' 'as a disaggregated assortment of "skills" and "services"'.[90]

Until 1988, the Law Society had been responsible for the administration of legal aid. However, the Thatcher government took the view that the duties of the Law Society as the representative body for solicitors conflicted with their responsibility for payment of lawyers' fees. The Legal Aid Board (LAB) was created, a non-departmental public body[91] and a manifestation of re-regulation in state services. Hynes and Robins viewed the creation of the LAB as the beginning of a period during which the government was increasingly unconcerned about policies related to publicly funded representation but were instead concerned about efficiency.[92] The Legal Action Group noted that 'no less than half the initial membership of the board came from business, while the role of the Law Society was reduced to putting forward the names of two solicitors'.[93] This is consistent with the Thatcher government's scepticism about the efficiency of state-funded institutions, alongside a more marketised, managerialist approach to funding in public services. This approach deprioritises the ability of parties to actively participate in the process of criminal justice.

There had been a significant rise in legal aid costs in summary criminal proceedings in the early 1990s.[94] The system had been, to an extent, demand led, in that solicitors were given broad discretion to certify a potential client's eligibility for legal aid via the green form scheme. This meant that the government lacked some degree of control over expenditure, and there is no doubt that some lawyers did exploit the green form scheme.[95] The government's cost

---

[87] Le Grand (n 83).
[88] See also discussion in Robins and Newman (n 68).
[89] H Sommerlad, '"I've Lost the Plot": An Everyday Story of the "Political" Legal Aid Lawyer' (2001) 28(3) *Journal of Law and Society* 335, 338.
[90] Sommerlad (n 39) 293.
[91] Department for Constitutional Affairs (n 49).
[92] Hynes and Robins (n 51).
[93] Legal Action Group (n 54).
[94] Goriely (n 44).
[95] See discussion in Robins and Newman (n 68).

reduction strategy at this time was to abolish an hourly rate payment system and reintroduce a payment system of fee per case in the magistrates' courts, and that system (as described earlier in this chapter) remains in place today. Furthermore, as public service professionals came to be seen as obstructive to government policy, greater (and more aggressive) regulation was introduced, and demands for greater efficiency were made. While the increased efficiency brought about by lawyers' greater presence in proceedings was appreciated, governments remained of the view that lawyers were, at least to an extent, self-serving professionals. One way that governments sought to manage that dilemma was to introduce specialist contracting requirements that closely monitored and regulated the way that lawyers were able to provide their services.

These actions were part of a wider project in which governments sought greater control over state-funded institutions. Efficiency was encouraged through measures that increasingly restricted lawyers' professional decision-making practices by juxtaposing business needs and professional practices. Such demands did, however, also increase defendant marginalisation as lawyers were required to balance business and professional needs against their clients' interests – a dilemma that now appears constant in the process of summary criminal justice (chapter five).[96]

VII. NEW LABOUR'S APPROACH TO LEGAL AID: MARKETISATION AND EFFICIENCY

There was an increase in summary criminal legal aid claims in the late 1990s.[97] At the same time, the supplier induced demand theory became popular in government. Proponents of the theory suggest that lawyers construct the need for legal assistance by providing unnecessary services.[98] The theory remains unproven, and Tata highlighted the problem of determining what constitutes 'need' in a quasi-market, which relies to a large degree on the complexities of professional decision-making according to the case details, ethical issues involved, particular clients' needs and lawyers' own interests.[99]

Nevertheless, the government remained distrustful of lawyer behaviour. In an attempt to restrict further expansion of legally aided services, New Labour decided that the number of firms providing legal aid in criminal cases should be limited by a franchising system.[100] In 2000, the LAB was replaced by the Legal

---

[96] Newman (n 79); Welsh (n 12).

[97] Hynes and Robins (n 51).

[98] Young and Wall (n 15); C Tata, 'In the Interests of Clients or Commerce? Legal Aid, Supply, Demand, and "Ethical Indeterminacy" in Criminal Defence Work' (2007) 34(4) *Journal of Law and Society* 489.

[99] Tata (n 98).

[100] The Lord Chancellor at the time, Lord Falconer, has recently stated his regret about New Labour's approach to curbing legal aid. See C Falconer 'Labour Helped these Devastating Legal Aid

Services Commission (LSC) under the Access to Justice Act 1999. The LSC was required to develop and then maintain criminal legal aid funds under new contracts, which required firms to meet certain contracting criteria in order to provide publicly funded criminal defence services. From 2001, firms who wished to provide publicly funded advice in criminal proceedings would have to hold a contract for those services issued by the LSC.[101] The idea to impose a franchising scheme can be traced to the 1980s, when politicians – guided by principles of neoliberalism – 'were beginning to 're-invent government' by contracting out services to private suppliers'[102] and re-regulating services that remained under state control. The introduction of new contracts resulted in an approximate 15 per cent drop in the number of firms providing legal advice in criminal proceedings because many small firms could not meet the contracting criteria.[103]

As franchising regimes were introduced, managerial influences took greater control over lawyers because the new contracts required firms to adopt specific working practices which the LSC (and not necessarily the firm) regarded as appropriate. As a result, legal professionals were faced with a choice between 'serving the interests of their clients and serving government interests',[104] the latter of which is promoted by contracting conditions. For example, the contract determines when claims for payment can be made and governs what tests are to be applied by lawyers when initially considering whether an accused qualifies for publicly funded representation. While recent research indicates that lawyers accept that there needs to be an appropriate test to ensure that public funds are spent appropriately,[105] the way in which the contracting criteria are applied undermines professional judgement (by surrendering responsibility to government), and this represents a challenge to the lawyer/client relationship.[106] In short, such measures were designed to 'infuse legal aid practice with business principles',[107] as efficiency and quality were targeted via processes of audit. Reduced trust in professional discretion has weakened the autonomy of defence lawyers,[108] and the relationship between legally aided defence lawyers and the government 'became increasingly fractious'.[109]

The government's desire to increase efficiency alongside the payment regime set out in the contract was likely to lead to conveyor-belt type procedures and

Cuts Along. Now It's time to Fix It' *The Guardian* (London, 31 Dec 2018); Fouzder, M, 'Falconer: My 'Regret' over Labour's Effort to Curb Legal Aid Budget' *Law Society Gazette* (London, 31 May 2019).

[101] Hynes and Robins (n 51).
[102] Goriely (n 44) 8.
[103] Hynes and Robins (n 51).
[104] Cape (n 39) 62.
[105] R Vogler, L Welsh, A Clarke, S Wiedlitzka and L McDonnell. 'The Criminal Cases Review Commission: Legal Aid and Legal Representatives. Final Report' (University of Sussex, 2021).
[106] Newman (n 79); Welsh (n 12).
[107] Sommerlad (n 14) 360
[108] Ibid; Cape (n 39).
[109] Smith and Cape (n 81).

de-skilling,[110] with significant reliance being placed on unqualified support staff[111] as firms attempted to remain profitable while also improving efficiency. Newman's study found that defence lawyers tended to adopt a factory-like approach to case progression in order to cope with government initiatives.[112] Such approaches (perhaps inadvertently) increase marginalisation experienced by defendants because they are increasingly provided with a routinised service. It should be noted here that studies of magistrates' court proceedings in the 1970s had already highlighted that defendants struggled to play an active role in the criminal justice process (discussed further in chapter three).[113] These changes can only have exacerbated the problem and emphasise governments' preference for policies that encourage efficiency over principled adversarialism in summary criminal courts. As we will see in chapters three and four, demands for efficiency have increased alongside complexity in the nature of legal provisions. Those demands interact with the already strong workgroup culture discussed in chapter three and the impact of legal aid cuts discussed here and in chapter five, so that it seems even less likely that defendants can effectively and meaningfully participate in modern summary proceedings than in the 1970s.

Despite New Labour's desire 'to regulate the cost and delivery of public services through market competition',[114] spending on criminal legal aid increased by 37 per cent between 1997 and 2005. In 2004, the total cost of criminal legal aid was £1.4 billion, but a significant proportion of those costs arose as a result of Crown and higher court proceedings.[115] Notably, the costs of work conducted at magistrates' courts and police stations did not grow at a rate that was disproportionate to other areas of economic production.[116] Over the same period, the costs of running other elements of the criminal justice system (in terms of the police, the prison service, the probation service and the Crown Prosecution Service) had, according to former Lord Chancellor Lord Falconer, increased by 46 per cent. The crime spend had taken off 'as a result of New Labour's promise to be "tough on crime and tough on the causes of crime"'.[117] At the same time, and as a result of misplaced attention about the source of rising costs, the government gave 'insufficient attention to the reasons why the state should provide access to justice'.[118] Two successive New Labour Home Secretaries (David Blunkett and Jack Straw) had blamed increased costs on defendants and 'their unscrupulous lawyers playing the system. Ministers developed an almost

---

[110] Young and Wall (n 1) 5.

[111] Goriely (n 44).

[112] Newman (n 79).

[113] P Carlen, *Magistrates' Justice* (Martin Robertson 1976).

[114] Hynes and Robins (n 51) 35.

[115] Smith and Cape (n 81).

[116] E Cape and R Moorhead, 'Demand Induced Supply? Identifying Cost Drivers in Criminal Defence Work' (Legal Services Research Centre, 2005).

[117] Hynes and Robins (n 51) 108.

[118] Smith (n 53) 3.

pathological refusal to accept that New Labour's relentless law-making could contribute to pressures to process high numbers of guilty pleas.'[119]

It seems, therefore, that increasing distrust of public service professionals and concerns with efficiency led to a greater focus on cost-cutting measures, which are less concerned with defendants' rights than traditional due process provisions. As such, principles relating to access to justice and defendant participation become invisible in the context of political debate about efficiency, consumerism and individual responsibility, thereby contributing to processes of defendant marginalisation. Despite recognising that legally aided representation makes a crucial contribution to both the effectiveness and fairness of criminal proceedings, New Labour's preference for marketisation in public services led the Lord Chancellor to the view that legal aid remuneration rates should be determined by the operation of market practices rather than by central government.

Lord Carter conducted a further review of legal aid, during which he formed the view that the government 'had to break the hold of criminal practitioners and force them to restructure so we could get more control over the costs of provision'.[120] Echoing earlier governments' fondness for market-based approaches, Carter viewed legal aid provision in criminal proceedings as a market that should be 'driven by competition based on quality, capacity and price'.[121] Carter recommended fixing fees for block contracted police station work, reform of Crown and magistrates' court fees and a system of Best Value Tendering for high-cost cases.[122] Carter's review was not well received by either professionals or the House of Commons Constitutional Affairs Committee, and the LSC's response (a failure to realise most of the recommendations) betrayed its 'half-hearted faith in market forces'.[123] Members of the Legal Action Group – a charity that campaigns on matters relating to access to justice – argued that Carter's recommendations were based on,

> [a]n overly simplistic belief in 'the market' being able to sort out the problem. But there was a failure to understand what 'the problem' was, that the publicly funded legal sector has evolved in a complex and haphazard fashion, and is one that will not withstand shocks.[124]

The Law Society asked economist Peter Grindley to assess the likely impact of Carter's recommendations. Grindley noted that the reforms would require major restructuring of firms providing legally aided advice and representation, 'making it unclear ... whether there will be enough capacity to provide services'.[125]

---

[119] Hynes and Robins (n 51) 115.

[120] Ibid 53.

[121] Department of Constitutional Affairs, 'Procurement of Criminal Defence Services: Market-Based Reform' (London, DCA, 2006).

[122] Ibid.

[123] Hynes and Robins (n 51) 60.

[124] Ibid 57.

[125] P Grindley, 'Legal Aid Reforms Proposed by the Carter Report – Analysis and Commentary' (LECG Corporation, 2006) 3.

His analysis found that, as the most stable aspect of legal aid expenditure, 'magistrates' court costs have fallen by 0.1% per year and per case by 0.5%. After allowing for inflation, these each represent net decreases in real per case costs'.[126] These findings demonstrate that profit margins in legally added work were falling. Coupled with the fact that there has been no rise in legal aid payment rates since the mid-1990s, and in the face of cuts discussed below, sustainability of service has become a grave issue in criminal defence work.[127] While, as this book shows, there is much more to access to justice and defendant participation than simply the provision of state-funded legal services, enabling defendants to have easy access to professional expertise in the same epistemic community as prosecutorial bodies and the courts (chapters three and four) is one important feature of enabling meaningful participation among the parties.

Persistent challenges to the structure and availability of publicly funded representation during this period reflect governments' desire to increase economy and efficiency in the criminal justice system but at the cost of adversarial criminal justice principles that have developed since the nineteenth century. Reductions in welfare provision can be politically justified through penal populism on the basis that precariat groups no longer have legitimate needs if they fail to follow nudges towards responsibilised behaviour.[128] This discourse also allowed New Labour to adopt greater use of criminalisation (and quasi-criminal measures)[129] and increase penalties, reflecting a 'sustained and substantial expansion into criminal law'.[130] That expansion actually justifies increased lawyer activity during this same period and could account for some of the rises in criminal justice expenditure generally, including legal aid funding. However, discourses that legitimise the roll back of welfare provision for 'undeserving' citizens (whose rights have been reclassified as 'weak'[131]) also justifies reductions in access to justice via legal aid. Arguments about the sustainability of service only appeared to be of minimal importance to policymakers.

---

[126] Ibid 4.

[127] A Gregory, 'British Justice is in Jeopardy': Legal Aid System is Doomed without More Criminal Defence Lawyers, Solicitors Warn' *The Independent* (London, 28 February 2020); J Thornton, 'Is Publicly Funded Criminal Defence Sustainable? Legal Aid Cuts, Morale, Retention and Recruitment in the English Criminal Law Professions' (2020) 40(2) *Legal Studies* 230–51.

[128] Those 'nudges', under New Labour's time in power, did include greater access to social welfare provision in other areas of society, such as the Sure Start programme for families with young children. See, eg, S Cattan, G Conti, C Farquharson and R Ginja, *The Health Effects of Sure Start* (Institute for Fiscal Studies, 2019).

[129] See generally, S Demetriou '*From the ASBO to the Injunction: A Qualitative Review of the Antisocial Behaviour Legislation Post-2014*' (2019) (April) *Public Law* 343–61.

[130] G Dingwall *and* T Hillier, *Blamestorming, Blamemongers and Scapegoats: Allocating Blame in the Criminal Justice Process.* (Policy Press, 2015) 140.

[131] Sokhi-Bulley (n 4).

VIII. AUSTERITY: THE COALITION AND CONSERVATIVE GOVERNMENTS

David Cameron, as leader of the 2010–15 Coalition government, advocated the use of 'nudging' to responsibilise citizens through public policy as part of the government's 'Big Society' agenda.[132] Having adopted the Big Society approach to public policy, Coalition politics then became dominated by austerity. It was clear that one of the 2010–15 Coalition government's key aims was 'to cut government expenditure in order to reduce the public spending deficit' via austerity measures.[133] Early on in the Coalition's time in government, the Ministry of Justice indicated that the government's 'first priority is to reduce the burden of debt by reducing public spending … Legal aid must, therefore, make a substantial contribution to the required savings'.[134] Through these measures, lawyers' behaviour became further instilled in political discourse, becoming more acute as greater pressure was placed on government spending targets.

In 2010, the Ministry of Justice acknowledged that the reintroduction of fixed fees and means-testing had stabilised legal aid spending but also stated that the way that services were delivered needed to be reorganised in order to be sustainable.[135] Means-tested eligibility for legal aid had been reintroduced in magistrates' courts in 2006 (via the Criminal Defence Service Act 2006) in light of the government's concerns that its abolition had caused an increase in criminal legal aid expenditure. The means-test was reintroduced despite evidence that means testing in criminal legal aid had previously proved overly bureaucratic, costly and raised little in the way of contributions from defendants.[136] Nevertheless, the government sought even greater control over the delivery of justice services, which further undermined the ability of lawyers to make autonomous, individualised case management decisions. One of the ways in which the government achieved greater control was through the abolition of the LSC, a non-departmental government body, and its replacement with the LAA as a department of the Ministry of Justice. Through this process, we can see that the governments gradually exerted greater regulatory control over legal aid expenditure by moving it away from the Law Society to a non-departmental public body (the LSC), to an executive agency sponsored by the Ministry of Justice. Since its inception, lawyers have raised concerns about how staff at the LAA make

---

[132] M Lister, 'Citizens, Doing It for Themselves? The Big Society and Government Through Community' (2014) *Parliamentary Affairs* 1–19.

[133] S Hynes, *Austerity Justice* (London, Legal Action Group, 2012).

[134] Ministry of Justice, 'Legal Aid Reform: Scope Changes. Impact Assessment' (2010) webarchive. nationalarchives.gov.uk/20111013060729/http://www.justice.gov.uk/downloads/consultations/ia-scope-changes.pdf. It is appropriate to mention that civil legal aid funds have suffered significantly in this regard (House of Commons Justice Committee, *Impact of Changes to Civil Legal Aid under Part 1 of the Legal Aid, Sentencing and Punishment of Offenders Act 2012* (HC 311, 2015)). See further Robins and Newman (n 67).

[135] Ministry of Justice, 'Restructuring the Delivery of Criminal Defence Services' (2010).

[136] Smith and Cape (n 81).

decisions, describing them as flawed and inconsistent.[137] Furthermore, lawyers report that it is a 'constant struggle'[138] to get legal aid granted and bills paid. This seems to have a negative effect on morale and feed into perceptions that there is a 'cult of refusal on the part of the Legal Aid Agency'.[139]

The Coalition government expressed a desire, through LASPO, to reduce criminal legal aid by eight per cent between 2009/10 and 2014/15,[140] and then reduce the criminal legal aid budget by £220m per year by 2018–19.[141] As Robins and Newman point out, LASPO represented the 'most radical package of reforms to the legal aid scheme' since publicly funded legal advice schemes were established.[142] The amendments set out in the Ministry of Justice's policy document, Transforming Legal Aid,[143] proposed reductions in criminal legal aid fees of 17.5 per cent across two years, along with reducing the police station fixed fees that had been introduced following Carter's review.[144] This led the campaign group JUSTICE to accuse the government of focusing too much on inputs (funds) rather than outputs (justice).[145] This dichotomy reflects the tension between (political) policy versus (legal) principles of adversarial justice, while the focus on inputs demonstrates the continued influence of marketised practices as manifested in austerity politics.

The introduction of contract tendering proposals had been repeatedly postponed because the government was 'persuaded that the scheme proposed was unlikely to lead to the efficient, re-structured legal services market envisaged by Lord Carter'.[146] The government rejected those proposals on the basis of efficiency rather than because they offended principled adversarialism, which demonstrates governmental priorities lay in efficiency and cost control. However, the Ministry of Justice stated that it remained committed to market restructuring

[137] See discussion in Welsh et al (n 21) ch 8 and Vogler et al (n 105). Similar concerns have been raised in relation to the cumbersome nature of LAA procedures in civil proceedings (Robins and Newman (n 68)), and especially immigration and asylum claims, raising serious concerns about quality and sustainability (J Wilding, *The Legal Aid Market: Challenges for Publicly Funded Immigration and Asylum Legal Representation* (Policy Press, 2021)).

[138] House of Commons Justice Committee, *Oral Evidence: (a) Court Capacity, HC 284; (b) The Future of Legal Aid* (HC 289. 9 February 2021; Q109). One barrister interviewed by Thornton said of the LAA, 'They just don't pay ... I mean, to be honest, they're a bit like a shady backstreet garage!' (Thornton (n 127) 237).

[139] Ibid. Robins and Newman (n 68) discuss that a culture of refusal also seems to exist concerning claims for legal aid in civil proceedings.

[140] C Baksi, 'No Extra Pay for "Speedy" Justice' *Law Society Gazette* (London, 19 July 2012) 1.

[141] Smith and Cape (n 81).

[142] Robins and Newman (n 68) 1.

[143] Ministry of Justice, *Transforming Legal Aid: Delivering a More Credible and Efficient System* (CP14/2013, 2013).

[144] Ministry of Justice, 'Transforming Legal aid – Next Steps: Government Response' (2014) consult.justice.gov.uk/digital-communications/transforming-legal-aid-next-steps.

[145] Smith (n 53).

[146] V Kemp, 'Transforming Legal Aid: Access to Criminal Defence Services' (Legal Services Research Centre, 2010).

and thus proposed a more rigorous form of price-based tendering.[147] While the price competition tendering element of the most recent restructuring proposals in Transforming Legal Aid was eventually abandoned, the government then required firms to bid for separate contracts to perform 'own' and duty solicitor work. 'Own' client work is when a suspect/defendant requests the services of a particular solicitor. Duty solicitor work is conducted when a suitably qualified solicitor is allocated cases according to a rota and generally has not previously represented the accused. Both types of work have traditionally been remunerated under different parts of a single contract. Additionally, there was to be a limited number of contracts offered per county, fee cuts and requirements to provide wider area coverage.[148]

In *R (on the application of London Criminal Courts Solicitors Association and Criminal Law Solicitors Association) v The Lord Chancellor*,[149] the High Court initially declared the consultation process unlawful, but the government, after a further brief period of consultation, pursued its position in relation to legal aid contracts. In January 2015, the High Court determined that the proposals were lawful.[150] Lawyers resorted to a series of protests and boycotts in an attempt to persuade the government that the proposed scheme would result in advice deserts and make the already fragile market unsustainable in the long term.[151] The 2015 Conservative Lord Chancellor, Michael Gove, initially indicated that the Ministry of Justice intended to proceed with the new contracting system and the new contracts were announced in mid-October 2015. However, a number of firms launched judicial review proceedings against the procurement process in light of a whistle-blower's allegations about the veracity of the tendering process, causing the government to ultimately abandon the new contracting procedures while continuing to implement fee cuts.[152] This was one of a number of rethinks performed by Gove as he tried to work through the 'ill-conceived policies introduced by his predecessor', Chris Grayling.[153] The contracting process remained somewhat uncertain until 2017,[154] leaving lawyers in a state of professional limbo to operate in an already fragile market.

---

[147] Ministry of Justice (n 143).

[148] Ministry of Justice (n 143).

[149] [2014] EWHC 3020 (Admin).

[150] O Bowcott, 'High Court Upholds Plan to Slash On-call Legal Aid Solicitors' *The Guardian* (London, 18 February 2015).

[151] O Bowcott, 'Legal Aid Cuts: Lawyers to Begin Boycott that Could See Courts Grind to a Halt' *The Guardian* (London, 30 June 2015).

[152] Ministry of Justice, 'Changes to Criminal Legal Aid Contracting' (2016), www.gov.uk/government/speeches/changes-to-criminal-legal-aid-contracting.

[153] R Garside, M Ford, H Mills and R Roberts, 'UK Justice Policy Review. Volume 6' (Centre for Crime and Justice Studies, 2017) 7.

[154] The contracts issued in 2017 are due for renewal in 2022 (www.gov.uk/government/news/crime-news-extension-of-2017-crime-contract-to-31-march-2022).

During the early 2010s, the government, in fact, achieved its proposed legal aid savings more than twice over.[155] At the same time, the Ministry of Justice acknowledged that firms were already asserting that criminal legal aid work is unsustainable and noted that 'we might, therefore, expect that suppliers would start to leave the market in significant number. We cannot predict ... the impact on the provision of services'.[156] In 2019–20, there were 300 fewer criminal legal aid firms operating than in 2014–15, and that figure declined by a further 91 firms according to 2021 data.[157] Many (57%) practitioners who left the market in 2018–19 were under the age of 35.[158] The number of defendants appearing without legal representation has increased in both Crown and magistrates' courts.[159] Additional research indicates that some areas of criminal practice are particularly prone to removal from the scope of services provided by firms.[160] It appears, therefore, that the impact of changes to legal aid funding on service provision are becoming clearer, and there does not appear to be any positive news for defendants or the integrity of the justice process.

In June 2016, the House of Commons Public Accounts Committee took the view that, in light of austerity measures and efficiency drives, the criminal justice system was nearing breaking point.[161] By the end of 2018, expenditure on criminal legal aid was £959m, amounting to just over 10 per cent of the Ministry of Justice's total expenditure.[162] In real terms, legal aid expenditure had fallen by 33 per cent between 2011 and 2018.[163] Nevertheless, the government continued to propose further cuts to criminal legal aid, which the Law Society described as untenable, unnecessary and damaging to the sustainability of service.[164] Although the Law Society instigated and won a legal challenge to the procedure through which those cuts were proposed to be made,[165] the government demonstrated its continuing commitment to market-based principles through funding

---

[155] The Fabian Society (n 71).

[156] Ministry of Justice (n 143).

[157] Ministry of Justice, (2020) Summary Information On Publicly Funded Criminal Legal Services assets.publishing.service.gov.uk/government/uploads/system/uploads/attachment_data/file/960290/data-compendium.pdf; M Fouzder, 'Landmark Report Paints Bleak Picture of Criminal Legal Aid' *Law Society Gazette* (London, 12 February 2021). See also the evidence given to the Justice Committee in 2021 (House of Commons Justice Committee, *Oral Evidence: (a) Court Capacity, HC 284; (b) The Future of Legal Aid, HC 289*. 9 February 2021).

[158] Fouzder (n 157).

[159] Law Society Gazette, 'Unrepresented Defendants Crowd Criminal Courts' Law Society Gazette (London, 2 May 2016); O Bowcott, 'Jump in Unrepresented Defendants as Legal Aid Cuts Continue to Bite' *The Guardian* (London, 24 November 2019). See further ch 5.

[160] Vogler et al (n 105).

[161] Garside et al (n 153).

[162] House of Commons Justice Committee, *Criminal Legal Aid. Twelfth Report of Session 2017–2019* (HC 1069, 2019).

[163] Ibid.

[164] J Van Der Luit-Drummond, 'Further Criminal Legal Aid Cuts Untenable and Short-sighted' *Solicitors' Journal* (London, 23 March 2017).

[165] *The Law Society, R (On the Application Of) v The Lord Chancellor* [2018] EWHC 2094.

cuts and streamlining measures discussed in the following chapter. Lawyers who conduct publicly funded defence work were – in mid-2021 – paid less than half of the hourly rate that they would receive if funding had risen in line with inflation. Lawyers argue that, in light of funding cuts, their engagement with case preparation suffers, as does equality of arms and the right to effective participation enshrined in Article 6 of the ECHR. This again highlights that recent governments have prioritised principles of efficiency and audit over principles of adversarial justice. Until the beginning of 2019, governments had appeared to ignore lawyers' concerns about equality of arms and the right to a fair trial, which may be considered unsurprising in the context of scepticism surrounding lawyers' motivation and behaviour detailed above. Furthermore, arguments about reduced defendant access to rights of participation and engagement in the process are undermined by the fact that many defendants have been situated as 'undeserving' citizens.

In October 2018, then Conservative Prime Minister Theresa May declared the end of austerity[166] and – at the time of writing – the government had begun a review of criminal legal aid in light of wider reforms to the criminal justice system. As the review progresses, current Conservative Prime Minster Boris Johnson has restated a commitment to avoid returning to austerity despite the challenges of the Covid-19 pandemic and continuing uncertainty around the impact of the UK's withdrawal from the European Union.[167] The review considers how criminal legal aid operates to ensure sustainability at each stage of a case – from the police station to the Criwn Court.[168] The timing of this review is interesting, albeit that it has been delayed by the December 2019 General Election and then by the Covid-19 pandemic. In the same way that legal aid expanded in the early 1980s following public concern about the legitimacy of the criminal process, the initial announcement of this review came at a time when state agencies were again criticised for increasing the risk of miscarriages of justice because the disclosure of material in criminal cases is not properly conducted by the police and Crown Prosecution Service.[169] A lack of funding for both state agencies and defence lawyers is also blamed for the increased risk of miscarriages of justice.[170] As the government recognises a need to take action to improve public confidence in the criminal process, so it seems, perhaps, tentatively, more willing to consider the needs of defence lawyers as an important check on the power of the state in the criminal justice system.

---

[166] H Stewart, 'Theresa May Pledges End to Austerity in Tory Conference Speech' *The Guardian* (London, 3 October 2018).

[167] A Woodcock, 'Coronavirus: Boris Johnson Promises Pandemic will not Lead to Return of Austerity' *The Independent* (London, 27 June 2020).

[168] Ministry of Justice *Criminal Legal Aid Review* (2019) www.gov.uk/guidance/criminal-legal-aid-review#who-were-working-with.

[169] HM Crown Prosecution Service Inspectorate, *Disclosure of Unused Material in the Crown Court* CP001:1267 (London: HMCPSI, 2020).

[170] House of Commons Justice Committee, *Disclosure of Evidence in Criminal Cases. Eleventh Report of the Session* 2017–19 (HC 859, 2018).

That said, the accelerated review proposals published at an early, expedited stage of the full review[171] caused widespread disappointment among the defence lawyer community.[172] The proposals suggested that an extra £32–51m of funding could be made available for the defence community, but this fell short of the £85m given to the Crown Prosecution Service the previous year.[173] Lawyers felt that the proposals would do little to address the concerns of the profession and improve access to justice. Thus, while there appears to have been some recent attempts to inject money into the criminal justice system, limited investment in criminal defence services has not matched the extent of cuts imposed by earlier governments, nor the level of investment provided to policing or prosecutorial services.[174] The limited funding that has been made available to defence services has not remedied the impact of earlier cuts in terms of ongoing concerns about the sustainability of publicly funded criminal defence services and poor morale among defence lawyers. Despite rejecting austerity at an ideological level, the fallout from significant cutbacks in state support of legal aid continues.

IX. SUMMARY

The present system of publicly funded representation developed throughout the last half of the twentieth century as initial concerns about the appearance of legitimacy and, later, welfarist approaches to government had the effect of increasing access to justice through participation by proxy. As liberal welfarism developed, interest in individual rights, due process in the criminal justice system and the provision of publicly funded representation, became increasingly important.

The pace of change to legal aid provision accelerated as more neoliberal, market-inspired politics became dominant. Lacey comments that the modern

---

[171] Ministry of Justice, 'Criminal Legal Aid Review: An Accelerated Package of Measures Amending the Criminal Legal Aid Fee Schemes' (London: Ministry of Justice, 2020) consult.justice.gov.uk/criminal-legal-aid/criminal-legal-aid-review/supporting_documents/criminallegalaidconsultationdocument.pdf.

[172] M Fouzder, 'Legal Aid Fees: MoJ Offer to Receive Resounding "No"' *Law Society Gazette* (London, 20 March 2020); R Atkinson, 'The New Legal Aid Settlement is an Insult' *The Times* (London, 5 March 2020).

[173] Following that financial injection, the CPS began to hire more lawyers in earnest. Anecdotally, and in evidence given to the Justice Committee, that recruitment drive appeared to negatively impact sustainability within criminal defence services, as many defence lawyers were tempted to move to the CPS with its more attractive salaries and benefits than private defence practice. See M Fouzder, 'CPS Embarks on Hiring Spree' *Law Society Gazette* (London, 13 January 2020) and associated comments online, and comments and in oral evidence to the Justice Committee: Justice Committee *Oral Evidence: (a) Court Capacity, HC 284 (b) The Future of Legal Aid, HC 289* 24 March 2021.

[174] While the CPS received an additional £85m in funding, in 2020, the police received its biggest funding injection – amounting to £1.1bn – in 10 years (www.gov.uk/government/news/policing-gets-biggest-funding-boost-in-decade-to-put-more-bobbies-on-the-beat).

political era, with its 'panoply of changes in the form of governance',[175] had significant repercussions for criminal law and criminal justice as both became tools of political competition. Neoliberal governments' preference for managerialism and increasing distrust of public service professionals led them to introduce regulatory measures designed to incentivise efficient working practices and cut costs.

In this context, lawyers have been encouraged to accommodate demands to cut costs because they depend on the government for funding, and various governments have paid insufficient attention to lawyers' ability to improve access to justice. The result is that the system of publicly funded representation is both complex and fragile. Such fragility arises because the system has developed in a haphazard fashion according to particular governments' interests. It seems that unless governments make an effort to understand the supplier base and regain trust in professional decision-making, legal aid provision will continue to suffer at the mercy of the next governmental crisis. Successive governments have attempted to manage the resources available to fund public services via austerity measures, but such decisions must not be made on the basis of 'flawed assumptions'[176] about the necessity and operation of publicly funded representation.

The measures introduced by governments have undermined the ability to have meaningful debates about the essence and significance of access to justice and the importance of defendant participation. While the responsibilisation rhetoric of 1979–97 Conservative governments had justified the marginalisation of defendant needs, New Labour aggressively re-regulated the provision of criminal legal aid. Re-regulation and funding cuts continued through the recent Coalition and Conservative governments. As austerity exerted greater influence over those agencies which remain funded by the state, greater tension arose between the competing rationales of the legal aid system, governments, courts, lawyers and client needs and expectations. In response, firms have tended to adopt a managerial approach to casework, reduced the time taken to deal with cases and take more risks with obtaining funding for representation (see discussion in chapters three and five). All of these factors tend to exacerbate defendants' inability to actively participate in the process of summary criminal prosecution.

Ultimately, the piecemeal and sometimes contradictory approaches adopted by different phases of government have created a system that is so fragmented that the providers of legally aided services, and their clients, are further marginalised from meaningful participation in access to justice. Such marginalisation undermines principles of due process discussed in the preceding chapter.

---

[175] Lacey (n 17) 86.

[176] C Storer, 'Legal Aid Practitioners Group Response to the Ministry of Justice Consultation: Proposals for the Reform of Legal Aid in England and Wales' (*Legal aid Practitioners Group* 2013) lapg.co.uk/wp-content/uploads/2014/.../LAPG-JR-consultation-response-FINAL.docx 4.

Austerity measures adopted by the 2010–15 Coalition government exacerbated the impact of earlier changes to legal aid provision, and the effects of austerity continue to have a negative influence on the provision of legal services to defendants in the criminal process even though austerity has been ideologically rejected since late 2018. Effectively, as concerns about reducing cost became the dominant discourse, debates about the meaning of access to justice appear to have been side-lined, if not lost altogether. While, at the time of writing, the government is undertaking a review of criminal legal aid, the outcome is uncertain. It may be that the landscape of legally aided defence service provision has already changed irrevocably. The impact of these issues on lawyers and, by implication, their clients, is discussed in chapter five. Before that discussion proceeds, it is important to examine the organisational culture context in which magistrates' courts operate. While that culture is undoubtedly influenced by funding issues, chapter three discusses the broader norms and practices which influence how defendants experience summary justice.

3

The Culture of Summary Criminal Justice

I. INTRODUCTION

THIS CHAPTER INTRODUCES some of the key socio-legal studies of summary justice and develops them with more recent data. These studies examined the behaviour of professionals who work in criminal courts and identified how workgroup culture and the behaviour of courtroom personnel could potentially affect defendants' experiences of the proceedings. In the previous chapter, I introduced some trends in political policy that have influenced summary criminal courts – most notably budget cuts (especially to publicly funded representation) and demands for efficiency. Organisational culture in public institutions presents a possible challenge to the implementation of policy: a strongly independent culture could create an 'implementation gap' by only conforming to limited aspects of policy, or by modifying, and therefore frustrating, the detail of a policy once applied in an institutional setting.[1] In turn, processes of cultural adaptation to the political policy have the potential to affect levels of marginalisation experienced by defendants and their ability to participate effectively in the proceedings.

Throughout this chapter, I use the term 'courtroom workgroup' when referring to the organisational culture of magistrates' courts.[2] The term was proposed by Eisenstein and Jacob to assist in explaining how low-level courts make decisions.[3] Occupational cultures are not fixed, and cultures can vary over time and place.[4] As organisational cultures are not fixed, criminal defence lawyers

---

[1] See, for discussion of implementation gaps in criminal justice, K Stenson and A Edwards, '*Policy Transfer in local Crime Control: Beyond Naïve Emulation*' in T Newburn and R Sparks (eds), *Criminal Justice and Political Cultures* (Willan Publishing, 2004) and J Terpstra and N Fyfe, 'Mind the Implementation Gap? Police Reform and Local Policing in the Netherlands and Scotland' (2015) 15(5) *Criminology & Criminal Justice* 527–44.

[2] See R Young, 'Exploring the Boundaries of Criminal Courtroom Workgroup' (2013) 42 *Common Law World Review* 203.

[3] J Eisenstein and H Jacob, *Felony Justice: An Organisational Analysis of Criminal Courts* (Little Brown, 1977).

[4] This can be especially true across different jurisdictions. As Hodgson found, inquisitorially-minded lower court judges in France tended to engage much more directly with defendants than magistrates in England, which facilitated greater space for defendants to speak for themselves and

(and prosecutors) are likely to experience different but overlapping cultural expectations according to whether they are working in their office, at different levels of court and/or prisons and the police station. However, the concept of a magistrates' courtroom workgroup is useful because this group is sufficiently small and homogenous for certain behaviours to form and perpetuate through generations of legal professionals.[5] The professional summary courtroom workgroup consists of magistrates, authorised court officers (also known as legal advisers),[6] prosecutors, defence lawyers, court staff (eg ushers), court cell staff and probation officers. According to Young, these 'court actors patrol and defend the boundaries of workgroup power'.[7] Those boundaries may be interrupted by policies that attempt to alter workgroup practices. The courtroom, therefore, becomes a potential site for struggle as actors negotiate the nature of their role within the proceedings. Once equilibrium is reached, the introduction of external pressures (such as efficiency drives) has the potential to upset the negotiated relationships as the site of struggle changes.[8]

Successive studies have demonstrated that the culture of magistrates' courts is powerful. Although many of those studies predate more marketised approaches to criminal justice, several cultural factors in the operation of summary justice (eg professional networking and the use of jargon) have proved enduring despite significant political change. The professional actors who participate in the criminal justice process in the magistrates' courts appear to work in such a way that the status quo is largely maintained, despite being subject to increasingly politicised intervention through re-regulation since the 1970s. Therefore, although the demands placed on and the composition of the workgroup may have changed, some features of summary criminal justice remain constant.

---

limited the role of defence lawyers more than in England. However, Hodgson also noted a 'general antipathy towards strengthening the rights of the accused' across both inquisitorial and adversarial traditions (J Hodgson, 'The Challenge of Universal Norms: Securing Effective Defence Rights across Different Jurisdictions and Legal Cultures' (2019) 46 *Journal of Law and Society* 95–114, 104). See further J Hodgson, *The Metamorphosis of Criminal Justice: A Comparative Account* (Oxford University Press, 2020). Of course, many different models and modes of engagement between lawyers, judges, suspects and defendants exist internationally. For an interesting discussion of some different models in Rwanda, eg, see C Bizimungu, 'An Examination of the Impacts of Rape Myths and Gender Bias on the Legal Process for Rape in Rwanda' (PhD thesis, University of Sussex, 2019).

[5] See generally on legal aid lawyer occupational cultures E Cooke, 'The Changing Occupational Terrain of the Legal Aid Lawyer in Times of Precariousness' (PhD thesis, University of Kent, 2019).

[6] There are different types of court legal advisers, some legally qualified while others are not. Court legal advisers have different powers depending on whether or not they are legally qualified: The Magistrates' Courts (Functions of Authorised Persons – Civil Proceedings) Rules 2020. As these rules have only relatively recently come into force, court authorised officers may also be referred to interchangeably (though not always entirely accurately) as court clerks, legal advisers and Justices' clerks.

[7] Young (n 2) 218.

[8] Young argued that change is most likely to be achieved by disrupting the relationships that constitute the workgroup itself because this would cause the most disturbance to pre-existing practices (Young (n 2)).

Two important features of magistrates' court workgroup behaviour appear to have a significant impact on defendants' experience of the proceedings: the networks that operate among court personnel and the speed at which cases progress. The marginalisation of defendants has been exacerbated by the political othering of precariat groups through legal aid cuts discussed in the preceding chapter. The resultant 'them and us' attitudes operate to strengthen the pre-existing court personnel networks from which the defendant is excluded. This is made worse by market-based demands for efficiency that have increased the speed at which proceedings take place, further undermining the ability of defendants to participate in a meaningful way.

In order to demonstrate this, the chapter begins by briefly explaining defendant experience in the context of the nature and structure of the work-groups in magistrates' courts. Features of magistrates' court workgroups and their effects on defendants are subsequently analysed through discussions about professional networks, efficient case progression, standardised work practices, cooperative workgroups practices and plea bargains.

II. DEFENDANT EXPERIENCES AND THE CULTURE OF SUMMARY JUSTICE

In 1976, Carlen argued that the culture of summary justice operates to prevent defendants from being able to engage properly in the criminal justice process.[9] There were three major contributory factors to this assessment. First, the volume of magistrates' court business requires the workgroup to manage cases strictly. Second, defendants lack understanding of legal rules and procedures and third, professional participants are concerned to preserve their own roles within the criminal justice system.[10] The second of Carlen's factors is discussed in the following chapter. Carlen had earlier noted that defendants in the magistrates' courts were required to behave in ways unfamiliar to normal social settings, such as the appropriate use of particular forms of language.[11] These factors, combined with nervousness, might have a paralysing effect on unrepresented defendants.[12]

It is clear that cuts to legal aid have resulted in greater numbers of unrep-resented defendants struggling to present their cases in court. Statistics on representation levels in magistrates' courts are not routinely produced for public access, but one survey indicated that levels of unrepresented defendants in magistrates' courts had risen to 30 per cent by 2017.[13] During the course of my

[9] P Carlen, *Magistrates' Justice* (Martin Robertson 1976).

[10] Another important study conducted shortly after Carlen's can be found in D McBarnet *Conviction: Law, the State and the Construction of Justice* (Macmillan 1981).

[11] Carlen (n 9).

[12] Ibid.

[13] Institute for Government 'Criminal courts' (Institute for Government, London 2019) www.instituteforgovernment.org.uk/publication/performance-tracker-2019/criminal-courts.

own magistrates' courtroom observations in 2013, 22 per cent of defendants appearing in person were unrepresented, suggesting an eight per cent increase in the number of unrepresented defendants in four years (see further chapter five).

Despite this recent and concerning drop in levels of representation in magistrates' courts, the majority of defendants appearing there continue to be legally represented. Levels of legal representation rose in the 1980s, which coincided with the increasing professionalisation of summary justice (discussed further in chapter four). Since the enactment of the Prosecution of Offences Act 1985, prosecutions are largely managed by legal professionals independent of the investigation process rather than by police officers, and there are more defence advocates in court. Therefore, while the English and Welsh system is unique in its extensive use of lay justices, the workgroup has become increasingly professionalised despite the challenges to professionalism posed by the adoption of strategies of New Public Management into criminal justice (chapter one). Ideological distrust of professionals led to the development of a closely regulated professional network. Magistrates' court proceedings have also increased in complexity since the 1970s,[14] and 'represented or not, greater complexity serves to further remove the defendant from active engagement in the criminal process'.[15]

In studies of the 1970s and 1980s,[16] there was an implicit argument that if defendants were legally represented, fewer issues with comprehension might exist because the defence lawyer's role would be to ensure equality of arms and enhance the defendant's understanding about and during the proceedings. That assumption remains operative today, with many rules of evidence designed to address issues of participation predicated on the belief that being legally represented enables an adequate level of understanding for defendants, and therefore at least partially protects their Article 6 right to a fair trial.[17] However, Carlen was concerned that the provision of defence advocates would not alleviate problems with summary justice, but rather a cultural shift would be necessary to ensure that defendants could properly have a role in the magistrates' courts.[18] McBarnet also thought that, because the institutions of criminal justice are workplaces, they create networks and routines that exclude the defendant[19] and,

---

[14] D Newman, *Legal Aid, Lawyers and the Quest for Justice* (Hart Publishing 2013). The Ministry of Justice also recognises that criminal proceedings have become more complex in recent years. See Ministry of Justice 'Criminal Legal Aid Review: An Accelerated Package of Measures Amending the Criminal Legal Aid Fee Schemes' (London, Ministry of Justice 2020). The increased complexity of summary justice is discussed in ch 4.

[15] Newman (n 14) 9.

[16] McBarnet (n 10); A Bottoms and J McClean, *Defendants in the Criminal Process* (Routledge, 1976); A Samuels, 'The Unrepresented Defendant in Magistrates' Courts' (London, Justice 1971).

[17] A Owusu-Bempah, 'The Interpretation and Application of the Right to Effective Participation' (2018) 22(4) *International Journal of Evidence & Proof* 321–41. This issue is explored further in ch 4.

[18] P Carlen 'The Staging of Magistrates' Justice' (1976) 16(1) *British Journal of Criminology* 48.

[19] McBarnet (n 10).

therefore, 'to simply prescribe lawyers on tap for the lower courts as a solution to the defendant's dilemma is ... to ignore the much more fundamental structural and ideological realities which lie behind the courtroom situation'.[20] Newman's work suggests that these predictions were correct. He observes that 'the legal system does not work for outsiders. It is a member's only club, the world of lawyers and jurists'.[21] Both Newman's and my findings suggest that there remains a strong culture of cooperation among magistrates' court personnel, which continues to marginalise defendants from proceedings.

III. THE INFLUENCE OF PROFESSIONAL NETWORKS

Defending and prosecuting advocates have very particular roles, but those roles are constrained by a broader pattern of courtroom procedure (in addition to their organisational working practices). Snipes and Maguire note that although actors in court 'are from different institutions, have different goals and are formally arranged in an adversarial relationship, they often bind together in mutually convenient informal networks'.[22] The networks that operate in magistrates' courts develop as a result of the existence of shared goals among the workgroup members. The goals that exist may provide symbolic meaning to activities (such as seeing that 'justice' is done or maintaining group cohesion), or they may exist to ensure the smooth functioning of the proceedings (ie, expeditious case handling and controlling uncertainty).[23] This analysis, while useful, is not necessarily straightforward because different types of goals may come into conflict. As Young notes, not only does 'doing justice' mean different things to different groups, but also for most defence solicitors

> while delay might help them win a case ... most clients bring with them only modest fees ... and a fast aggregate turnover is the only way to make a living and/or to cope with the caseload. At the same time their institutional and market position requires them to maintain a reputation for effective representation.[24]

As such, while instrumental goals of reducing uncertainty and dealing with cases expeditiously are usually complementary, the goals of maintaining group cohesion and 'doing justice' may come into conflict, and the balance performed between core principles of crime control and due process (of which understanding and participation are part, to enhance procedural fairness) may vary on a case-by-case basis. This leads Young to hypothesise that 'expressive goals are

---

[20] D McBarnet, 'Two Tiers of Justice' in N Lacey (ed), *A Reader on Criminal Justice* (Oxford University Press, 1994) 203.

[21] Newman (n 14) 10.

[22] J Snipes and E Maguire, *Foundations of Criminal Justice Theory* (Routledge, 2007) 30.

[23] Eisenstein and Jacob (n 3).

[24] Young (n 2) 209.

merely rhetorical notions that are invoked by courtroom actors to legitimise their roles and activities'.[25] Even though it is a useful term here, the idea that these 'goals' are fixed or immutable should be avoided.

That said, there seem to be high levels of cohesion and stability among magistrates' court actors, even though there is also evidence to support that the people who make up the court workgroup differ in the way they prioritise and attach importance to varying goals. Overall, defence advocates tend to adopt cooperative rather than confrontational roles[26] and are prepared to modify their behaviour according to the needs of the workgroup as a whole.[27] One element of my research also suggested that when they feel that their hand is forced, defence advocates will prefer solidarity with their clients to solidarity with their workgroup (see below). The way that this type of resistance occurs is likely influenced by 'the relationships and norms that develop between those working repetitively together in these settings, in particular, judges, prosecutors and defence lawyers'.[28] In other words, there exists an '*internal politics of the profession*, which exercises its own specific and pervasive influence on every aspect of the law's functioning'.[29] While each professional group will differ in the working cultures adopted outside the courtroom,[30] the subsequent discussion focuses on the impact of workgroup culture within the court itself.

IV. EFFICIENT (AKA SPEEDY) CASE PROGRESSION

The demands for efficiency partially described in the preceding chapter provide a stark example of when professional and policy-related goals might come into conflict. Concern to ensure efficiency was manifest in the introduction of the Criminal Procedure Rules (Cr.PR) in 2005.[31] Their provisions mean that magistrates are under pressure to avoid delay and to be wary of granting adjournments.

---

[25] Young (n 2) 210. This is a significant point to remember in the context of interviewing advocates about their actions.

[26] Young (n 2); Carlen (n 9).

[27] Young (n 2).

[28] Young (n 2) 204.

[29] P Bourdieu, 'The Force of Law: Toward a Sociology of the Juridical Field' (1987) 38(July) *The Hastings Law Journal* 805; 806. Emphasis in original.

[30] On prosecutorial working cultures, see L Soubise (2015), 'Prosecutorial Discretion and Accountability: A Comparative Study of France and England and Wales' (Doctoral thesis (PhD), University of Warwick, 2015); L Soubise, 'Regulating Prosecutorial Discretion: Professional Identity, Legitimacy and Managerialism at the CPS' (Gordon Seminar in Criminal Law, Glasgow (online), 8 June 2021); A Porter, 'Prosecuting Domestic Abuse in England and Wales: Crown Prosecution Service "Working Practice" and New Public Managerialism' (2019) *Social & Legal Studies* 493–516 and A Porter, *Prosecuting Domestic Abuse in Neoliberal Times* (Palgrave Macmillan, 2020). On defence lawyer working cultures, see Newman (n 14) and Cooke (n 5). There are some notable overlaps between the two groups, highlighted where relevant.

[31] Updated versions of the Cr.PR are available on the Ministry of Justice website: www.gov.uk/guidance/rules-and-practice-directions-2020.

Those rules require that the parties identify issues in the case at an early stage and place a duty on the court to actively manage cases,[32] as adjournments at the trial stage are likely to be resisted.[33] This reflects a shift in adversarial approaches to criminal justice, which would have previously allowed a defendant to simply make the prosecutor prove the case against them without disclosing the nature of the defence, particularly in the magistrates' court.[34] The shift began before the commencement of the Cr.PR, as reflected in *Gleeson*,[35] which identified a duty on the parties to ascertain issues in a case at an early stage in the proceedings, and asserted that the same duty did not conflict with rules that protected the defendant from self-incrimination, nor did it offend solicitor-client privilege. These measures have explicitly required members of the courtroom workgroup to cooperate, thereby prioritising efficient, cooperative working practices over adversarial principles.[36]

A further initiative, specific to magistrates' courts, was introduced during 2006 and 2007 to try and combat perceived delay – Criminal Justice: Simple Speedy Summary (CJ: SSS).[37] At the time, the Department for Constitutional Affairs[38] said that magistrates' courts ought to be 'a platform from which we deliver simpler, speedier justice for our communities'.[39] The policy was designed to reduce the workload of magistrates' courts by advocating greater use of out of court disposals (eg police cautions) in minor offences.[40] Measures that diverted low-level offending away from the court process were advocated on the basis of economic efficiency, but this approach does not recognise the procedural safeguards attached to the criminal court process. Evidence suggests that diversionary penalties are administered on occasions when behaviour would previously have merited no more than an informal warning.[41] The result is that

---

[32] See also *R v Chaaban* [2003] EWCA Crim 1012. That duty extends to the defence, who the Court will now expect to indicate the likely issues at trial and confirm which parts of the prosecution case are not in dispute because justice does not allow 'people to escape on technical points or by attempting … an ambush' (Thomas LJ in *DPP v Chorley Justices and Andrew Forrest* [2006] EWHC 1795 at para 27).

[33] Criminal Practice Directions 2015, Amendments No 8 [2019] EWCA Crim 495.

[34] As a result of the Criminal Procedure and Investigations Act 1996, defendants in the Crown Court have been obliged to disclose their defence in a Defence Case Statement or face adverse inferences for failing to do so for many years. On obligatory participation, see A Owusu-Bempah, *Defendant Participation in the Criminal Process* (Routledge 2017). See further ch 4.

[35] [2003] EWCA Crim 335.

[36] Cr.PR 3.3 of the Cr.PR 2020 explicitly states that the parties are expected to cooperate and assist the court.

[37] Office for Criminal Justice Reform 'Delivering Simple Speedy Summary Justice. An Evaluation of Magistrates Court Tests' (London, 2007).

[38] The Department for Constitutional Affairs has now been subsumed into the Ministry of Justice.

[39] Department for Constitutional Affairs *Supporting Magistrates' Courts to Provide Justice* (Cm 6681, 2005) 4.

[40] M Zander, *Cases and Materials on the English Legal System* (Oxford University Press, 2007).

[41] R Roberts and R Garside, 'Punishment before Justice? Understanding Penalty Notices for Disorder' (Centre for Crime and Justice Studies, 2005); A Ashworth and L Zedner, 'Defending the Criminal Law: Reflections on the Changing Character of Crime, Procedure and Sanctions' (2008) (2) *Criminal Law and Philosophy* 21. Instead, police officers can exercise considerable discretion in

the powers of criminal justice agencies have been enlarged 'with little protection afforded to the vulnerable or innocent'.[42]

CJ: SSS discouraged adjournments at the first hearing, as all necessary documents should be with the court and the defence advocate before the hearing, thereby allowing appropriate early advice to be given.[43] There was some difficulty reconciling this with simultaneous changes to legal aid provision, which meant that funding for representation was uncertain, meaning that timely advice could not always be provided. Despite this, CJ: SSS appeared to have been successful in reducing the number of court hearings that occurred per case. For example, when I interviewed Defence solicitor D, they said that the number of hearings per case had reduced since the introduction of CJ: SSS, and there have been positive effects 'in terms of focusing people's minds at an early stage'. Several other interviewees also commented that case management is useful to help focus the issues. Young observed that on the basis that the incentives of the workgroup are not drastically altered, the workgroup is likely to modify their behaviour to absorb sporadic attempts at reform.[44] Perhaps the fact that court groups have always striven for efficiency explains why there has been relatively little coordinated pushback from lawyers, who instead noted the benefits of the policy. Young also notes how familiarity among a workgroup has a tendency to produce relatively stable workgroups who frequently and easily negotiate case outcomes.[45] Through this analysis, we begin to see the importance of the structural/cultural intersection that affects defendants' experience of the criminal justice system: the way in which initiatives are actually implemented is dependent on the behaviour of the courtroom workgroup. As Garland observes, 'a new configuration does not finally and fully emerge until it is formed in the minds and habits of those who work in the system'.[46] Thus it may be that it is the cohesion in the workgroup, rather than any efficiency drives, that has the greatest influence on courtroom productivity.

---

deciding whether or not to issue a caution or penalty notice. For discussion, see L Welsh, L Skinns and A Sanders, *Criminal Justice* 5th edn (Oxford University Press, 2021) and A Ashworth and M Redmayne, *The Criminal Process* 3rd edn (Oxford University Press, 2005)).

[42] Roberts and Garside (n 41). Ashworth and Zedner (n 41) do, however, express the view that diversionary methods might have a number of advantages for would-be defendants, such as avoiding the stigma of conviction, while Morgan notes that diversionary processes 'arguably avoid expensive, slow and arcane court proceedings, thereby freeing up the courts to deal more effectively with serious matters'. (R Morgan 'Austerity, Subsidiarity and Parsimony: Offending Behaviour and Criminalisation' in A Silvestri (ed), 'Lessons for the Coalition: An End of Term Report on New Labour and Criminal Justice' (Centre for Crime and Justice Studies 2010); 19.

[43] Office for Criminal Justice Reform, 'Delivering Simple Speedy Summary Justice. An Evaluation of Magistrates Court Tests' (London, 2007). The prosecutors' duty to serve initial case details on the defence is found in Cr.PR, part 8.

[44] Young (n 2).

[45] Ibid.

[46] D Garland, *The Culture of Control: Crime and Social Order in Contemporary Society* (University of Chicago Press, 2002) 24. Garland further notes, at 26, that 'socially situated, imperfectly knowledgeable actors stumble upon ways of doing things that seem to work, and seem to fit with their other concerns'.

In essence, the provisions of CJ: SSS were designed to increase efficiency and reduce cost. The need to deal with cases efficiently was also restated by the Administrative Court in *Persaud*.[47] However, as Jones predicted, justice may give way to speed as lawyers are given insufficient time to prepare cases properly.[48] The courts have attempted to cope with this conflict by means of 'a stale application of generalised procedures'[49] (discussed below).

Generalised procedures direct the exercise of control over cases so that 'routinised courses of action will seem appropriate and be facilitated'.[50] As Tata notes, it has long been established that the lower criminal courts are

> orientated to the high-volume throughput and disposal of cases, standardisation, and speed; the minimisation of uncertainty; the value of court workgroups or communities; the maintenance of inter- and intra-professional relations; and the avoidance of conflict. Speed and routinisation seem to be privileged over the unique stories of individuals. What is important to everyone is the 'efficient' disposal of cases (i.e. disposing of as many cases as possible with as little effort as possible).[51]

Consequently, 'bureaucratisation of decision-making ... emerges in opposition to norms of 'individualised' treatment'.[52] The result is that defendants are less able to play a distinctive role in the proceedings.

Building on CJ: SSS, the Ministry of Justice introduced the Stop Delaying Justice policy in 2012. The policy documents criticise the judiciary for failing to properly implement CJ: SSS, even though the number of hearings per case had reduced and the speed at which cases were progressed had increased.[53] The government's view in 2012 was that the defence community benefited from causing a delay in the system,[54] despite the fact that, as the Law Society pointed out,

> Defence practitioners have no interest in prolonging cases. Defence lawyers have been subject to significant reductions in legal aid fees, and are paid on the basis of a fixed,

---

[47] [2010] EWHC 1682 (Admin), *Hereford Magistrates' Court (ex parte Rowland)* [1998] QB 110 also stressed the need for efficiency alongside fairness. These cases follow a long line of precedent, including *R v Aberdare Justices (ex parte DPP)* [1990] 155 JP 324, *R (ex parte Walden and Stern) v Highbury Corner Magistrates' Court* [2003] EWHC 708 and *CPS v Picton* [2006] EWHC 1108. Similarly, these cases have reinforced a requirement for the defence to cooperate with the prosecution process. See, eg, *Malcolm v DPP* (2007) EWHC 363 (Admin).

[48] C Jones, 'Auditing Criminal Justice' (1993) 33 *British Journal of Criminology* 187.

[49] G Howard and J Freilich, 'Durkheim's Comparative Model and Criminal Justice Theory' in D Duffee and E Maguire (eds), *Criminal Justice Theory: Explaining the Nature and Behaviour of Criminal Justice* (Routledge, 2007) 61.

[50] C Hosticka, 'We Don't Care About What Happened, We Only Care About What is Going to Happen: Lawyer-Client Negotiations of Reality' (1979) 26(5) *Social Problems* 599; 607.

[51] C Tata, 'Ritual Individualisation': Creative Genius at Sentencing, Mitigation and Conviction. (2019) 46(1) *Journal of Law and Society* 112–40; 118.

[52] L Tepperman, 'The Effect of Court Size on Organisation and Procedure' (1973) 10(4) *The Canadian Review of Sociology and Anthropology* 346; 346.

[53] B Waddington, 'Is Stop Delaying Justice! working?' *Law Society Gazette* (London, 2012).

[54] Ministry of Justice, *Swift and Sure Justice: The Government's Plans for Reform of the Criminal Justice System* (Cm 8388, 2012).

standard or graduated fee scheme for criminal cases. The incentive on them is for cases to proceed quickly.[55]

One of the key provisions of the 2012 initiative was that case management should occur at the first hearing. Riddle noted that lawyers were concerned that legal aid applications would not be processed in sufficient time for the first hearing, adequate prosecution case papers would not be available and trying to conduct case management at too early a stage in the proceedings could breach lawyer-client privilege if instructions are unclear.[56] Waddington went on to describe the position in the magistrates' courts, which appears to undermine traditional adversarial principles, as follows:

> The Crown makes inadequate disclosure on the day the defendant appears at court. Within a short period of time thereafter, the defendant (in person or through his lawyer) is required to: identify the issues in the case (in effect advise the court and prosecution where the Crown's case might need more work to have the best or any chance of success); identify which prosecution witnesses are required to attend at trial (explaining why this should be permitted by the court); give an adequate account of his defence; identify his witnesses (at least in general terms) and be able to give a time estimate for any trial.[57]

By April 2012, defence lawyers complained that service of evidence in magistrates' courts was inadequate, but defendants were still expected to enter a plea.[58] Nonetheless, the next policy designed to further streamline criminal cases in magistrates' courts was introduced in 2015: Transforming Summary Justice. That initiative was again designed to encourage fewer hearings per case, greater cooperation among the parties, more effective trials and increase the speed at which cases progress through the magistrates' courts. A Crown Prosecution Service Inspectorate report about the initiative concluded, in 2017, that although the time taken to complete a case had reduced, and good working relationships among the parties were noted, prosecutors were still struggling to disclose adequate case papers, and there was a lack of consistency in the way trial preparation documents were handled.[59] As Ashworth had argued,

---

[55] The Law Society, 'Response of the Law Society of England and Wales to "Swift and Sure Justice": The Government's Plans for Reform of the Criminal Justice System' (London, The Law Society, 2012).

[56] H Riddle, 'Advancing the Case for Swift Action' *Law Society Gazette* (London, 18 October 2012) 32. The cases of *Firth v Epping Magistrates' Court* [2011] EWHC 388 (Admin) and *R v Rochford* [2010] EWHC 1928 have effectively undermined this claim.

[57] B Waddington, 'Rules of Engagement. Stop Delaying Justice!' *Law Society Gazette* (London, 29 November 2012) 21; 22.

[58] R Cave, 'Lawyers Claim New Policy Causes Miscarriages of Justice' www.bbc.co.uk/news/uk-17690404.

[59] HM Crown Prosecution Service Inspectorate, 'Business as Usual? A Follow-up Review of the Effectiveness of the Crown Prosecution Service Contribution to the Transforming Summary Justice Initiative' (London, 2017). See generally, J Ward, *Transforming Summary Justice* (Routledge, 2017).

'the appearance of haste quickly becomes the appearance of unfairness, and of 'summary justice' at its worst'.[60]

Three of the defence solicitors I interviewed felt that the court applies a desire to conclude cases at speed with too much rigidity because demands for efficiency legitimised the view that defendants know whether or not they are guilty of a crime regardless of the need for legal advice. That view of defendant knowledge is contrary to the evidence that they are often bewildered by the process itself, let alone the legal provisions behind it, and tend to assume a passive role in court.[61] Furthermore, one interviewee alluded to the burden and standard of proof in response to the court's views about defendant knowledge, noting that a client

> ... may well know whether he did it or not but that's not really what the criminal procedure's about is it? Otherwise they would just get people into the dock and say 'hello, what have you done?' That's not the way it works. You've got to know and understand the case against your client ... and unless they're going to suddenly change the way in which the court operates to become an inquisitorial system there is no reason for the defence to change that as being their starting point (*Defence solicitor F*)

All of the above initiatives have been designed to ensure a speedy throughput of cases in magistrates' courts, based on management techniques in public services.[62] As argued in chapter two, government policies employed management techniques in light of political perceptions about inefficiency in state-funded services. However, Carlen,[63] Bottoms and McClean[64] and McBarnet[65] had earlier noted that summary proceedings were often conducted at speed, which left defendants confused. Measures designed to increase speed are likely to leave more defendants more confused. The Law Society also voiced its concern that, by placing emphasis on speed, the courts risk increasing the likelihood of miscarriages of justice.[66] It seems that greater value is placed on lawyers' ability to improve efficiency than their ability to improve access to justice through enabling and enhancing defendant participation.

---

[60] A Ashworth, 'Magistrates and the Right to a Fair Trial' in D Faulkner (ed), *The Magistracy at the Crossroads* (Waterside Press, 2012) 31.

[61] See generally Carlen (n 9), M McConville et al, *Standing Accused. The Organization and Practices of Criminal Defence Lawyers in Britain* (Oxford University Press, 1994); J Jacobson and P Cooper (eds), *Participation in Courts and Tribunals: Concepts, Realities and Aspirations* (Bristol University Press, 2020).

[62] Other initiatives are also being pursued to streamline proceedings, such as the use of virtual courts and greater reliance on technology (C Baksi, 'Lawyers Must Embrace IT, Says Minister' *Law Society Gazette* (London, 25 February 2013) 3; Ministry of Justice, 'Criminal Justice System Efficiency Programme' (2012), www.justice.gov.uk/about/justice/transforming-justice/criminal-justice-efficiency-programme. Virtual courts are discussed later in this chapter. On the relationship between management techniques and neoliberal approaches to criminal justice, see ch 1.

[63] Carlen (n 9).

[64] Bottoms and McClean (n 16).

[65] McBarnet (n 10).

[66] C Baksi, 'Speeding Up Cases "Risks Miscarriages"' *Law Society Gazette* (London, 29 November 2012) 3.

V. REMOVING DEFENDANT PRESENCE TO IMPROVE EFFICIENCY

Another way to increase the speed of proceedings is to take cases outside of the physicality of magistrates' courts altogether, which is what happened through the enactment of the Criminal Justice and Courts Act 2015. The provisions of that Act introduced the Single Justice Procedure (SJP), which removed many low level (in purely doctrinal legal terms) offences from the magistrates' court as it has traditionally been understood. The SJP allows (encourages) adults who have been charged with non-imprisonable offences to enter pleas without attending court at all. Once a plea has been entered, and if it is a plea of guilty, the case will then be dealt with by a single magistrate and legal adviser without lawyers attending court for either party. It is left to prosecuting authorities to identify which cases are suitable for that procedure, while defendants should be sent a notice that advises them about the procedure and their options. While a defendant is able to request that the case be dealt with by way of a 'traditional' hearing in open court,[67] it seems likely that only the most confident defendants will not be put off by the time, cost and bureaucracy involved in asking for the matter to be dealt with in a traditional court setting. This also acts as a disincentive to plead not guilty.

An assumption that defendants both receive and understand the procedural notice is built into the procedure: defendants who do not respond are likely to be convicted and sentenced in their absence through this procedure. Transform Justice reported that over 80 per cent of people who sent a SJP notice entered no plea at all[68] and are punished by way of a fine administered via the Courts Service.[69] In 2018, the Courts and Tribunals Judiciary Service confirmed that if defendants 'do not engage, the case will be judged online on the papers by a single magistrate, working with a legal adviser to record the decision and sentence digitally'.[70] Furthermore, the administrative case progression powers of legal advisers have recently been increased to improve efficiency.[71]

In 2019, 57 per cent of magistrates' courts cases were disposed of using the SJP, and the vast majority of those cases concluded in a single day without any plea entered.[72] Conducting cases administratively behind closed doors literally

---

[67] See generally J Sprack and M Sprack, *A Practical Approach to Criminal Procedure* (Oxford University Press, 2019).

[68] Transform Justice, 'The Right to Know You are Accused of a Crime' 19 August 2019 www.transformjustice.org.uk/the-right-to-know-you-are-accused-of-a-crime/.

[69] The Criminal Procedure Rules allows magistrates' courts to proceed with cases in the absence of the defendant, which, in practice, means that the defendant will be taken to have entered a not guilty plea, and the prosecutor is allowed to present the evidence (in these cases, on the papers alone) and invite the court to find that the defendant is guilty in a streamlined hearing.

[70] Courts and Tribunals Judiciary, 'Judicial Ways of Working – 2022. Crime' (2018) www.judiciary.uk/wp-content/uploads/2019/01/jwow-2022-crime-survey.pdf.

[71] See The Magistrates' Courts (Functions of Authorised Persons – Civil Proceedings) Rules 2020.

[72] Ministry of Justice, 'Criminal Court Statistics (Quarterly): October to December 2019 (tables)' (2020) www.gov.uk/government/statistics/criminal-court-statistics-quarterly-october-to-december-2019; Ministry of Justice, 'Criminal Court Statistics Quarterly, England and Wales, January to

removes the defendant from physical participation in the process of summary justice and is unlikely to increase confidence in, or public understanding of, magistrates' courts. The chair of the Magistrates' Association raised concerns about this issue, commenting that '… it is essential that openness and transparency are not compromised. How the Single Justice Procedure can be opened to public scrutiny must be addressed'.[73]

Another way defendants have been (further) removed from active participation in the physical surroundings of magistrates' courts is via the rise of 'virtual' hearings. In these cases, defendants remanded into custody following charge appear in court via a TV live link between the court and the prison or, in some cases, the police custody area instead of being physically transported to the court building. The lawyer, if the defendant has one, is either at the court (and able to consult with the client via another video link in a private consultation room) or at the police station. Also, in 2015, the Chief Executive Officer of HM Courts and Tribunals Service set out a vision for streamlining summary criminal justice, which included reliance on virtual court hearings to save time and money.[74] While this is often referred to as a way of 'modernising' the summary court process, it is congruent with an overarching desire to 'improve efficiency' and reduce cost.

The use of remote live links for use by vulnerable and/or intimidated witnesses had been in place for some time, following the provisions of the Youth Justice and Criminal Evidence Act 1999. For witnesses, the provision of those facilities might make the difference of being prepared to give evidence or not and are undoubtedly a useful tool. Two things can, however, be criticised about this. First, vulnerable defendants are entitled to far less protection under the same provisions than vulnerable victims, highlighting the presumed lower status of the defendant in the criminal process.[75] Second, the fact that live links are appropriate for victims, who are often able to choose whether they participate or not, does not automatically mean that the same facilities are appropriate for use with defendants who are compelled to be present and for whom the consequences of conviction can be far-reaching, yet they have a muted role.

March 2019' (2019), assets.publishing.service.gov.uk/government/uploads/system/uploads/attachment_data/file/812556/ccsq-bulletin-q1-2019.pdf.

[73] J Bache, 'Magistrates Association Comment on the Single Justice Procedure' 20 August 2019, www.magistrates-association.org.uk/News/magistrates-association-comment-on-the-single-justice-procedure. Other magistrates have raised a range of concerns, such as the SJP becoming a rubber stamp exercise. See House of Commons, 'Role of the Magistracy within the Criminal Justice System' (2016), publications.parliament.uk/pa/cm201617/cmselect/cmjust/165/16505.htm.

[74] J Ward, *Transforming Summary Justice* (Routledge, 2017). Virtual courts had operated as a pilot scheme in a region of Kent since 2010 but were quite slow to develop.

[75] S Fairclough, 'It doesn't Happen … and I've Never Thought It was Necessary for It to Happen': Barriers to Vulnerable Defendants Giving Evidence by Live Link in Crown Court Trials' (2017) 21(3) *International Journal of Evidence and Proof* 209; S Fairclough, 'Speaking Up for Injustice: Reconsidering the Provision of Special Measures Through the Lens of Equality' (2018) *Criminal Law Review* 4–19.

The use of virtual magistrates' courts was expanded during the Covid-19 pandemic, meaning that members of the courtroom workgroup did not need to leave home to participate in proceedings. Supporters of remote court hearings hope that the pandemic was the catalyst that will lead to greater adoption of virtual court processes to increase efficiency and – for certain populations – access to justice.[76] Provisions to permanently expand the use of live links in criminal cases have been included in Part 12, Police, Crime, Sentencing and Courts Bill 2021. Benefits reported from the use of virtual courts include quickening 'the time from police charge to first hearing. The number of failures to appear in court for first hearings was also lessened'.[77] But, operationally, the use of virtual courts have caused numerous practical difficulties in summary criminal courts. Magistrates have complained about adjournments caused by malfunctioning equipment. Defence lawyers have expressed concern about due process and procedural fairness being undermined, lower levels of defence representation (and more guilty pleas among that group), and higher rates of imprisonment. Prison staff are often overstretched yet are relied on to provide the live link at their end of proceedings. Police complained about the greater risk and responsibility imposed on their services.[78] Lawyers also face a predicament about where they are best placed; at home (which might be best for their business in terms of reduced overheads), with the workgroup in court, or with their client outside the court.[79] Defence lawyers further complain that it is more difficult to take instructions and build a rapport with a client who appears via video link.[80] Fielding et al asked a small sample of defendants about their experiences of appearing via video link, who reported that they experienced greater difficulty communicating with their lawyers and felt unable to participate in proceedings properly.[81] That defendants felt unable to participate properly is unsurprising when attempts to engage with the court that are incongruent with the court's expectations can result in defendants simply being literally muted during proceedings.[82] Additionally, lawyers particularly struggled to obtain case

---

[76] R Susskind, 'Covid-19 Shutdown Shows Virtual Courts Work Better' *Financial Times* (London, 7 May 2020); R Susskind, *Online Courts and the Future of Justice* (Oxford University Press, 2019).

[77] Ward (n 74) 35.

[78] Ward (n 74).

[79] E Rowden, 'Virtual Courts and Putting "Summary" Back into "Summary Justice": Merely Brief, or Unjust?' in J Simon, N Temple and R Tobe (eds), *Architecture and Justice: Judicial Matters in the Public Realm* (Ashgate, 2013).

[80] J Ward, 'Transforming "Summary Justice" Through Police-led Prosecution and "Virtual Courts"' (2015) 55 *British Journal of Criminology* 341. See further N Fielding, S Braun and G Hieke, 'Video Enabled Justice Evaluation' (Guildford, University of Surrey 2020) Online at spccweb.thco.co.uk/our-priorities/access-to-justice/video-enabled-justice-vej/video-enabled-justice-programme-university-of-surrey-independent-evaluation/. See further V Long, 'Online Courts: Re-assessing Inequality in the "Remote' Courtroom"' (2021) 11(1) *Excursions* 77–102.

[81] Fielding et al (n 80). See also (Justice Committee Oral Evidence: (a) Court Capacity, HC 284; (b) The Future of Legal Aid, HC 289. 9 February 2021).

[82] P Gibbs, 'Defendants on Video – Conveyor Belt Justice or a Revolution in Access?' (Transform Justice, 2017). I had also experienced this as a practitioner.

papers at short notice for video link hearings.[83] Ward persuasively argued that these matters 'point to issues of procedural rights and principles of open justice becoming weakened within virtual court styles of delivery',[84] particularly as no one has the right to refuse an appearance via video link.[85] While, in light of the accelerated use of virtual hearings since 2020, the Judicial College has issued guidance that aims to improve the experience of all parties to virtual hearings,[86] the issue of muting participants is not addressed in the document. Additionally, the Equality and Human Rights Commission found 'that opportunities to identify impairments and make adjustments are lost or reduced when a defendant appears in court by video-link rather than in person'.[87] If defendants are less able to participate in and properly understand hearings conducted via video link, this might further undermine their right to effective participation under Article 6 ECHR.[88] The use of virtual court facilities also appears to have accelerated a reduction in the court estate: by late 2017, the court estate had shrunk to 350 magistrates' courts from 605 in 2010, and further closures were planned.[89]

Through the continued use and further implementation of these measures, successive governments have expressed their wish to increase efficiency despite recognising that 'target chasing has replaced professional discretion and diverted practitioners' focus from delivering the best outcomes using their skill and experience'.[90] Defendants' needs appear to be further marginalised through the implementation of efficiency drives in summary justice. Interviewed defence advocates seemed to be more likely to express these issues through their view that demands for efficient case management remove discretion so that court procedures become routine. For example, one Defence solicitor said

> I always taunted them that they often forget that there's a 'J' in there and what does that stand for and, you know, they're so obsessed with this bureaucratic machine and moving it on ... It made the thing less case sensitive and it was very much a one size fits all mentality (*Defence solicitor K*)

[83] Criminal Justice Joint Inspection 'Delivering Justice in a Digital Age' (2016) www.justiceinspectorates.gov.uk/cjji/inspections/delivering-justice-in-a-digital-age/.

[84] Ward (n 74) 38. See also Ward (n 80).

[85] Crime and Disorder Act 1998 as amended by the Coroners and Justice Act 2009. The small sample of former defendants referred to above expressed the desire to choose whether or not to appear in person (Fielding et al (n81)).

[86] Judicial College, 'Good Practice for Remote Hearings' (Judicial College ETBB Committee, 2020).

[87] Equality and Human Rights Commission, 'Inclusive Justice: A System Designed for All' (Equality and Human Rights Commission, 2020).

[88] Gibbs (n 82).

[89] R Garside et al, 'UK Justice Policy Review. Vol 8' (Centre for Crime and Justice Studies, 2019); L Cameron 'Do Our Buildings Make Us? Covid-19 and the Courts Reforms' *Counsel Magazine* (London, May 2020).

[90] Ministry of Justice, *Swift and Sure Justice: The Government's Plans for Reform of the Criminal Justice System* (Cm 8388, 2012) 5.

This lack of case sensitivity reflects a desire to process cases rather than to promote individualised participation.

VI. SPEED THROUGH STANDARDISATION

Carlen noted, in 1976, that the volume of business that passes through the magistrates' courts means that the proceedings need to be carefully managed.[91] This meant that prosecutors made value judgements about which cases were worthy of being dealt with early in the day. Those judgements were often based on whether the defendant was pleading guilty – meaning the case could be disposed of quickly – alongside an assessment of the defendant's behaviour based on certain court accepted typecasts, which limited the ability of the defendant to present themselves in any other way.[92]

These situations occur because the volume of court business requires a quick, routinised approach to case management, legitimising institutional power.[93] The volume of cases that make their way through the magistrates' courts means that the workgroup is concerned 'to progress through the work of the day with minimum levels of confrontation and maximum levels of speed'.[94] In light of cuts to legal aid, volume processing is implicitly encouraged, and Johnston reports that some defence lawyers he interviewed have actively embraced further calls for cooperation ushered in through the new managerial style discussed in this and the preceding chapter.[95] Lawyers are also encouraged to act speedily by judges, who are drawn further into active case management roles encouraged by the efficiency drives discussed above. Darbyshire noted that District Judges sitting in magistrates' courts favoured 'the speed of the proceedings, the *summary* nature of summary proceedings'.[96] The speed at which the proceedings operate coupled with low levels of publicly-funded remuneration for defence lawyers means that defendants are, in Newman's view, offered fragmented access to legal services.[97]

---

[91] Carlen (n 18).

[92] For example, 'nuts'. This technique means that when a defendant does something regarded as inappropriate (ie something which threatens the legitimacy of the proceedings), remedial methods classify defendants as acting out of time, place, mind or order (Carlen (n 9)).

[93] Carlen (n 9); L Welsh and M Howard, 'Standardization and the Production of Justice in Summary Criminal Courts: A Post-Human Analysis' (2019) 28(6) *Social and Legal Studies* 774–93.

[94] F Leverick and P Duff, 'Court Culture and Adjournments in Criminal Cases: A Tale of Four Courts' (2002) 39 *Criminal Law Review* 44.

[95] E Johnston, 'The Adversarial Defence Lawyer: Myths, Disclosure and Efficiency – A Contemporary Analysis of the Role in the Era of the Criminal Procedure Rules' (2020) 24(1) *International Journal of Evidence & Proof* 35–58.

[96] P Darbyshire, *Sitting in Judgment: The Working Lives of Judges* (Hart Publishing, 2011); 154. Indeed, until the early 1950s, magistrates' courts were known as courts of summary jurisdiction (D McBarnet, 'Two Tiers of Justice' in N Lacey (ed), *A Reader on Criminal Justice* (Oxford University Press, 1994)).

[97] Newman (n 14).

The speed of the proceedings also creates an air of informality which, to McBarnet, 'would seem to be rather one-sided: the defendant's *role* ... is still governed by formal procedures, but the defendant's *rights* are greatly reduced'.[98] Specialist practitioners allow cases to progress at greater speed because they are equipped with the tools for negotiating case outcomes and understand the procedural issues involved in case management (see chapter four). This further adds a degree of specialisation to the proceedings, which allows the workgroup to routinise procedures.[99] Routinisation thus appears as a by-product of demands for efficiency and is manifested by a desire to process cases in standardised ways.[100] Bourdieu presented the concepts of habitus, field and capital to examine the behaviour of any group, including lawyers.[101] Habitus consists of people's understanding of how a particular world works and their experiences of that world. The ideas underpinning the habitus play out in the field – in this case, the courtroom and rules pertaining to it. Finally, each person has varying levels of power – or capital – concerning the way in which the principles and rules attaching to the habitus play out in the field. All three interact to inform the culture of any group. Practices that encourage standardisation become an important part of the habitus, providing actors with a sense of appropriate actions to take in particular circumstances.[102] Howard and Freilich are of the view that advocates when dealing with large caseloads, increase efficiency via 'a stale application of generalised procedures'.[103] I have taken generalised procedures to mean those that encourage particular routines through standardisation, reduce discretion and are applied to cases regardless of the particular features of each case. Further, and of particular relevance to the local context, familiarity and cooperation among a workgroup are likely to lead to standardised practices.[104]

As Leader notes, standardisation of practice is also key to professional identity in that it excludes the untrained newcomer from the commonalities woven into roles through repetition and negotiation in organisations, not least

---

[98] McBarnet (n 10) 140. O'Barr and Conley have similarly noted that the level of formality affects how participants behave, often to the detriment of the non-professional participant who is unable to utilise the formal language of dispute. Thus 'a litigant who is unable to structure his or her case in this familiar format may be at a serious disadvantage' (W O'Barr and J Conley, 'Litigant Satisfaction Versus Legal Adequacy in Small Claims Court Narratives' (1985) 19(4) *Law and Society Review* 661; 686).

[99] U Castellano, 'Beyond the Courtroom Workgroup: Caseworkers as the New Satellite of Social Control' (2009) 31(4) *Law and Policy* 429.

[100] Soubise (n 30) also identified a working culture among Crown prosecutors in which managerial practices created a tendency to adopt fragmented but routinised case progression procedures.

[101] P Bourdieu, *The Logic of Practice* (Stanford University Press, 1990).

[102] J Thornton, 'The Way in Which Fee Reductions Influence Legal Aid Criminal Defence Lawyer Work: Insights from a Qualitative Study' (2019) 46 (4) *Journal of Law and Society* 559–85; L Welsh, 'The Effects of Changes to Legal Aid on Lawyers' Professional Identity and Behaviour in Summary Criminal Cases: A Case Study' 44(4) *Journal of Law and Society* 559–85.

[103] Howard and Freilich (n 49) 61.

[104] Young (n 2).

the courts.[105] This is taken a step further through the introduction of management measures that are designed to limit professional discretion and closely regulate working practices.[106] Standardisation has the effect of undermining individual rights in favour of speed and reconfigures our understanding of 'justice' in a way that means efficiency is given greater priority in case management decisions than individual cases and circumstances.[107]

In the criminal courts, those management measures are supported by rules of evidence. As Owusu-Bempah highlights, many rules force defendants to subjugate their traditional rights (eg attenuation of the privilege against self-incrimination, the rules on admissibility of previous convictions) to the demands of the court,[108] fuelled by a 'toxic political atmosphere concerning due process rights of the defendant'.[109] Along with procedural demands for efficiency, the cultural shift implemented by statutory provisions, Cr.PR and criminal justice policy has pushed defence lawyers in summary courts even further away from the popular notion of a fervent defender of adversarial rights and more towards delivering a homogenised form of justice that allows defendants only limited opportunities (or requirements) for participation. Through these processes, case facts become normalised and translated into particular types of knowledge to be managed throughout the criminal process.[110] For example, Defence solicitor O expressed the view in an interview that 'it's purely tick boxes at the moment … it's just so bureaucratic'. This provides an example of how speedy case progression dehumanises defendants, whose cases are all managed subject to the same procedures even though they are likely to involve different issues and defendants have different priorities.

Newman also noted that, by focusing on a need to be efficient and meet targets, clients are often offered standardised services.[111] One of his interviewees commented, '[t]here's no time for access to justice … the client loses out in the need to get through the list'.[112] The standardisation that follows 'entails that both action and speed are utilised to undermine individual identity'.[113] Four interviewed defence solicitors and one interviewed prosecutor expressed the opinion that too many issues are reduced to 'yes' or 'no' answers on standardised forms. This exemplifies a desire for rigidity to encourage expeditious case progression. Defence solicitor K explained during an interview that 'everyone's

---

[105] K Leader, 'From Bear Gardens to the County Court: Creating the Litigant in Person' (2020) 79(2) *Cambridge Law Journal* 260–87.
[106] Garland (n 46).
[107] Welsh and Howard (n 93); Johnston (n 95).
[108] Owusu-Bempah (n 34).
[109] Johnston (n 95) 39.
[110] C Tata, *Sentencing: A Social Process* (Palgrave Macmillan, 2020).
[111] Newman (n 14).
[112] Ibid, 96.
[113] Ibid, 98.

got to fill in a form; everyone's got to tick a box to be audited and assessed to why you did that'. The same interviewee went on to describe policy designed to reduce the number of hearings per case as dehumanised and standardised bureaucracy, which removed personal discretion at all levels. That standardised bureaucracy can manifest itself through the use of forms during summary proceedings.[114]

At least 16 types[115] of form were regularly referred to (either implicitly or explicitly) in the magistrates' courts that were studied. Across 183 cases observed, there were a total of 220 references to forms, but only 49 of those references were explicit.[116] This demonstrates that forms operate to regulate the behaviour of the workgroup without necessarily directly involving the person who is actually subject to the proceedings. The alienating effects of this linguistic process are discussed in chapter four. My observations suggested that the most frequent explicit references to forms involve case management preparation for effective trial forms. Those case management forms are used when a defendant pleads not guilty. The advocates are required to record the matters that are in dispute and evidential requirements and then fix a trial date accordingly. The use of case management forms is further discussed in chapter four because they represent how the law has come to be expressed in magistrates' court proceedings.

Six of the seven prosecutors interviewed felt that case management is useful to focus on the issues in the case, but only three of 12 defence advocates expressed a similar view. Defence advocates seemed to be more likely to state that case management removes discretion and routinises casework, undermining the particular features of individual cases. That approach supports Brenneis's[117] view that the way forms are produced provides 'frameworks for guided response',[118] making it possible to detect a move towards standardised procedures associated with the perceived need to process cases quickly. As Defence solicitor G noted during the interview, 'the system really is being forced through … for the sake of expediency as opposed to justice'.

All of the above is not, however, to say that defendants would necessarily prefer the proceedings to be conducted at a slower pace. Bottoms and McClean

---

[114] This issue is discussed extensively in Welsh and Howard (n 93).

[115] Police bail notices, MG5 (police prepared case summary), MG10 (prosecution witness availability), Court bail notice, case management forms, sentencing reasons forms, trial reasons forms, means forms, cracked and ineffective trial forms, interpreter's timesheets, legal aid applications, form certifying committal procedures, TIC schedules, special measures applications, bad character and hearsay applications. These practices have also been discussed in L Welsh, 'Are Magistrates' Courts Really a "Law Free Zone"? Participant Observation and Specialist Use of Language' (2013) 13 *Papers from the British Criminology Conference* 3–16.

[116] I have taken implicit references to mean when it is clear that a form will be used, but it is not actually referred to during proceedings.

[117] D Brenneis, 'Reforming Promise' in A Riles (ed), *Documents. Artefacts of Modern Knowledge* (University of Michigan Press, 2006).

[118] Ibid, 49.

noted that many defendants seek swift case conclusion for a number of reasons, including issues with employment, the trouble of attending court and the anxiety it causes.[119] There is consequently a balance to strike between the swift conclusion of cases and enabling defendants to be included in the process while protecting their rights and enabling their participation through understanding. Ultimately, though, the process of case management is dependent on continued cooperation between the parties. We turn to a discussion of these phenomena and the extent to which they might marginalise defendants below.

VII. COOPERATION WITHIN THE WORKGROUP

Negotiation is commonly used to meet the court workgroup objectives of doing 'justice', maintaining cohesion, controlling uncertainty and efficient case progression. The relationship between advocates and the court seems to consist of both common and differing goals. While prosecutors will be concerned with securing a conviction,[120] organisational issues and victims' interests, defence advocates will be concerned with their duties towards clients, business interests and securing the best outcome for their client. All parties have an interest in maintaining cooperative relationships and dealing with cases expeditiously.[121] Lawyers in Newman's study also commented that there is a need to cooperate to ensure swift case progression.[122] Specific provisions in the Cr.PR are designed to encourage more early discussion about cases.[123] This means that all courtroom behaviour is characterised by high degrees of negotiation alongside routinisation, which enable the 'courtroom workgroup to move through its long list of cases at great speed'.[124]

All of the prosecutors interviewed felt that there is a good deal of cooperation between defence advocates, the court and Crown prosecutors, demonstrating that actors tend to avoid provocative forms of behaviour. However, there was a tendency to think that cooperation among advocates has always been good,[125] and the requirements of efficiency drives appeared to have antagonised those relationships, although prosecutor M said, 'we've probably fallen into, not deliberately, but accidentally, some sort of compromised way of working'. This supports Young's view that external influences are likely to result in an initial

---

[119] Bottoms and McClean (n 16).

[120] Porter (n 30) found that the managerially-driven desire to secure a conviction (that has restricted prosecutors' professional discretion) tended to create a working practice that resulted in the routine issue of witness summons in cases of domestic abuse where the complainant withdrew support for the prosecution.

[121] Eisenstein and Jacob (n 3).

[122] Newman (n 14).

[123] See, eg the overriding objective in Pt 1 Cr.PR.

[124] Young (n 2) 229.

[125] As evidenced by Carlen (n 9) and Bottoms and McClean (n 16).

period of resistance resulting in conflict and uncertainty, followed by acceptance of a need to make changes resulting in the establishment of amended norms for processing cases.[126] It also supports the notion that 'groups only have social structure to the extent that individuals act in regular and fairly predictable ways, while action is only possible because each individual has a certain amount of socially structured knowledge'.[127] External disruption, such as the introduction of policy designed to alter workgroup patterns, causes a degree of tension until the new material has been absorbed and, where the group feels it appropriate, adapted. One interviewee was of the view that there had never been any problem with cooperation and then 'the Criminal Procedure Rules came in and seem to be ordering people to do this and do that and get down to the issues in the case but I think we pretty much got that anyway' (prosecutor J). This interviewee described an initial period of disruption to stable work patterns followed by acceptance and adaptation.

Interviewed defence solicitors were of the view that while schemes designed to increase efficiency did encourage cooperation, they also imposed unrealistic timetables on defence advocates who, in line with concerns expressed above, were unlikely to have access to case papers before the first hearing date. Part 8 Cr.PR requires the prosecution to supply 'initial details' of its case, including a summary of the circumstances of the offence, a summary of any account given by the defendant in an interview, any written witness statement or exhibit that the prosecutor then has available and considers crucial to decisions about plea and case management, the defendant's criminal record, if any, and any available statement of the effect of the offence on a victim or others. The initial details supplied must contain enough information to allow the parties, at the first hearing, to make informed decisions about the plea, trial venue (if applicable), case management and/or sentencing. Despite these provisions, it is a common complaint in magistrates' courts that the defence does not have sufficient case details to enable defendants and their representatives to make informed decisions, supporting Frost's view that criminal justice reform is usually done 'dragging the defence along in its trail, rather than consulting in any meaningful way'.[128] Campbell, in his study, also recorded frequent delays in magistrates' court case progression as a result of incomplete service of case papers by the prosecution.[129] In 2018, the Justice Committee reported that

> The Magistrates' Association stated in its written evidence to us that it 'is aware of issues involving poor time and file management which result in delays and non-compliance with the duty to disclose—both initially and throughout the criminal

---

[126] Young (n 2).

[127] Newman (n 14) 27.

[128] T Frost, 'A Simple Solution' *Law Society Gazette* (London, 7 September 2007) 1.

[129] J Campbell, *Entanglements of Life with the Law: Precarity and Justice in London's Magistrates Courts*. (Cambridge Scholars Publishing, 2020).

justice process. ... The Defence Practitioners' Working Group also raised a number of issues specific to the Magistrates' Courts, including: prosecutors only serving a summary of the case; blank or incomplete schedules of unused material; unused schedules which were 'routinely' unsigned by the prosecutor; and defence requests for disclosure not being responded to. The Criminal Bar Association stated in their evidence that 'Transforming Summary Justice' has not delivered the results that may have been anticipated [in the Magistrates' Courts]. The approach to disclosure is cursory at best.[130]

The participants in this research felt that cooperation and the progress of cases are hindered because Crown prosecutors struggle to comply with disclosure within appropriate time periods. Eight of the 12 defence solicitors, and three of the seven prosecutors, interviewed expressed the view that the Crown Prosecution Service (CPS) either fails to comply with the required time limits for the service of case papers or simply fails to prepare cases thoroughly and in good time. By way of example, one Defence solicitor said:

> The Crown Prosecution Service, because of their staffing levels, is incapable of doing it [complying with service of papers] anyway. So literally within a couple of months [of policy implementation] it's all but forgotten about yet when it suits they'll bring it out and say that this is what you're supposed to abide by because the police and the CPS can't get their house in order and run it effectively. (*Defence solicitor I*)

Another defence lawyer said

> The prosecution have no ability any more to deal with summary only cases within the Criminal Procedure Rules. In fact, I think, because of the cuts, the CPS cannot comply with Criminal Procedure Rule time limits. It is impossible for them and therefore directions made have no bearing whatsoever in criminal trials and I think the prosecution know that, from a line of recent cases that suggest as long as there's some time for the defendant to give instructions, that's OK. (*Defence solicitor R*)

Significantly, nearly half of the prosecutors interviewed expressed similar opinions. One stated the opinion that economies of scale have meant insufficient staff to complete the work, which means file preparation is often subject to delay. Furthermore, thorough case preparation is time-consuming, so 'the whole system is grinding slower and slower and justice is suffering as a result' (prosecutor H). Another prosecutor expressed almost identical sentiments,

---

[130] House of Commons Justice Committee, 'Disclosure of Evidence in Criminal Cases Eleventh Report of Session 2017–19 HC 859' (London 2018) 42. Also, in 2018, the Secret Barrister wrote (about magistrates' court trials) 'For reasons I have never understood, and can only attribute to resourcing, the files are delivered to the agent on the night before or the morning of the big day. Whether on paper (as when I first started) or emailed (as now), they are guaranteed to be incomplete, disordered and missing the latest vital information' (The Secret Barrister *Stories of the Law and How It's Broken* (Macmillan, 2018) 75). A local area report of Wales in 2019 noted continuing problems with the timeliness and completeness of case details being served by the prosecution (HM Crown Prosecution Service Inspectorate, 'Area Assurance Inspection of CPS Cymru-Wales. CP001:1261' (London 2019)).

while another said that efficiency drives did not work because 'you never really get everything you need for the first hearing ... for that reason it failed miserably' (prosecutor J). The National Audit Office also found that the CPS often failed to oversee cases sufficiently and that CPS lawyers often did not have enough time to prepare for hearings properly.[131] This trend seems to have at least continued, if not worsened, though the effect of an £85m cash injection in 2019 remains to be seen.[132] Defence solicitor F felt that problems involving the late service of case papers were less acute before policies that encouraged efficiency sought to reduce the average number of hearings per case to two (ie a plea hearing and a trial where there has been a not guilty plea). That lawyer felt that defence solicitors often do not receive what they require from the CPS and then have to ask for cases to be listed for a court hearing to resolve those issues, whereas the previous system of allowing pre-trial review hearings allowed for necessary discussion to take place, which saved a lot of time and, therefore, money. Fragmented case progression practices and lack of file ownership at the CPS exacerbates this problem.[133] It also delays and complicates the process for defendants. Unrepresented defendants might especially struggle to remedy problems with disclosure.

Further tension between the parties was reported because once initial details were disclosed, the court's demands to proceed immediately to plea and, where necessary, a trial preparation hearing meant that defence lawyers 'are expected to assimilate gigantic amounts of information in a very short period of time and then make decisions for which you can be criticized at a later date' (Defence solicitor F). These comments provide evidence of the effect of external pressures on the courtroom workgroup as a whole. Those pressures might mean that defendants and their lawyers are pressured into making decisions at speed and without complete and/or accurate information about their case. As the primary objective of magistrates' courts becomes volume processing, the individual needs and rights of defendants (and victims) are side-lined in order to 'crank up the speed machine' (Defence solicitor K).

Half of the advocates interviewed felt that pleas are forced when the appropriate evidence is not available. One prosecutor said,

> We are trying to deal with case management quicker. Ultimately, whether this is improving cases or not ... I personally, I don't think it is improved. I think there is

---

[131] National Audit Office, 'Effective use of Magistrates' Court hearings' (London, The Stationery Office 2006). Further support for the issue is found in Grove's comments that, in his experience, CPS lawyers were often ill-prepared for hearings and often sought adjournments (T Grove, *The Magistrate's Tale* (Bloomsbury Publishing, 2003)).
[132] See www.bbc.co.uk/news/uk-49314259 and www.cps.gov.uk/cps/news/cps-response-additional-ps85m-funding.
[133] Soubise (n 30).

some benefit in stepping back allowing for enquiries to be made for perhaps a more informed decision to be made. (*Prosecutor L*)

Several defence lawyers felt the same way, with one saying:

> … they force it through and that is just again pointless. Just so they can say they've got a plea. Well, great but that plea could change in three weeks' time when I get that CCTV …. They'll say, 'your client knows if he did it'. 'Well my client says he didn't do it. Shall we just walk out of court and dispense with you lot? Because that's what, if you're saying that's how much trust you put in my client's word, well, let him go, drop the charges because he said he didn't do it'. (*Defence solicitor G*)

In addition, half of the defence solicitors and half of the prosecutors interviewed felt that the court's insistence on making progress at an early stage in cases leads to problems as the case moves through the court. There appear to be two problems. The first problem is a rise in the number of unrepresented defendants, which reduces the speed at which cases can be conducted. One interviewee commented on this, stating that while the courts are being told to avoid adjourning cases for legal aid to be resolved, 'all they're doing is building up longer proceedings for the court, taking up more time because people are unrepresented' (Defence solicitor E). Several interviewees felt that cases involving unrepresented defendants take longer to be processed, and those views appear to be supported more widely by barristers[134] and the judiciary.[135] Such delay appears to result from the inability of unrepresented defendants to understand both legal issues and the nuances of courtroom behaviour, which confirms that the defendant is at a greater disadvantage as an 'outsider' in the proceedings. This is discussed further in chapter four.

The second problem raised by participants in my research concerned how the desire to process cases at speed restricts the ability of advocates to conduct cases in the way they might wish.[136] Perhaps influenced by this, defence advocates were less likely to speak of cooperative relationships in a favourable way compared to the prosecutors interviewed. Only three of the 12 interviewed defence lawyers indicated that they felt there is a good degree of cooperation among advocates. Defence advocates tended to express the opinion that cooperation among advocates is important in order to maintain credibility with the court and CPS and, therefore, be in a stronger position to negotiate. Similarly, Newman found that lawyers regarded good relationships with prosecutors as beneficial to clients.[137] Carlen had noted the existence of compromise between lawyers many years

---

[134] O Bowcott, 'Jump in Unrepresented Defendants as Legal Aid Cuts Continue to Bite' *The Guardian* (London, 24 November 2019).

[135] J Thomson and J Becker, 'Unrepresented Defendants: Perceived Effects on the Crown Court in England and Wales – Practitioners' Perspectives' (Ministry of Justice 2019).

[136] Similar criticisms were made by lawyers interviewed by Johnston (n 95) and in relation to some CPS working practices (Soubise (n 30)).

[137] Newman (n 14).

ago,[138] and that behavioural pattern appears to persist. In his more recent study, Young noted that courtroom workgroup behaviour tended to be characterised by evidence 'that much decision-making was the product of shared expectations'.[139] One defence lawyer did acknowledge the difficulty of this position, saying that the defence advocate's role is not really to facilitate the proceedings, yet there seems to be a lot of scope for discussion and finding the best outcome even though 'crime is not something that you can mediate' (Defence solicitor A).

Difficulties at the CPS were not the only things that advocates criticised. One lawyer stated that those who design policies intending to improve efficiency do not understand the causes of delay in magistrates' court proceedings, saying that such initiatives are imposed 'in the flawed belief that delay in the court is caused by defence solicitors ... most delay in my experience is caused by the CPS not being held to account for their time limits' (Defence solicitor C). Ashworth and Redmayne previously noted that courtroom workgroups tend to view externally imposed change as reflective of a lack of understanding by those who are not part of the workgroup.[140] In the workgroup's mind, this may serve to justify adaptation through cooperation or could be an example – as Thornton identified – of minimising responsibility through the use of cognitive shielding.[141] This can mean that 'the form that 'justice' takes may depend on who has the most power within the ongoing flow of interactions, itself subject to the influence of a web of relationships and factors reaching well beyond the court'.[142]

The networks and routines operating in magistrates' courts provide an example of the different relationships between one's 'knowledge of the rules ... and their ability successfully to employ them to achieve a variety of ... meanings'.[143] In seeking to employ various legal rules, Carlen noted the existence of an uncomfortable compromise between court personnel.[144] Similarly, Sudnow reported a high degree of interaction and negotiation among prosecuting attorneys and public defenders in American criminal courts.[145] During an adversarial hearing itself, the advocates must usually 'temporarily step outside their typical modes of mutual conduct and yet, at the same time, not permanently jeopardise the stability of their usual team like relationship'.[146] One way this seems to occur is via the adoption of particular routines and processes that the workgroup is a party to, meaning that the rules can be understood and followed by the workgroup without upsetting its overall cohesion. The defendant, as a comparatively

---

[138] Carlen (n 9).

[139] Young (n 2) 229.

[140] A Ashworth and M Redmayne, *The Criminal Process* 3rd edn (Oxford University Press, 2005).

[141] Thornton (n 102).

[142] Young (n 2) 214.

[143] Carlen (n 9) 10.

[144] Ibid.

[145] D Sudnow, 'Normal Crimes: Sociological Features of the Penal Code in a Public Defender Office' (1965) 12(3) *Social Problems* 255.

[146] Ibid, 275.

fleeting participant in these relationships, is in a weak position of power. Newman found that the firms in his study all exhibited a factory-like approach to case processing, with one lawyer stating that business needs get in the way of idealism.[147] While magistrates' court workgroup behaviour seems to have been disturbed by external pressure for increased speed in case disposal, patterns of negotiation appear to remain strongly influential in summary proceedings. A prime example of cooperative workgroup practice arises when we consider plea negotiations.

VIII. PLEA AND CHARGE NEGOTIATIONS

One way in which the networks manifest themselves and interact with a desire for speedy case progression is via the use of plea negotiations.[148] McConville and Marsh describe the principal aim of plea negotiations as increasing 'control over output through consistency of production methods',[149] highlighting a further relationship between efficiency, plea negotiations and standardisation. In the 1980s, McBarnet was concerned about 'bureaucratic pressures pushing the police into acceptable arrest rates, lawyers into negotiating pleas, court officials into a speedy rather than necessarily a just through-put of cases'.[150] Such speed denies defendants the opportunity to understand the proceedings and consequently does not necessarily persuade them that just procedures are followed.[151] Further, Carlen noted that the police were aware that a less serious charge would be more likely to elicit a guilty plea and pressure to save police time was evident.[152] This meant that less serious charges might be offered to speed up the court process. Courts have themselves noted that prosecutors might prefer summary charges in the name of expedition but also in order to elicit early guilty pleas.[153] Conversely, defendants often spent protracted periods of time waiting for their cases to be called, which only increased their anxiety.[154] It is via processes such as these that 'the ideal of adversary justice is subjugated to an organisational efficiency'[155] as legal ideology becomes subordinate to economic

---

[147] Newman (n 14).

[148] A Mulcahy, 'The Justifications of "Justice": Legal Practitioners' Accounts of Negotiated Case Settlements in Magistrates' Courts' (1994) 34(4) *British Journal of Criminology* 411.

[149] M McConville and L Marsh, 'Factory Farming and State-Induced Pleas' in J Hunter, P Roberts, S Young and D Dixon (eds), *The Integrity of Criminal Process. From Theory into Practice* (Hart Publishing, 2016) 102.

[150] McBarnet (n 10) 3.

[151] Carlen (n 9).

[152] Ibid.

[153] Bottoms and McClean (n 16).

[154] Carlen (n 9).

[155] Ibid, 20.

and bureaucratic ends.[156] Campbell's view is that summary justice 'is notable for the absence of due process rights'.[157]

Both prosecutors and defence advocates that I interviewed spoke in favour of plea negotiations. Interviewees, whether prosecuting or defending, mentioned that plea negotiations were helpful to improve the speed of proceedings, reduce unnecessary cost and improve outcomes for both parties. Both prosecutors and defence solicitors mentioned that plea negotiations could be valuable to both victims and defendants. Defence solicitor N spoke of the need to be respectful to victims during negotiations, and prosecutors H and P both felt that plea negotiations could be beneficial to victims. Interviewee P was proud of the stance they took in plea negotiations:

> I'm not one of those prosecutors who would never accept a basis or a lower plea, or a mixture of pleas for example, particularly where you've got vulnerable victims, people who don't want to give evidence that have to come to court. If you can get another conclusion that will give the same sentence or near enough and it reflects the offence then I don't think that's a bad thing.[158]

Another prosecutor expressed the view that

> If a defendant is willing to plead guilty to some offences and it's quite clear that the other offences that are left aren't going to affect his sentence at all, then clearly, a plea negotiation with the defence is going to be useful … At the end of the day, it's all statistics driven for the court and the CPS. At the end of the day you just want to get a guilty plea, a good result on the file. (*Prosecutor J*)

Newman noted that most defence advocates tended to consult prosecutors about cases before speaking to their clients,[159] and I also found this common-place (including as a practitioner myself). From my own perspective, speaking to the prosecutor before speaking to the client enabled me to attend to the client with all the information I could have about a case and some understanding of the prosecutor's approach. Yet, these practices might also operate to prioritise the issue of 'getting a deal' or that 'good result on the file'. These practices seem to be a significant concern in light of both that prosecutor's comment and Soubise's study, in which recording an expeditious guilty plea appeared to be a significant concern for prosecutors.[160] Plea negotiations of this nature increase the likelihood that guilty pleas are 'not always or even typically consensual admissions of guilt, but are rather tactical decisions based on forecasting the probability of conviction at trial and the likely outcomes of trial, and evaluating potential discounts in exchange for pleading guilty'.[161]

---

[156] McBarnet (n 10).

[157] Campbell (n 129).

[158] A 'basis' in this sense is an amendment to the facts of the case – eg that a punch was provoked rather than unprovoked. Interviewee H felt there could be a midway point; it could be beneficial for the victim not to go to court if the 'right' result can still occur following a negotiation.

[159] Newman (n 14).

[160] Soubise (n 30).

[161] R Helm, 'Conviction by Consent? Vulnerability, Autonomy and Conviction by Guilty Plea' (2019) 83(2) *Journal of Criminal Law* 161–72; 162.

While plea negotiations often place undue pressure on defendants to plead guilty[162] (as does the system of credit, or 'reward'[163] through a sentencing discount for entering an early guilty plea and provisions which allow for an advance indication of sentence)[164] they may also 'allow the defendant to return to a normal routine ... provide the prosecution with the desired conviction, and allow the defence to claim success in the form of a sentence discount or other concession'.[165] While all advocates who spoke about plea negotiations appreciated the opportunity to foreshorten the proceedings, defence advocates also mentioned that plea negotiations could be beneficial to clients in resolving the issues as soon as possible and limiting the nature or number of charges. As prosecutor M put it:

> ... the defendants themselves like to feel as though they've got something. So even if it's just a slight movement they would've felt like they've won something and so would be more open to pleading to something, however little they got at the end of the day.

Prosecutor J further indicated that plea negotiations tick the right boxes for the CPS while issues for the victims seem to be undermined because 'statistics seem to be the important thing'. However, as Mulcahy[166] notes, plea negotiations also fulfil a desire for swift case resolution, which may favour bureaucratic procedures over adversarial due process aims, including the ability of defendants to participate as an element of due process. Among these bureaucratic 'necessities' is keeping not guilty pleas at a manageable level.[167] In 2019, magistrates' courts dealt with 1.48m cases, compared to the 103,000 cases received by Crown Courts in 2018.[168] As Mulcahy notes, heavy workloads encourage routine, minimal practices in which plea bargaining is a useful tool that may subordinate the needs of defendants to managerial imperatives.[169] Recently, 90 per cent of surveyed legal professionals 'said that they do think that some defendants plead

[162] R Helm, 'Constrained Waiver of Trial Rights? Incentives to Plead Guilty and the Right to a Fair Trial' (2019) 46(3) *Journal of Law and Society* 423–47.
[163] Grove (n 131) 32. See s 73 Sentencing Act 2020, and Sentencing Council, 'Reduction in Sentence for a Guilty Plea' (2017), www.sentencingcouncil.org.uk/overarching-guides/crown-court/item/reduction-in-sentence-for-a-guilty-plea-first-hearing-on-or-after-1-june-2017/. For discussion, see McConville and Marsh (n 149).
[164] See *R v Goodyear* [2005] 2 CrAppR 20.
[165] Mulcahy (n 148) 414.
[166] Mulcahy (n 148).
[167] Bottoms and McClean (n 16). Roach Anleu and Mack also found that judges were more inclined to adjourn proceedings if there was a likelihood an adjournment would elicit a guilty plea (S Anleu and K Mack 'Intersections Between In-Court Procedures and the Production of Guilty Pleas' (2009) 42(1) *Australian & New Zealand Journal of Criminology* 21–23).
[168] G Sturge, 'Court Statistics for England and Wales Briefing Paper Number CBP 8372' (House of Commons Library, 2019).
[169] Mulcahy (n 148). Mulcahy noted that plea negotiations tend to take place at Pre Trial Review hearings, which have been reformed as Case Management Hearings in recent years. The resort to plea bargaining and system of credit for the entry of an early guilty plea is considered by Bibas to be an example of insiders in the criminal justice system redirecting standard practices in order to dispose of more cases in less time (S Bibas, *The Machinery of Criminal Justice* (Oxford University Press, 2012)).

guilty just because it is quicker and easier than going to trial'.[170] Innocent people who belong to marginalised populations tend to suffer more adverse effects from plea bargaining than privileged defendants.[171] As rules and policies introduced by the state seek to encourage as many early guilty pleas as possible, the aim of efficiency in criminal justice is in direct conflict with the presumption of innocence, burden and standard of proof and needs of defendants. Demands for cooperation of this nature, especially in an era of problematic levels of prosecution disclosure, have further undermined the traditional view of the defence lawyer's role[172] as a zealous advocate for their clients' interests[173] and pushed defendants themselves more towards the margins of participation.

Similarly, Sudnow noted, in the context of the American Public Defender, that explicit forms of plea bargaining are used to manage cases and produce 'normalised' or common types of offending.[174] As Baldwin and McConville noted, such practices operate to exclude defendants from the process,[175] while producing, via negotiation, 'a set of unstated recipes for reducing original charges to lesser offences'.[176] This strips defendants of their individuality in favour of efficiency[177] and effectively excludes defendants from participation in the process because they are unaware of the 'ingredients' necessary for the recipe, exacerbating the process of marginalisation. Similar patterns emerge in English and Welsh courts, and the consequent use of plea negotiations reinforces the cooperative networks that operate in summary criminal courts at the expense of the 'outsider' defendant to whom 'justice' is done.

Worryingly, McConville, Sanders and Leng noted that weak cases also tended to elicit guilty pleas via bargaining techniques.[178] They suggested that this occurs because the defence advocates are a '*part of*, rather than challenger to, the apparatus of criminal justice ... As officers of the court they are captured by crime control, not due process'.[179] Bottoms and McClean were less critical of the advocates' behaviour in this regard, suggesting that lawyers advise possibly innocent people to plead guilty not

> because of any commitment to a crime control ideology, nor because they are the subservient hacks of the court system ... they are operating within a system heavily

---

[170] Helm (n 152), 443; See further R Nobles and D Schiff, 'Criminal Justice Unhinged: The Challenge of Guilty Plea' (2018) 39 *Oxford Journal of Legal Studies* 100.

[171] J Peay and E Player, 'Pleading Guilty: Why Vulnerability Matters' (2018) 81 *Modern Law Review* 929.

[172] Johnston (n 95).

[173] T Smith, 'The "Quiet Revolution" in Criminal Defence: How the Zealous Advocate Slipped into the Shadow' (2013) 20:1 *International Journal of the Legal Profession* 111–37.

[174] Sudnow (n 145).

[175] J Baldwin and M McConville, *Negotiated Justice: Pressures on Defendants to Plead Guilty* (Martin Robertson, 1977).

[176] Sudnow (n 145) 262.

[177] McConville and Marsh (n 149).

[178] M McConville, A Sanders and R Leng, *The Case for the Prosecution* (Routledge, 1991).

[179] Ibid, 167. Emphasis in original.

imbued with liberal bureaucratic rules and values, and they know that their clients might indeed receive heavier penalties if they are found guilty rather than plead guilty.[180]

It should also be noted that Bottoms and McClean found that the majority of defendants who had pleaded guilty said they had done so because they were, in fact, guilty or because the police had a good case.[181] While Newman's more recent study would support Baldwin and McConville's observations[182] in that he similarly considered that defence solicitors placed pressure on defendants to enter negotiated guilty pleas, neither he nor I interviewed defendants.[183]

Carlen had earlier noted that court personnel presented coercive tactics (such as plea negotiations) as no more than the routine and mundane way of conducting court business because those who regularly work within the courts can exercise greater control over the social space than those who pass through the system.[184] The exercise of such control 'infuses the proceedings with a surreality which atrophies defendants' abilities to participate in them'.[185] Furthermore, the design of the courtroom (including poor acoustics and the use of the dock) along with the use of jargon[186] and intra-personnel signalling ostracise the defendant, which leaves defendants unable to understand or follow proceedings.[187] All parties are aware that such compromises exist while simultaneously trying to preserve their professional integrity, which is itself undermined by the very existence of inter-professional compromise.[188] Again, these problems appear to persist in summary criminal justice.

Compromise has, therefore, always been a significant feature of professional relationships among advocates and, as Carlen noted, 'the tacit knowledge among all players that strict adherence to the formal rules would slow down and ... probably stop play altogether puts those who are prepared to put the game at risk ... in a very strong position'.[189] However, strict adherence to rules might also damage professional relationships and, in turn, affect negotiating

---

[180] Bottoms and McClean (n 16) 231.

[181] Bottoms and McClean (n 16).

[182] Baldwin and McConville (n 175).

[183] Newman (n 14).

[184] Carlen (n 18); Carlen (n 9). Young points out that 'routine' should not, however, be conflated with superficial (R Young 'Managing the List in the Lower Criminal Courts: Judgecraft or Crafty Judges?' (2012) 41(1) *Common Law World Review* 29–58).

[185] Carlen (n 9) 19.

[186] That is not to say that court personnel did not attempt to explain the rules to unrepresented defendants, although this often simply added to the confusion (Carlen (n 9)). On courtroom design, especially the use of the dock, see L Mulcahy, 'Putting the Defendant in Their Place: Why Do We Still Use the Dock in Criminal Proceedings?' (2013) 53 (6) *The British Journal of Criminology* 1139–56; Campbell (n 129). See also the example of the defendant in the dock in ch 1.

[187] Carlen (n 18); For more recent work by Carlen which indicates little has changed since her earlier study, see also P Carlen, 'Struggling for Justice' (2018) 27 (2) *Griffith Law Review* 176–81 and P Carlen and L França (eds), *Justice Alternatives* (Routledge, 2019).

[188] Carlen (n 9).

[189] Carlen (n 9) 69.

powers and reputation. In a more recent study, Young referred to the literature supporting the notion that defence lawyers tend to refrain from performing 'legal manoeuvres that would aggravate other members of the workgroup'.[190] As budgets have been cut and demands for efficiency have increased, lawyers have become further alienated from their role as active advocates, which means they are further disempowered and more dependent on a cooperative workgroup.[191]

When discussing plea negotiations, half of the interviewed defence lawyers felt that delegation of work to Associate Prosecutors[192] inhibited the ability to conduct plea negotiations because Associate Prosecutors had less case owner-ship and fewer powers than Crown prosecutors. Defence solicitor F said

> It's very difficult to get them to go behind a decision that has already been made even when you are drawing attention to evidence that might not properly have been considered in context when the original decision to prosecute was made.

Comments of this nature and the favourable view of plea negotiations taken by prosecutors and defence lawyers alike highlights how important cooperation and negotiation is to the magistrates' court workgroup. At best, defence lawyers are bargaining for their clients (and at their instruction) when the prosecutor is unable to prove the case, but a different charge would be appropriate to all parties. In the middle of the spectrum, they have insufficient time and fund-ing to challenge the workgroup desire for swift case progression. At worst, they have little motivation to defend properly, especially if they develop an expecta-tion that cases will conclude via a plea negotiation.[193] But the defendant, as a transient bystander to the group, is unlikely to be able to participate in these processes fully and meaningfully. As McConville and Marsh say of plea nego-tiations, all '[p]articipants in the process today have become entrapped in an elaborate charade in which they act out prescribed roles'.[194]

IX. CHALLENGING EFFICIENCY THROUGH DUE PROCESS AND PROCEDURAL FAIRNESS

When the ability to negotiate is challenged, defence lawyers were quick to express their distaste for work practices that they felt were designed to push cases through the process inflexibly. An interesting example of this distaste arose when discussing plea advice and decisions in the context of demands for

[190] Young (n 2) 232.
[191] D Newman and L Welsh, 'The Practices of Modern Defence Lawyers: Alienation and its Implications for Access to Justice' (2019) 48(1–2) *Common Law World Review*. 64–89; Smith (n 173).
[192] Associate Prosecutors are not lawyers but are legally trained by the CPS to conduct a range of hearings in magistrates' courts. See further L Soubise, 'Prosecuting in the Magistrates' Courts in a Time of Austerity' (2017) 11 *Criminal Law Review* 847–59.
[193] McConville and Marsh (n 149).
[194] Ibid, 99.

efficiency. Almost half of the interviewed defence lawyers commented that when relevant papers are unavailable at the first hearing, defence solicitors will advise their clients to plead not guilty but later, when the relevant evidence has been received and reviewed, approach the prosecutor with a view to negotiating pleas. This increased the number of ineffective trial bookings and increased delay and uncertainty for both defendants and victims. Two interviewed prosecutors also noted that forcing the entry of a plea tended to mean that defendants entered not guilty pleas, which had a knock-on effect for case management and trial listings. Six of the defence solicitors and three of the prosecutors interviewed were of the view that this situation forces people into premature decision-making that might not be in the client's best long term interests, as well as leading to more trial listings that are ineffective. The advocates' views are supported by the courts' statistics which indicated that the number of ineffective trial bookings had increased following demands to streamline the case management and trial process into two hearings.[195]

The entry of a not guilty plea in such circumstances appeared to be one of the few ways in which defence solicitors resisted demands for efficiency. The evidence may demonstrate that, while the adversarial nature of the proceedings is largely eroded by high degrees of cooperation accompanied by judicial chastisement for failure to cooperate,[196] defence advocates will ultimately (albeit in extreme circumstances) demonstrate loyalty to their clients above all else. This issue may arise because, in Young's view, while 'Judges and prosecutors value high disposition rates in order to transmit an aura of accomplishment ... The position of defence lawyers is less clear cut'.[197] That lack of clarity results from issues such as modest fees, a need to maintain both institutional and marketplace reputation and different outcome goals among prosecutors and defence lawyers.

Defence lawyers indicated that they exercised a right to rely on legal provisions – the burden and standard of proof, both of which generally lie with the prosecutor – when they felt their client was being forced into an unfavourable situation. Interestingly, interviewees repeatedly used the words 'force' or 'push' when discussing this trend, as if the provisions represented a symbolic attack on principles relating to fair procedures. One defence solicitor echoed those sentiments in explaining that advocates do not like to be told that a plea must be entered and generally react by telling the client to plead not guilty and require the attendance of all of the witnesses at the trial because the regime forces

> ... you into a position from where you take the safest line for your client ... whereas if they gave you a little bit of time to engage with your client, get some proper

---

[195] Her Majesty's Court Service, 'CJ: SSS Project Defence Questions' (London, 2008).

[196] M McConville and L Marsh, 'Adversarialism goes West: Case Management in Criminal Courts' (2015) 19(3) *International Journal of Evidence & Proof* 172–89. See further McConville and Marsh (n 149).

[197] Young (n 2) 209.

> instructions, look at the paperwork … you may be pleading guilty or you may be saying 'alright it is a trial but these are the issues, it's only going to take two hours and we only need one witness.' (*Defence solicitor E*)

Therefore, when forced into what they regard as premature decision-making, defence advocates may be less likely to behave in a cooperative way and encourage defendants to enter not guilty pleas.

As Carlen[198] and Young[199] have noted, the smooth operation of summary criminal courts is dependent to a large extent on the ability of defence advocates to influence or control clients for the majority of the time. Thus, when they feel sufficiently threatened, advocates will reject their usual conciliatory behaviour in favour of strict legal provisions, which, in turn, disrupts the proceedings. It is unclear when and what causes advocates to feel sufficiently threatened to behave in that way. The behaviour does, however, suggest that, while working in congruence with instrumental goals of efficiency and cooperation most of the time, the expressive nature of justice via broad principles of procedural fairness and due process are, in fact, considered to be the most valuable goal – a kind of 'trump card'. As Carlen noted, a willingness to disrupt proceedings via strict adherence to legal principles places the challenger in a very powerful position.[200] For example, one defence lawyer, when speaking about being questioned over witness requirements, said:

> if you think as a defence lawyer that you need a witness then why should you be questioned about … why you should have your witness? You want the witness, you're a professional and you should be treated as one who is competent to make that decision for yourself … It [demands for efficiency] has changed the way they work – the magistrates and even the DJs because they do that very proactively even these days, they say 'well why do you want this person?' You know and the truth is actually can they actually stop you if you put your foot down? They can't so it's wasting the next five, 10 minutes arguing about something that they can't actually stop you if you say 'actually as a defence lawyer, I do want this witness'. (*Defence solicitor O*)

Unfortunately, interviewees did not explain further what it was about these cases that made them take a less cooperative approach to case management. It could be that they were cases in which they had a genuine belief in their client's innocence, that they felt affronted about the way the case was brought in, that it challenged principles of procedural fairness, that there were concerns about either missing or inappropriately obtained evidence or simply that they felt their or their client's, position was being unreasonably undermined. There could, of course, be several of these issues at work in any one case. Newman[201] and Young[202] may take the view that this forms part of a pretence performed by

---

[198] Carlen (n 9).
[199] Young (n 2).
[200] Carlen (n 9).
[201] Newman (n 14).
[202] Young (n 2).

advocates in an attempt to persuade clients that they are acting in their best interests. However, it should be noted that the entry of a not guilty plea is not necessarily in the advocates' interests. It means that more work is required, which may affect the profitability of the case. Additionally, the advocate concerned may be seen as 'difficult' and, therefore, undermine their reputation and work-group stability, inviting censure as a barrier 'to the mass disposition of cases [...] exploiting the system's weak spots'.[203] The consequences of entering a not guilty plea in these circumstances mean that it is unlikely to be only performative.

However, as a result of the need to balance their own competing interests of reputation, business interests and workgroup cohesion, advocates may only be prepared to exercise such rights in extreme situations. Newman also found that the lawyers he interviewed spoke of being forced into situations not in anyone's best interests, but the preference is for speed over justice.[204] Lawyers who I interviewed appeared to distinguish how they would like to act while also referring to constraints placed upon them by, among other things, funding and the court's desire for efficiency above all else. In this way, they demonstrated some insight into their behaviour and how it might influence the way in which a defendant does, or does not, participate in the process (or their ability to do so).

Carlen's concern about the absurdity of 'the judicial rhetoric of an adversary justice'[205] clearly remains relevant today. The system may be designed to be adversarial, but – in these magistrates' courts at least – cooperation (rather than adversarialism) is regarded as key to getting a 'good' result for all parties. Consequently, due process procedural safeguards (including the defence right to participate) become a 'gloss'[206] used to legitimise proceedings rather than actually allowing the defendant a fair opportunity of comprehension and participation. This situation is exacerbated when one considers the speed at which cases are processed, which is also dependent on cooperative networks among the workgroup and knowledge of routine case handling procedures.

X. SUMMARY

Magistrates' courts have, since the latter half of the twentieth century at least, operated with voluminous caseloads. This has required either greater investment in the process or techniques that encourage efficient case progression. A high degree of cooperation among courtroom personnel is central to those techniques, which not only adds to the speed at which cases are progressed but also creates an air of informality. This operates to exclude defendants from

[203] McConville and Marsh (n 149) 107.
[204] Newman (n 14).
[205] Carlen (n 18) 49.
[206] Carlen (n 9) 87.

effective participation in the proceedings along with the specialised use of language and technical decision-making (see chapter four).

It is clear from this and the preceding chapter that there has been an increased focus on the perceived need for efficiency in magistrates' courts over the last two decades. Advocates' responses to policies designed to meet demands for efficiency demonstrate how the magistrates' courtroom itself is a site of struggle among actors. However, professionals are likely to 'employ a set of established procedures for the resolution of any conflicts'.[207] Given that summary criminal courts have always relied on a good degree of cooperation among actors in order to process cases smoothly, it is unsurprising that the established procedures resorted to by the workgroup consist largely of adaptation via compromise rather than aggressive forms of non-cooperation. Once a point of equilibrium is reached, it has the potential to become unbalanced by external influences (such as efficiency drives), which create new struggles.

Resolving those struggles through cooperation means that increased levels of representation can act as a 'double-edged sword' for defendants. Increased levels of representation are beneficial in that unrepresented defendants were previously excluded from participation in the proceedings by lack of specialist knowledge in relation to law, procedure and jargon. However, the advocate's presence serves to strengthen networks and allow for increased routinisation, greater degrees of professional negotiation and compromise and quicker case progression, which may leave defendants confused and alienated. This, in turn, reinforces the othering process in relation to defendants as they are excluded from effective participation in the process. As a result of her observation of a magistrates' court in 2017, Carlen noted that despite the passage of 40 years since her initial study, defendants remain outsiders to the process through taken-for-granted practices of the courtroom workgroup.[208]

Maintaining and adapting relationships of compromise appears to exacerbate marginalisation experienced by defendants. In this case, there is some evidence that actors will resort to strict legal provisions to exercise power in the event of a conflict, but only when they feel that attempts at compromise fail (such as refusals to adjourn) or that there is a power imbalance (such as the CPS having more time to prepare). In the majority of instances, conflict may be resolved via compromise learnt by way of 'professional tools developed in response to ... practice'.[209] It seems that recent concerns with efficiency in summary proceedings have been a possible site of struggle within the courtroom as workgroups grapple with their competing agendas. However, all parties seem to favour efficiency as a goal in itself for instrumental reasons. This, combined with a culture of cooperation among the parties, seems to have led advocates

---

[207] Bourdieu (n 29) 819.
[208] P Carlen, 'Struggling for Justice' (2018) 27(2) *Griffith Law Review* 176–81.
[209] Bourdieu (n 29) 824.

to acquiesce to the demands of policies designed to increase efficiency, both in terms of its existence and intensity. This occurs despite the fact that those initiatives appear to further undermine procedural fairness and the traditionally adversarial nature of the proceedings. The marginalisation of defendants, therefore, appears to have been exacerbated by a culture of cooperation which has allowed efficiency drives to be successful in further promoting the volume processing of cases. That process has been assisted by the standardisation of case management, which has encouraged implicit reference to legal principles among professional court users. Therefore, the culture of summary justice can actually intensify the effects of policies that marginalise defendants through demands for ever more efficient case progression. Coupled with the specialised nature of proceedings discussed in the following chapter, defendants are in a vulnerable position of marginalisation, which significantly limits their ability to actively participate in magistrates' court processes. Representation is thus important to improve the descriptive element of access to justice through the meaningful operation of the right to legal assistance. However, the normative element of access to justice through meaningful and effective participation is undermined by the culture of the court itself.

4

The Legalisation of Summary Criminal Justice

I. INTRODUCTION

T HIS CHAPTER CHALLENGES the notion that magistrates' courts are essentially the courts of common sense and highlights how the legalised nature of the proceedings impacts the ability of defendants to participate in proceedings. Governments have placed much value on the ability of lay magistrates to come to common-sense conclusions about cases,[1] but this rhetoric should not blind us to the fact that magistrates' courts remain places in which people are required to comply with the complex legal procedures in which the criminal justice system is grounded. It may be that the English tradition of common law, through its reliance on 'the perfection of human reason',[2] elevated the importance of adjudication through common sense despite its inherently flexible and variable nature. Psychologists have long criticised the criminal law's reliance on the common sense of jurors to assess the credibility of witnesses,[3] though the presence of lay participants does appear to improve the democratic legitimacy and accountability of the law itself.[4] It is, perhaps, easier to think that common sense approaches are more relevant in the magistrates' court than in the Crown Court because magistrates are arbiters of both law and facts and because the offences dealt with are generally less serious. Adopting this 'ideology of triviality'[5] about magistrates' courts should, however, be

[1] See generally Department for Constitutional Affairs, *Supporting Magistrates' Courts to Provide Justice* (Cm 6681, 2005); Transform Justice, 'Why have a Lay Magistracy? The Magistrates' View' (Transform Justice, 2014) www.transformjustice.org.uk/why-have-a-lay-magistracy-the-magistrates-view/.

[2] W Renwick Riddell, 'Common Law and Common Sense' (1918) 27(8) *The Yale Law Journal* 993–1007, 995.

[3] See generally S Friedland, 'On Common Sense and the Evaluation of Witness Credibility' (1989) 40 *Case Western Reserve Law Review* 165.

[4] See generally N Finkel, 'Commonsense Justice, Culpability, and Punishment' (2000) 28(3) *Hofstra Law Review* 4; V Whittington, 'The Role of the Common Law Jury as Direct Deliberative Mechanism for the Democratic Self-legitimation of Law' (2015) 24 *Studies in Social and Political Thought* 15–40.

[5] D McBarnet, 'Magistrates' Courts and the Ideology of Justice' (1981) 8(2) *British Journal of Law and Society* 181–97.

counselled against in favour of recognising both the ways in which legal provisions are used by the magistrates' court workgroup and how the use of the provisions can exacerbate the marginalisation of defendants and reinforce their status as outsiders.

Summary criminal justice has become subject to more complex legal provisions, but the subtleties with which those provisions are deployed means that it is difficult for a participant who is not a member of the court workgroup to understand what the provisions entail, let alone be able to meaningfully (and voluntarily) participate in the process. Kirby noted that the ability of court users to understand both judicial processes and outcomes is perceived among legal practitioners as an important element of participation in court processes,[6] yet the way that practitioners discuss and apply legal provisions undermines the ability of court users to understand those same processes and outcomes. As discussed in chapter one, the ability of a defendant to effectively participate in the process of summary justice is important to avoid the further disempowerment of people who are likely already socio-economically marginalised in some way and increase access to justice through the normative aspect of facilitated yet autonomous decisions about engagement with the process.

This chapter begins with a review of the idea that magistrates' courts are 'law-free zones', followed by a discussion about the professionalisation of magistrates' courts and the complexity of magistrates' court proceedings. The discussion then moves on to provide specific examples of the ways in which legal and procedural issues manifest themselves in summary criminal proceedings, as they became apparent during periods of observation. These are connected to observations about issues that arose during interviews, which helped provide both explanatory factors and insights into how practitioners view the use of law in magistrates' courts. The examples provided below illustrate that those points of law arise more frequently in summary proceedings than previously observed. Greater complexity resulting from recent legislative and procedural provisions justify an increase in levels of legal representation, and that representation has been increasingly professionalised.

Practitioner insights will be set within the context of literature that considers how magistrates' courts operate, and examines the ability of court users to participate in proceedings. I will then consider the context in which defendants are now obliged to cooperate with the process of prosecution through increasingly legalised processes. Obligations to cooperate do not, ultimately, enable effective participation in the process and could, in fact, act as a barrier to effective participation.[7] This leads me to identify two ways in which the legalisation of summary justice serves to exacerbate defendant marginalisation: how the

---

[6] A Kirby, 'Conceptualising Participation' in J Jacobson and P Cooper (eds), *Participation in Courts and Tribunals* (Bristol University Press, 2020).

[7] On the meaning of effective participation, see ch 1.

workgroup uses legal provisions, and forcing the engagement of defendants in ways that are contrary to their interests.

II. MAGISTRATES' COURTS AS 'LAW-FREE ZONES'

There is no doubt that magistrates' courts process cases quickly and have – as illustrated in the preceding chapter – been pressed to increase the speed at which cases progress in recent years. Socio-legal scholars have noted that the speed at which cases progress means that there are often minimal due process protections and give the impression that those advocates who refer to points of law are dismissed as inexperienced and/or time-wasting.[8] According to Darbyshire,[9] lawyers who raise so-called spurious legal issues are unwelcome as they are regarded as a threat to what Carlen described as the uncomfortable compromise, which typifies the relationships between members of the court workgroup.[10] Consequently, there is a perception that points of law are seldom referred to in magistrates' courts or, alternatively, that when legal issues are raised, they are treated like an inconvenience that delays the volume processing of cases.[11] As McConville et al reported, '. . . magistrates' court cases are not argued on legal issues, usually assumed to be inappropriate in such a forum'.[12] When conducting her study, Carlen was told that she would not see much law in a magistrates' court because they only dealt with 'rubbish'.[13]

In 2011, Darbyshire reported that judges took the view that legal argument should not be raised in magistrates' courts because it is the place of common sense, describing it as a 'law free zone'.[14] This resonates with Carlen's view (as noted in chapter three) that advocates prepared to contest the proceedings by raising legal issues were in a strong position to challenge the usual process of case management.[15] However, Darbyshire acknowledges that relatively infrequent use of legal argument does not mean that the law is not applied in summary proceedings but rather that it is applied in routinised ways. She referred to the fact that the District Judges (DJ) who commented that summary criminal justice is 'law free' also carried a file containing case law with him.[16] Application of

---

[8] P Carlen, *Magistrates' Justice* (Martin Robertson, 1976); A Bottoms and J McClean, *Defendants in the Criminal Process* (Routledge, 1976); D McBarnet, *Conviction: Law, the State and the Construction of Justice* (Macmillan, 1981).

[9] P Darbyshire, *Sitting in Judgement: The Working Lives of Judges* (Hart Publishing, 2011).

[10] Carlen (n 8).

[11] McBarnet (n 8). For an example, see L Welsh et al, *Criminal Justice* (Oxford University Press, 2021) ch 8.

[12] M McConville et al, *Standing Accused* (Clarendon, 1994) 225.

[13] P Carlen, 'Struggling for Justice' (2018) 27(2) *Griffith Law Review* 176–81, 178.

[14] Darbyshire (n 9) 171.

[15] Carlen (n 8).

[16] Darbyshire (n 9). See also L Welsh, 'Are Magistrates' Courts Really a "Law Free Zone?" Participant Observation and Specialist Use of Language' (2013) 13 *Papers from the British Criminology Conference* 3–16.

the law in routinised ways is entirely consistent with the culture of summary justice, but, as discussed in chapter three, routinisation is a way of obscuring and dehumanising procedural decision-making and potentially shrouding the law in mystery.

My findings suggest that complex legal issues frequently arise in summary criminal proceedings, albeit in routine ways. More than half of all advocates interviewed felt that proceedings involving unrepresented defendants (likely around 30 per cent of magistrates' court cases – see chapter five) take longer to conduct *because* the legal provisions and courtroom etiquette involved need to be explained.[17] Both prosecutors and defence solicitors spoke of unrepresented defendants in embarrassed terms,

> I think that the court is always a little afraid of self-represented defendants because they're a loose cannon. You don't know what they're going to say, you don't know whether they're going to address the court appropriately, and so there's very often – and I tend not to be in court when self-represented defendants are there because I find it so excruciating – but when you are there very often if anybody starts saying something and was immediately told 'no, no, no you can't say that now, you've got to sit down and wait and it's always done perfectly courteously but everyone's paranoid that the defendant is going to blurt something out that he shouldn't or address the court inappropriately. And it is silly things like defendant starts talking to the court and is told 'stand up when you are talking to the magistrates, take your hands out of your pockets when you are speaking to the magistrates'. All of that sort of thing leaves one feeling rather uncomfortable, which is why, as I've said, I tend to leave the room because I just find it uncomfortable. (*Defence solicitor F*)

> There's obviously certain defendants who really want to have their say, and the Bench is constantly trying to keep them quiet in the court room because they know, if they open their mouth, that they're going to stitch themselves up and probably say something that they shouldn't do. (*Prosecutor J*)

> It's rare that an unrepresented defendant says 'no I don't understand', they will just say 'yes', and there's that heart sinking feeling for me of 'do you really understand?' and then the question of the plea and then the, the position on the law … it's the agony of watching the conversation that you would be having outside in consultation. (*Defence solicitor A*)

A study of unrepresented defendants by Transform Justice noted that lack of understanding about criminal charges and rules of evidence were a significant impediment to participation,[18] which highlights that magistrates' courts are far from law-free. Unrepresented defendants in earlier studies were also seen to be unaware of the relevant legal rules and often silenced by magistrates because they would not take the same tactical or professional routes to cross-examination as

---

[17] This finding is supported by the research presented in J Jacobson and P Cooper (eds), *Participation in Courts and Tribunals* (Bristol University Press, 2020) and research conducted by Transform Justice; P Gibbs, 'Justice Denied? The Experience of Unrepresented Defendants in the Criminal Courts' (London, Transform Justice, 2016).

[18] Gibbs (n 17).

a defence advocate.[19] This created 'the paradox of a legal system which requires knowledge of procedural propriety in making a case and a legal system that denies access to it'.[20]

The concerns expressed about unrepresented defendants also indicate that these practitioners – in concert with practitioners spoken to in other studies – view managing defendants to avoid disruption as a significant part of their professional role.[21] Predictably, the majority (nine of 12) of defence advocates interviewed in this study reported that they attempt to explain the law and procedure to clients before going into court. One such defence advocate commented that those explanations are 'a major part of the job … and it's a part of the job that saves a lot of time' (Defence solicitor G). Thus, represented defendants ought to be better equipped to effectively participate in proceedings than unrepresented defendants, though the extent of any defendant's ability to participate is still hindered by how the workgroup operates (chapter three). This suggests that, in the same way that professional practices become standardised via routinisation in order to cope with managerial demands for increased efficiency, the use of law also becomes routinised to assist speedy case progression and preserve the status of the workgroup (discussed below). As discussed in chapter three, this form of standardisation also serves to undermine individual defendant status and freedom of choice because '[s]tandardised treatment entails that both action and speech are utilised to undermine individual identity'.[22]

All this means that, while it may be correct to say that detailed or complex legal argument arises infrequently compared to in higher court settings, it is a step too far to describe magistrates' courts as 'law free'. Although the routine use of legal provisions may mean that 'there is little room for argument',[23] it does not mean that references to particular legal provisions are insignificant. As defence solicitor F explained:

> I can entirely understand where that criticism comes from because sometimes you do sort of think to yourself, 'oh people are just freewheeling here', but I think in reality a lot of the day to day slog of criminal litigation is so well known to all the parties in the court that you don't stand up and say 'let's have a look at the Bail Act' or something like that, but no, it's not law-free zones.

The research presented in this book was conducted following a period during which governments introduced a disproportionate amount of new statutory

---

[19] D McBarnet, 'Two Tiers of Justice' in N Lacey (ed), *A Reader on Criminal Justice* (Oxford University Press, 1994).

[20] McBarnet (n 8) 124.

[21] Kirby (n 6); V Long, 'Online Courts: Re-assessing Inequality in the "Remote" Courtroom' (2021) 11(1) *Excursions* 77–102.

[22] D Newman, *Lawyers, Legal Aid and the Quest for Justice* (Hart Publishing, 2013), 98. For discussion in relation to sentencing practices, see also C Tata, 'Ritual Individualisation': Creative Genius at Sentencing, Mitigation and Conviction. (2019) 46(1) *Journal of Law and Society* 112–40.

[23] Darbyshire (n 9) 171.

criminal offences and criminal justice legislation.[24] Robert Marshall-Andrews QC, MP, described governments of the late 1990s and early 2000s as suffering from 'legislative hyperactivity syndrome in respect of criminal justice matters'.[25] Many of those legal provisions were created to avoid proceedings being trans-ferred to the Crown Court as part of the political desire for magistrates to retain jurisdiction in cases in the name of efficiency.[26] Sanders,[27] and Ashworth and Zedner,[28] noted that a significant number of new offences created in the last two or three decades are of a type usually confined to summary-only proceedings.[29] So, while Darbyshire asserts that lawyers who wish to raise legal argument will, where possible, try to have the case dealt with in the Crown Court,[30] there are measures that seek to deter committal to the Crown Court.

Six of the 19 interviewees said that more cases are being dealt with in magistrates' courts rather than sent to the Crown Court. Three of those six interviewees attributed this change to charging policy within the Crown Prosecution Service (CPS). One prosecutor told me when asked if there had been any change in sending cases to the Crown Court,

> Yes, definitely. I think a lot of that is to do with CPS policy and where we were kind of being instructed that, … to be very careful when, even at pre charge stage, if it's the case that clearly the person isn't going to receive more than 6 months in prison then don't bother charging them with an either way offence. … I think probably we've been charging lesser offences … from a CPS point of view, because we were charging at a lower level to try and keep things in the magistrates' court because the magistrates' have sufficient powers. (*Prosecutor J*).

Prosecutors P, Q and M similarly mentioned changes to CPS charging policy in order to explain that more serious cases are staying in magistrates' courts,[31]

---

[24] J Chalmers and F Leverick, 'Tracking the Creation of Criminal Offences' (2013) *Crim LR* 543–60; J Chalmers 'Frenzied law making': Overcriminalization by Numbers. (2014) 67(1) *Current Legal Problems* 483–50; J Chalmers, F Leverick, and A Shaw, 'Is Formal Criminalisation Really on the Rise? Evidence from the 1950s' (2015) 3 *Crim LR* 177–91.

[25] See www.publications.parliament.uk/pa/cm200708/cmhansard/cm071107/deb/text/71107-0009.htm.

[26] P Darbyshire, 'Strengthening the Argument in Favour of the Defendant's Right to Elect' (1997) (Dec) *Criminal Law Review* 911. On Crown Courts, where professional judges and lay juries tend to deal with more serious offences than magistrates' courts, see Welsh et al (n 11) ch 9 and J Jacobson, G Hunter and A Kirby, *Inside Crown Court* (Bristol University Press, 2016).

[27] A Sanders, 'What was New Labour Thinking? New Labour's Approach to Criminal Justice' in A Silvestri (ed), 'Lessons for the Coalition: An End of Term Report on New Labour and Criminal Justice' (London, Centre for Crime and Justice Studies 2010).

[28] A Ashworth and L Zedner, 'Defending the Criminal Law: Reflections on the Changing Character of Crime, Procedure and Sanctions' (2008) (2) *Criminal Law and Philosophy* 21.

[29] Many of these offences are classed as 'strict liability'. Strict liability offences require no proof of the defendant's state of mind when the behaviour occurred and are usually dealt with in magistrates' courts.

[30] Darbyshire (n 9).

[31] There may, however, be certain CPS priority issues where over- rather than under-charging occurs. See generally M Walters, S Wiedlitzka and A Owusu-Bempah, *Hate Crime and the Legal process: Options for Law Reform. Project Report.* (Brighton, University of Sussex 2017).

but also mentioned changes to solicitor's fees as an explanatory factor – the intimation being that there is no longer a financial incentive for lawyers to send cases to the Crown Court.

Alongside a desire to avoid sending cases to the Crown Courts, legislation that allows a number of low level, uncontested offences to be diverted from the criminal court process via the use of fixed penalty notices and conditional cautions has been enacted,[32] meaning that the cases which do come before the court are more likely to be complex or contested in some way. Defence solicitor D explained that mid or low level offending is not being dealt with in the magistrates' courts.[33] All this means that the types of cases the magistrates' courts are dealing with are likely to be more complex than prior to the introduction of a greater range of diversionary measures and with greater recourse to (more varied and complex) legal provisions. However, this does not mean that magistrates' courts take on the features of Crown Courts, but rather that the courtroom workgroup is likely to absorb these trends and standardise them (chapter three). In fact, similar patterns emerge in relation to Crown Court practices, where the additional formality of lawyers wearing wigs and gowns does nothing to assist defendants (or victims and witnesses) who are also confused and alienated by the language and processes used there.[34]

III. PROFESSIONALISING MAGISTRATES' COURTS

The passivity of a defendant's role in criminal proceedings has waxed and waned over time. In the Middle Ages, the defendant was expected to be an active participant in the trial process (as it then was) and expected to speak to defend themselves.[35] Lawyers became more involved in criminal trials from the 1730s,

---

[32] R Morgan, 'Austerity, Subsidiarity and Parsimony: Offending Behaviour and Criminalisation' in A Silvestri (ed), Lessons for the Coalition: An End of Term Report on New Labour and Criminal Justice (London, Centre for Crime and Justice Studies, 2010).

[33] Nine of the 12 defence solicitors interviewed believed that diversion was increasingly used, and six of those interviewees were concerned that diversion was used inappropriately for serious (and sometimes indictable only) offending. Defence solicitor B felt that diversions were used for serious offences while defence solicitor E used the example of diversion for an offence of unlawful sexual intercourse with a minor, G of diversion for rape and O of diversion for arson and robbery. Defence solicitors C and I both said that numerous cautions were being given rather than a single caution, following which any offenders would be sent to court for the commission of further offences. While, since this research was conducted, there has been a decrease in the use of most types of diversion (Ministry of Justice 'Criminal Justice Statistics Quarterly, England and Wales, July 2019 to June 2020' (2014) assets.publishing.service.gov.uk/government/uploads/system/uploads/attachment_data/file/934391/criminal-justice-statistics-quarterly-june-2020.pdf), a 2019 report indicated that diversion remains popular and a majority of police forces were piloting or developing new diversion schemes (C Robin-D'Cruz and S Whitehead, 'Pre-court Diversion for Adults: An Evidence Briefing' (London, Centre for Justice Innovation, 2019).

[34] Jacobson et al (n 26) A Kirby 'Effectively Engaging Victims, Witnesses and Defendants in the Criminal Courts: A Question of "Court Culture"?' (2017) 12 *Criminal Law Review* 949–68.

[35] A Owusu-Bempah, *Defendant Participation in the Criminal Process* (Routledge 2017); J Langbein, *The Origins of Adversary Criminal Trial* (Oxford University Press, 2005).

and 'there was a definite increase [in representation] from the mid-eighteenth century, even though the majority of defendants remained unrepresented'.[36] Lawyers began to represent their clients more aggressively, giving effect to the defendant's interests but also making it easier (and perhaps beneficial) for defendants to assume a more passive role in proceedings.[37] It was through the active role of the lawyer that defendants were enabled to engage with the law pertaining to their case and engage their rights, such as the right to silence.[38] Consequently, '[i]mportant defence rights became workable within a system which effectively discouraged defendant participation, and it was these rights which, in turn, facilitated the lack of participation'.[39]

While the above discussion indicates that a 'legal culture which discourages active participation has developed over a long period of time',[40] especially in relation to more serious types of offending, professionalising the courts is not just about the legal language through which defence rights are invoked, but also about the creation of the court workgroup as a particular epistemic community (chapter three). When Carlen,[41] McBarnet[42] and Bottoms and McClean[43] conducted their studies, defendants in the magistrates' courts tended to appear without the assistance of a solicitor and the police (rather than qualified legal professionals) were the prosecutors. The CPS took over state-led prosecutions in 1986 and, by 1986/87, four-fifths of defendants appearing in magistrates' courts were legally represented.[44] Earlier socio-legal studies of summary justice have drawn attention to marginalisation consequent to courtroom layout and signalling between personnel.[45] These issues, coupled with the strong professional network operating in the magistrates' court, exacerbate the marginalisation of defendants by situating them as outsiders who are not privy to the relevant legal provisions and not afforded the opportunity to voluntarily engage with them because they are used in standardised and implicit ways. As Dehaghani and Newman state, 'the criminal justice system is confusing, self-referential, and alienating'.[46] In this way, 'vulnerability can relate as much to the nature of the legal system as to individual personal circumstances'.[47]

---

[36] Owusu-Bempah (n 35) 62.

[37] Ibid.

[38] Sections 34–38 Criminal Justice and Public Order Act 1994. For discussion, see H Quirk, *The Rise and Fall of the Right of Silence* (Routledge, 2016).

[39] Owusu-Bempah (n 35) 65.

[40] Owusu-Bempah (n 35) 68.

[41] Carlen (n 8).

[42] McBarnet (n 8).

[43] Bottoms and McClean (n 8).

[44] Legal Action Group, *A Strategy for Justice: Publicly Funded Legal Services in the 1990s* (Legal Action Group 1992).

[45] Carlen (n 8). These issues are discussed in ch 3.

[46] R Dehaghani and D Newman, 'Criminal Legal Aid and Access to Justice: An Empirical Account of a Reduction in Resilience' (2021) *International Journal of the Legal Profession Online First*: 16.

[47] G Hunter, 'Policy and Practice Supporting Lay Participation' in J Jacobson and P Cooper (eds), *Participation in Courts and Tribunals* (Bristol University Press, 2020) 24.

Leader noted that, in relation to County court proceedings, displacing self-representation in favour of increasing the role of legal professionals brings with it 'a desire for greater formality of procedure and content, and this makes it harder and harder for individuals to act without lawyers'.[48] There is no reason to think that a similar issue has not arisen in magistrates' courts, especially as – like in County courts – the venue can become a

> ... battleground for attorneys to claim their place in a legal profession that actively discriminates between the 'higher' calling of the Bar and the 'lower' rungs of the rank-and-file practitioners. This battle is a battle for distinction that takes place through the marking out of legal representatives from laypersons, the normalisation of legal expertise ...[49]

In criminal cases, the 'higher' calling of the Bar is most frequently represented in the Crown Court, with barristers who are mainly at the early stages of their careers appearing in magistrates' courts. This battleground is, of course, all part of the culture of summary justice too, creating a field of practice that creates its own norms and accepted practices.[50] This creation of norms perhaps allows people to describe the court as a place of common sense but obscures the professionalised discourses and routines that operate to keep magistrates' courts running at a fast pace. As such, the way in which the role of the defendant has waxed and waned over time can be characterised as moving from early active participation to the greater presence of lawyers who create a specialised workgroup to invoke defence party rights, to passive participation coupled with demands for efficiency, to the co-option of lawyers into those demands for efficiency. The co-option of lawyers into efficiency drives (chapter three) creates practices that either require the defendant to participate whether or not they wish to do so (see discussion below) or remove a defendant's choice to participate by the invocation of a normative culture which is particular to the professional workgroup. An important part of those accepted practices is standardisation (chapter three), including legal rules, through which professionals develop their epistemic community. This then serves to maintain the professional autonomy of the courtroom workgroup. As the professional autonomy of the courtroom becomes normalised, so do implicit references to legal provisions. These performative aspects of magistrates' courts create a barrier which means the court is 'fully accessible only to those duly consecrated'.[51] This arguably creates

---

[48] K Leader, 'From Bear Gardens to the County Court: Creating the Litigant in Person' (2020) 79(2) *Cambridge Law Journal* 260–87.

[49] Ibid.

[50] P Bourdieu, 'The Force of Law: Towards a Sociology of the Juridical Field' (1987) 38 *Hastings Law Journal* 805.

[51] T Smejkalová, 'Legal Performance: Translating into Law and Subjectivity in Law' (2017) 22 *Tilburg Law Review* 62, 63.

a power monopoly among lawyers, which somewhat contrasts with the sense of altruism that Cooke found lawyers rely on to sustain/improve morale.[52]

Despite a general political trend towards professional distrust since the 1980s and the former Prime Minister Cameron's appeal to a Big Society involving local forms of governance (see chapter one), a more recent development in the professionalisation of magistrates' courts is the increased use of legally-qualified DJs. This trend is illustrative of a desire to improve efficiency in criminal justice above other ideological demands. The institution of magistracy dates back many hundreds of years, with the first statutory recognition of the role in the Justice of the Peace Act 1361. Magistrates' courts themselves were formalised as an institution in 1971.[53] The role of magistrate has undergone many iterations throughout the centuries, but the essence of the lay magistracy is that it consists of legally unqualified, volunteer members of the general public who sit as members of a Bench consisting of three Justices of the Peace in magistrates' courts for at least 26 half days per year. The value of involving lay magistrates is reportedly in their application of common sense,[54] and 'the value of a lay magistracy as an embodiment of citizen participation in justice is a cornerstone of the philosophical underpinnings of the magistracy in England and Wales'.[55]

However, alongside the professionalisation of advocacy in the magistrates' courts, there has been increasing debate about the role of lay magistrates – especially in the last decade or so. The closure of magistrates' courthouses,[56] and some reductions in the numbers of cases processed through magistrates' courts have led to debates about what the appropriate role of magistrates should be, and the issue of inefficiency was considered in the government's 2012 White Paper, *Swift and Sure Justice*.[57] Against this backdrop, the number of magistrates in England and Wales has declined dramatically. Donoghue reported a 20 per cent drop in the number of magistrates in 2014,[58] while official figures indicate a drop from 29,419 magistrates in 2008 to only 13,177 in 2020.[59]

The number of DJs (and part-time Deputy DJs), who each sit alone to hear cases in the magistrates' courts, had not declined so dramatically up to 2014,

[52] E Cooke, 'The Changing Occupational Terrain of the Legal Aid Lawyer in Times of Precariousness' (Doctor of Philosophy (PhD) thesis, University of Kent, 2019).

[53] J Campbell, *Entanglements of Life with the Law: Precarity and Justice in London's Magistrates Courts* (Cambridge Scholars Publishing, 2020).

[54] See generally Department for Constitutional Affairs (n 1); Transform Justice, 'Why have a Lay Magistracy? The Magistrates' View' (2014) www.transformjustice.org.uk/blog/ 1 April.

[55] J Donoghue, 'Reforming the Role of Magistrates' (2014) 77 *Modern Law Review* 928–63; 932.

[56] Fifty-one per cent of magistrates' courts closed between 2010 and 2020 (commonslibrary.parliament.uk/home-affairs/justice/courts/constituency-data-magistrates-court-closures/).

[57] Donoghue (n 55).

[58] Donoghue (n 55).

[59] M Fouzder, 'Magistrate Numbers Worse than Thought Due to HR Error' *Law Society Gazette* (London, 18 September 2020).

despite being subject to the same issues of declining court business and court-house closures. Nineteen per cent of cases observed in this study were dealt with by a DJ, while the remainder were conducted by magistrates. In 2013, there were 315 DJs and Deputy DJs sitting in magistrates' courts, and that number had been relatively stable since 2006.[60] For some time, lay magistrates were increasingly replaced by DJs.[61] More recently, though, the number of DJs in magistrates' courts has also declined. By 2016, their number was 234 judges,[62] and 125 judges by 2020.[63] The reason for the lag in reducing the number of DJs might be connected to their perceived greater levels of efficiency. Ministry of Justice research indicated that DJs were 'viewed as transacting cases more quickly and considered to be more adept at case management' than lay magistrates.[64] The greater speed with which DJs conduct proceedings has long been documented by, among others, Zander[65] and Morgan and Russell.[66]

In line with other research, interviewees in this research almost unanimously agreed that the presence of a DJ increases the speed at which proceedings are conducted. All seven prosecutors and eight of 12 defence solicitors interviewed asserted that the DJ is much more efficient than lay magistrates. Prosecutor Q asserted, 'DJs are way more efficient. I think they get through more work. I find magistrates retiring so laborious, it's just so tedious'. Similarly, another prosecutor believed that the DJ 'is a lot swifter. He's less indecisive. He makes decisions and goes with it. He will get through a list in half the time' (prosecutor N). The majority of defence solicitors were of the same opinion, with defence solicitor R going so far as to say, 'if they want to save money, get rid of magistrates and employ DJs'. My observations also suggested that the DJ appeared to conduct proceedings with greater speed, perhaps because they rarely retired to make decisions, presumably at least partially influenced by the fact that they do not have to seek the agreement of at least one of two other colleagues in decision-making. Another influence may be that they do not often have to pause to seek legal advice from the court clerk, who assumes a much more administrative role in the proceedings by performing tasks such as fixing hearing dates and

---

[60] P Gibbs and A Kirby, 'Judged by Peers? The Diversity of Lay Magistrates in England and Wales' (Howard League What is Justice? Working Papers 6/2014, 2014).

[61] K Hall, 'Lay Magistrate Numbers Continue to Fall' (2014) www.lawgazette.co.uk/practice/lay-magistrate-numbers-continue-to-fall/503938.

[62] House of Commons Justice Committee, 'The Role of the Magistracy' Sixth Report of Session 2016–17 (HC 165, 2016).

[63] Courts and Tribunals Judiciary, 'List of Members of the Courts Judiciary. DJs (Magistrates' Courts)' (2019) www.judiciary.uk/about-the-judiciary/who-are-the-judiciary/judicial-roles/list-of-members-of-the-judiciary/dj-mags-ct-list/.

[64] House of Commons (n 62); 10. See also Ministry of Justice, 'The Strengths and Skills of the Judiciary in the Magistrates' Courts' (Ministry of Justice, 2011).

[65] M Zander, *Cases and Materials on the English Legal System* (Oxford University Press, 2007).

[66] R Morgan and N Russell, 'The Judiciary in the Magistrates' Courts' (Home Office 2000). See further ch 1. On balancing time and legitimacy in Australian magistrates' courts, see K Mack and S Roach Anleu '"Getting Through the List": Judgecraft and Legitimacy in the Lower Courts.' (2007) 16 *Social & Legal Studies* 341–61.

completing forms. The case management hearings that I observed provide an interesting case in point. If magistrates were presiding over a case management hearing, the court clerk tended to go through the case management form methodically with the advocates, confirming each part completed but with little challenge to the issues raised. Conversely, the DJ did not go through the case management form openly but only discussed issues contained thereon when they wished to challenge or clarify a point raised by the advocate.

Interviewed advocates spoke favourably about appearing before a DJ. For example, one defence solicitor said,

> Appearing before magistrates is like appearing before an inept jury without proper guidance whereas appearing before a DJ is how it should be. Preparing for somebody who understands and knows how to apply the law in correct factual circumstances. (*Defence solicitor R*)

Another interviewee also said of DJs, 'they're much more robust, much more direct but also are professional lawyers and are therefore not going to say or do anything to leave them exposed to a complaint or an appeal' (Defence solicitor K), while a third said that they preferred appearing in front of a DJ 'because one of the most frustrating things in the world is when you know something is right in law but the magistrates just don't get it' (Defence solicitor E).

Both prosecutors and defence solicitors interviewed tended to attribute the expediency of proceedings to the DJ's ability to direct the proceedings to the issues they feel are important and the fact that the DJ is legally qualified. The perception that legal knowledge increases the speed of the proceedings does, however, undermine the suggestion that magistrates' courts are places of common sense. One defence advocate explained,

> … you're addressing a professional Judge who knows the law and you don't need to address him about the law in any significant detail. He will know the Guidelines. Whereas if you're addressing three lay people you've got to take them through it I think in much more detail. No, there's certainly a very different approach and DJs get through the work much much faster and more efficiently. (*Defence solicitor F*)

It also seems that this is, at least in part, because cases are progressed more efficiently by someone who has specialist legal knowledge, and advocates seemed more confident that DJ would make a legally correct decision. For example, one prosecutor was of the view that the decisions made by the local DJ seem 'much more sensible and they're more consistent with the law' (Prosecutor N). But the addition of another lawyer in the proceedings may exacerbate defendants' inability to engage in the process because the law is more likely to be referred to in fleeting terms. A minority of interviewees expressed a contrary viewpoint when discussing the behaviour of the DJ towards unrepresented defendants,

> I go again and say that the DJ … who has been appointed down here, is in my limited experience extremely helpful to unrepresented defendants. He really goes out of his

> way to make sure they understand the, [sic] they are given the opportunity, if he thinks they need to seek legal advice he will give them time. (*Defence solicitor B*)

> I've dealt with many unrepresented defendants when he really will sit and talk to them and engage with them. There's even been times after the sentence where he's almost invited them up to the Bench he can speak to them properly. (*Prosecutor J*)

> ... they give more time to explaining what's happening in court to them [defendants]. (*Prosecutor M*)

Furthermore, in some observed cases, the DJ actually appeared to interact more directly with defendants than magistrates did. While these comments are both important and encouraging, remarks of this nature were only made by three of the 19 interviewees, and the remainder spoke largely of the benefits to themselves and their client in terms only of securing a speedier, more legally refined outcome in relation to appearing before a DJ. The comments were relevant only to unrepresented defendants, as there seemed to exist an often unstated assumption that represented defendants would have the procedure and legal provisions explained to them by their lawyers outside the courtroom (above). The DJ, as a legally qualified professional, is also arguably located more within the professional courtroom workgroup than lay magistrates, and therefore more likely to adopt the same implicit references to shared legal knowledge than lay magistrates,[67] though this could be moderated by greater levels of direct interaction between the DJ and defendant themself. Indeed, in Ward's study, magistrates felt that they mitigated the issue of legalese by communicating 'with defendants in a way that is understandable to them by speaking in layman's language'.[68] The ability of lay magistrates to relate to defendants in an inclusive way is questionable in light of a lack of diversity among that group,[69] though magistrates are more diverse (and therefore perceived as fairer by some court users) than DJs.[70] As with my own experiences with other courtroom actors, the way magistrates spoke to defendants was variable. Some did their best to be empathic and encouraging, while others assumed a more patronising, disciplinarian role.

Regardless of whether a case is being adjudicated upon by magistrates or a DJ, it seems likely that with increased professionalisation in magistrates' courts comes increased reference to legal provisions and greater use of legalese (though the effects might be more pronounced when a DJ is sitting). Professionalisation leads to the creation of an epistemic community that views the application of the law in an efficient manner as beneficial to proceedings. It is partly for the sake of expediency that the Ministry of Justice considers DJs more suitable than lay magistrates to deal with complex cases.[71]

---

[67] See also Campbell (n 53).
[68] J Ward, *Transforming Summary Justice: Modernisation in the Lower Criminal Courts* (Routledge, 2017) 89.
[69] See also Gibbs and Kirby (n 60); Ward (n 68); Campbell (n 53).
[70] Ministry of Justice (n 64).
[71] Ministry of Justice (n 64).

IV. CASE COMPLEXITY IN THE MAGISTRATES' COURTS

Case complexity in summary criminal proceedings has increased since the 1990s.[72] Approximately half of the defence advocates and half of the prosecutors interviewed cited the Criminal Justice Act 2003 (CJA) and Criminal Procedure Rules (Cr.PR) as responsible for increased evidential and case complexity.

The CJA introduced significant amendments to the rules concerning evidence of previous convictions[73] and hearsay.[74] Both were previously subject to common law provisions that tended to weigh against admissibility, but the statute introduced complex guidelines and an application process in relation to the admission of both types of evidence. Those provisions enabled the Crown to apply to admit these types of evidence much more frequently than prior to the introduction of the CJA. Furthermore, the way that hearsay and character evidence are managed in the courts through the Cr.PR,[75] means that the defence must engage with these types of evidence in a much more frequent, structured and formalised way than before the enactment of the CJA. Defence solicitor B made this point, saying 'increasingly there are matters of law coming into [magistrates' courts]'. Defence solicitor C also talked of being asked to argue points about hearsay and character evidence with 'more and more' frequency, while defence solicitor D said that the changes to rules about hearsay and character evidence 'introduced legal points in many cases that previously weren't there at all'. The defence also suffers the prospect of penalties for failure to engage with these provisions of the CJA.[76]

One defence advocate described evidential changes in the following way: 'that's changed immeasurably. Bad character, obvious example. Hearsay, another clear example' (Defence solicitor F). Another defence advocate described proceedings as 'pretty, sort of, straightforward' (Defence solicitor I) before the enactment of the CJA. Prosecutors appeared equally perturbed by the complexity introduced by increased statutory intervention in summary criminal proceedings. Prosecutor J expressed the opinion that, since the introduction of the CJA, 'it's all got a hell of a lot more complicated,' which means that cases probably take longer to prepare for trial. Another prosecutor asserted that the same statute

> … is a hideous Act with its, I forget how many sections and schedules it has, but it's a, it was a badly thought through piece of legislation … it is getting more complicated because of the way Parliament produces its Acts. (*Prosecutor H*)

---

[72] E Cape and R Moorhead 'Demand Induced Supply? Identifying Cost Drivers in Criminal Defence Work' (Legal Services Research Centre, 2005). On increased complexity in criminal courts generally, see G Atkins et al, 'Performance Tracker 2019' (Institute for Government 2019).
[73] Section 101 Criminal Justice Act 2003.
[74] Section 114 Criminal Justice Act 2003.
[75] Parts 20 and 21 Cr.PR.
[76] Owusu-Bempah (n 35). This issue is expanded upon below.

Additional legislation introduced has not only created a number of summary-only offences and complicated evidential issues but has also complicated sentencing proceedings. For example, between 1997 and 2020, several mandatory minimum sentences had been introduced under the Powers of Criminal Courts (Sentencing) Act 2000[77] alongside the introduction of extended sentences for 'dangerous' offenders (replaced by indeterminate life sentences under Legal Aid, Sentencing and Punishment of Offenders Act 2012 (LASPO)), as well as amendments to provisions relating to suspended sentence orders of imprisonment contained in the CJA. This may explain interviewees' opinions that sentencing provisions and guidelines are of increasing importance in magistrates' court cases. In *South East Surrey Youth Court (Ghanbari, interested party)*,[78] Rose LJ considered statutory amendments in relation to those classified as dangerous offenders and stated,

> Yet again, the courts are faced with a sample of the deeply confusing provisions of the Criminal Justice Act 2003, and the satellite statutory instruments to which it is giving stuttering birth … we find little comfort or assistance in the historic canons of construction for determining the will of Parliament which were fashioned … at a time when elegance and clarity of thought and language were to be found in legislation as a matter of course rather than exception.

The complexity of sentencing provisions introduced in a fragmented way led the Law Commission to conclude – after this research was conducted – 'It is simply impossible to describe the current law governing sentencing procedure as clear, transparent, accessible or coherent'.[79]

While statutory provisions have become more complex, interviewees also attributed increased complexity to the Cr.PR. These were designed to increase efficiency in the criminal justice process[80] but also appear to have encouraged greater reference to points of law. As discussed in chapter three, the procedures introduced by the Cr.PR were also established to encourage cooperative case management practices[81] amid (unfounded) fears that defence advocates were ambushing prosecutors with a legal argument at trial.[82] While the Cr.PR also require the courts to facilitate defendant participation, the increased level of legal complexity is likely to have increased references to points of law to assist

---

[77] The provisions of which have now been replaced under the Sentencing Act 2020.

[78] *South East Surrey Youth Court (Ghanbari, Interested Party)* [2005] EWHC 2929.

[79] Law Commission, 'The Sentencing Code: A Report. Summary' (Law Com No 382 (Summary), 2018) 7. This eventually resulted in the codification of sentencing law in the Sentencing Act 2020.

[80] R Auld, 'Review of the Criminal Courts of England and Wales: Executive Summary' (2001) www.criminal-courts-review.org.uk/auldconts.htm. For discussion, see E Johnston, 'The Adversarial Defence Lawyer: Myths, Disclosure and Efficiency – A Contemporary Analysis of the Role in the Era of the Cr.PR.' (2020) 24(1) *International Journal of Evidence and Proof*, 35–58; Owusu-Bempah (n 35).

[81] See eg Cr.PR 1.1 and 1.2.

[82] See eg *DPP v Chorley Justices and Andrew Forrest* [2006] EWHC 1795. See further commentary in Owusu-Bempah (n 35).

in navigating the provisions efficiently. To explain those complex rules to all defendants might assist effective participation by avoiding assumptions about understanding or overlooking the processes that exclude defendants, assuming that they are explained properly and in a way that is appropriate to aid defendants. But full explanations and checking understanding would take time that many members of the courtroom workgroup do not have (chapter three). In one study, Jacobson noted a tendency among legal practitioners to fall back on legalese when attempting to explain complex legal provisions.[83] This likely exacerbates the marginalisation of all defendants, though unrepresented defendants will likely experience marginalisation in different ways and/or to a different extent than represented defendants.

If the law is referred to using legalese and is assumed to be a mundane part of legal practice in summary criminal proceedings, its implicit use is likely to mean that it is less detectable to people who are not members of the professional workgroup. The process of translating complex legal provisions into legalese by the workgroup creates a (further) divide between defendants and the professionals in court.[84] Indeed, the classification of cases as straightforward and/or uncontested is itself based on legal construction.[85] The implication of customary, often implicit, use of the law is that it at best perpetuates, and at worst exacerbates, practices that exclude defendants from effective participation in the proceedings. Thus, McBarnet's assessment of the lower court as 'permeated by legalistic and professional consciousness'[86] is reflected in my findings, which is demonstrated in relation to three separate types of hearing below.

V. EVIDENCE OF (IMPLICIT) LEGALISATION

My observations suggested that there are frequent implicit and explicit references to particular points of law during the course of summary proceedings.[87] These practices manifest in the ways that advocates support the representations that they make to the court. The observations suggested that references to points of law were much more likely to be made when defendants were represented. Furthermore, the majority of both prosecutors and defence advocates interviewed indicated that they do refer to points of law in the magistrates' court on a relatively frequent basis and acknowledged that they would tend to refer to the principles stated in authorities rather than the actual case or statute that is

---

[83] J Jacobson 'Observed Realities of Participation' in J Jacobson and P Cooper (eds), *Participation in Courts and Tribunals* (Bristol University Press, 2020).

[84] Smejkalová (n 51).

[85] It is telling that a barrister interviewed in another study described evidential matters as 'simple' issues (Kirby (n 6)).

[86] McBarnet (n 19) 198.

[87] These findings are also the subject of in-depth discussion in Welsh (n 16).

relevant to their case.[88] This supports the observational finding that legal issues tend to be referred to in implicit terms but still employ specialist language.[89] This has exacerbated the marginalisation of defendants and highlighted their role as dummy players in the proceedings. An example of this issue was provided by one prosecutor who stated,

> So, for example, when a suspended sentence is to be triggered I would say 'you should do that unless it is unjust to do so' and I know that's the wording in the statute. I couldn't tell you actually now what that statute was but do you know what I mean? So yeah, I am trying to be technically accurate. (*Prosecutor Q*)[90]

While some interviewees commented that points of law rarely arise in magistrates' courts, they also talked about changes to evidential provisions and sentencing guidelines as if they are part of routine rather than specialist legal provisions. By way of example, one advocate stated that it would be easy to go through the magistrates' court without the law as long as the person concerned understood the 'admin and the tactics and the procedure' (Defence solicitor C).[91] There was also a tendency for interviewees to suggest that legal issues are more likely to arise at trial, which is logical in the sense that a trial involves contested points. However, with reference to my observation findings discussed below, these comments betray the way that specialist issues become part of professional routines and are ingrained in the workgroup culture.

On the other hand, some interviewees seemed to be almost offended at the suggestion that magistrates' courts are law-free zones.[92] Defence solicitor B described the idea that magistrates' courts are law-free zones as 'rubbish'. Interviewees perceived the implicit use of legal provisions as appropriate to avoid bombarding a lay Bench with complex provisions on the basis that magistrates simply want to hear about the principles rather than the authorities.[93] Defence solicitor G said – apparently somewhat inaccurately – 'of course there's law, it's not a law free zone but it's a legalese free zone' while defence solicitor R described the law as being the 'trade' so failing to use the law would be like a surgeon failing to use their surgical instruments.

The best evidence of references to legal provisions tended to arise when a particular outcome was sought, such as a particular sentence or release on bail. My observations suggested that points of law were most likely to be referred to

---

[88] Ten of the 12 defence solicitors and five of the seven prosecutors interviewed stated that they tend to refer to the principles rather than the authorities, particularly in front of a lay Bench.

[89] As one defendant in Jacobson et al's study commented, 'If you are a bit common, you are going to find it very hard to understand what they are saying'. (Jacobson et al (n 26) 93).

[90] Campbell (n 53) also found that the speed with which proceedings were conducted frequently meant that statutory provisions and/or charges were not clearly stated to defendants.

[91] Defence solicitor I also talked about bad character and hearsay provisions, while also stating that law is used relatively infrequently.

[92] For example, defence solicitor E said, referring to law, 'I don't see how you can do the job without it really'.

[93] This was expressed in interviews with defence solicitors D and K.

during sentencing proceedings. Furthermore, the provisions of the Bail Act 1976 were often implicitly referred to, while both implied and explicit references to the construction of charges and required evidence were also relatively common in the course of case management. These three circumstances are discussed further below.

A. Sentencing

When dealing with sentencing, points of law seemed likely to arise via reference to sentencing guidelines. In the early 2000s, Wilcox and Young observed that sentencing had become tougher and that legal proceedings had become more complex.[94] Courts are now obliged to follow sentencing guidelines unless considered contrary to the interest of justice to do so.[95] Sentencing guidelines are produced by the Sentencing Council,[96] consisting of judges, legal practitioners and legal academics. The sentencing guidelines are formulated according to research, policy investigations and legal investigations. A policy cycle approach is adopted to assess and evaluate new guidelines.[97] Thus, while the guidelines are not strictly points of law, they represent a distillation of legal opinion about what factors are important in determining the severity of offences. As the use of the guidelines is generally mandatory for sentencers, working knowledge of the guidelines is advantageous to advocates – either highlighting specific aggravating and/or mitigating features or arguing that it would not be in the interests of justice to apply a particular guideline.

The sentencing guidelines also represent an example of measures designed to combat inconsistent decision-making practices.[98] Magistrates are required to complete a sentencing reasons form to state which factors they considered most relevant in reaching their decision. Using a form in this way both standardises the process and encourages implicit or fleeting reference to the sentencing guidelines in favour of efficient decision-making. The way in which standardised forms contribute to such behaviours is discussed further below.[99]

---

[94] A Wilcox and R Young, 'Understanding the Interests of Justice: A Study of Discretion in the Determination of Applications for Representation Orders in Magistrates' Courts' (Legal Services Commission, 2006).

[95] When the research was conducted, that obligation arose as a result of s 125 Coroners and Justice Act 2009. The same provisions are repeated in s 59 Sentencing Act 2020.

[96] See www.sentencingcouncil.org.uk.

[97] See HM Treasury, 'The Green Book' (London, 2020), which provides guidance about how policies, programmes and projects should be appraised, as well as guidance on evaluation throughout the policy implementation process.

[98] P Darbyshire, 'An Essay on the Importance and Neglect of the Magistracy' (1997) (September) *Criminal Law Review* 627; M Davies, 'A New Training Initiative for the Lay Magistracy in England and Wales – A Further Step Towards Professionalisation?' (2005) 12(1) *International Journal of the Legal Profession* 93.

[99] For an excellent discussion about how documents shape expertise, see A Riles (ed), *Documents. Artifacts of Modern Knowledge* (University of Michigan Press, 2006). In relation to magistrates'

In observation, sentencing hearings involved frequent implicit references to sentencing guidelines. Interview data supported this finding; interviewees indicated that they tended to refer to principles contained in sentencing guidelines during the course of mitigation. Some interviewees specifically highlighted the increased need to refer to sentencing case law and guidelines. For example, defence solicitor A said they referred to points of law 'more so since the sentencing guidelines came in'. As if to exemplify this, there was a stark difference between how unrepresented defendants and lawyers addressed sentencing. When unrepresented defendants were asked, during sentencing hearings, if they wanted to say anything to the court about the offence, they tended to provide extremely brief answers to specific questions asked of them, in clear contrast to the speeches made by defence solicitors that were often directed to offence mitigation in terms of sentencing guidelines and offender personal mitigation. In one instance, an unrepresented defendant essentially admitted that he had committed the same offence on several previous occasions even though there was no record of the commission of those offences. Although the court did not act on that admission (and the defendant did not actually suffer any adverse consequences), it is highly unlikely that it would have occurred if the defendant had been represented.

Of 37 observed references to the sentencing guidelines,[100] nearly half were made implicitly by, for example, stating that a theft was opportunistic or that an assault was provoked. Both lack of planning in relation to theft, and provocation in relation to assault, are factors that the Sentencing Council has indicated lead to lower levels of culpability,[101] so it seems likely that advocates were aware of the legal impact of their submissions at the point of making them. As such, sentencing guidelines not only represent a coordinated effort to ensure greater consistency, but they also appear to introduce a greater degree of specialised legal knowledge into summary proceedings than has previously been noted. However, unless a person is aware of the guidelines, where to find them and how to use them (which in itself requires a particularly formulaic approach), it would be easy to miss indirect references to provisions that influence the outcome of a case and that a non-member of the workgroup would struggle to both identify and participate in. In several cases observed during this study, offences that were adjourned for sentencing to take place at a later date were described as a 'category two assault' or a 'category three case', which are references to offence severity within sentencing guidelines, but the term was not explained

---

courts, see L Welsh and M Howard, 'Standardization and the Production of Justice in Summary Criminal Courts: A Post-Human Analysis' (2019) 28(6) *Social & Legal Studies* 774–93.

[100] There were 70 hearings in which sentencing could have been considered.

[101] Sentencing Council, 'Theft from a shop or stall' (2016) www.sentencingcouncil.org.uk/offences/magistrates-court/item/theft-from-a-shop-or-stall/; Sentencing Council, 'Common Assault / Racially or Religiously Aggravated Common Assault' (2011) www.sentencingcouncil.org.uk/offences/magistrates-court/item/common-assault-racially-religiously-aggravated-common-assault/.

to a defendant in court. This is an example of how individual hearings become a discursive space where the real-life problem of punishment is translated into the language of the law.[102] This practice allows the workgroup to maintain its professional autonomy while also (inadvertently or unconsciously) limiting the ability of defendants to participate in the process.

B. Bail

The defendant generally has a right to be granted unconditional bail at their first appearance in the magistrates' court.[103] The complex provisions of the Bail Act 1976 are beyond the scope of this work,[104] but it is important to know that the fact of being placed on bail (subject to conditions or otherwise) allows any criminal court to prosecute an individual who fails to attend court while subject to bail under section 6 Bail Act 1976. Therefore, every time a defendant is released on bail, at whatever stage in proceedings, they are effectively put on notice that there will be further charges if they fail to attend court as directed.

Although most defendants have a right to be released on bail, Part I, Schedule 1 of the Bail Act 1976 states that bail may be refused or bail with conditions may be imposed to ensure attendance at court, to ensure the defendant does not commit an offence while on bail, or to ensure that the course of justice is not obstructed (such as through interference with witnesses). Those exceptions to the right to (unconditional) bail appear to be referred to in implicit terms when prosecutors make applications to remand defendants into custody and when defence advocates apply for bail to be granted with conditions because any conditions that are suggested are designed to meet concerns about the statutory exceptions to the right to bail. Examples include suggesting a condition to report to the local police at designated times to ensure a defendant does not abscond or a condition not to enter retail premises to limit the risk of further offending in a shoplifting case.

Furthermore, provisions of LASPO state that the prosecutor can only apply for a remand into custody if there is a realistic prospect of a custodial sentence on conviction.[105] Not only does this suggest that knowledge of sentencing guidelines is advantageous, but also observations suggested that it is now common to hear prosecutors stating that there is or is not a realistic prospect of a custodial

---

[102] Smejkalová (n 51). See also Tata (n 22).

[103] Section 4, Bail Act 1976. There are some exceptions to this right, such as in relation to allegations of murder or manslaughter and serious sexual offences where the person has previously been convicted of a serious offence.

[104] For some discussion, see Welsh et al (n 11) ch 8.

[105] There are certain limited exceptions to these provisions, such as where the allegation involves domestic violence.

sentence when addressing the court about a defendant's remand status. In doing so, the prosecutors did not refer to the particular statutory provision which highlights the relevance of that statement, meaning that it was an implicit reference to particular legal provisions. The significance of that terminology may not be understood by a defendant (or anyone who does not have legal training/experience). Another example was to refer to the defendant's 'record' as shorthand for their record of previous convictions.

These matters post-date earlier socio-legal studies of magistrates' courts proceedings discussed in chapter three and are particular legal provisions, of which knowledge is advantageous in framing submissions to the magistrates. An implicit reference to the provisions in LASPO or the Bail Act 1976 dealt with the practicalities of translating the defendant's circumstances into their place within particular legal categories by, for example, references to residential addresses or the likely sentence that would be imposed on conviction. Translating legal principles to cater to individual client's circumstances is a significant part of a legal representative's role and enables ritualised individualisation to occur within the parameters of a courtroom that requires the efficient disposal of cases.[106] The tacit use of legal provisions is consequently significant in summary proceedings but could result in misunderstanding to the untrained ear. As Campbell reported, the language spoken during proceedings by legal actors differs greatly from the everyday language of defendants.[107] The disconnect between legal linguistic and everyday language interactions was illustrated on several occasions during the course of observations. In one case, when asked whether they were guilty or not guilty, a defendant replied, 'yes, I was taking the drugs'. This was not, however, a good enough indication of guilt for the court, and the court legal adviser felt it necessary to clarify and confirm that the defendant was, in fact, pleading guilty. In another case, a legal adviser again had to confirm whether 'yes' meant a guilty plea was being entered. There is some logical sense to this, in that answering 'yes' to the question 'are you guilty or not guilty' strictly appears to be equivocal. But here, the issue is not so much about the substance of the conversation as about the language that the court finds acceptable. In another instance, a defendant responded by saying 'lovely, cheers' as they were told they could leave the court, much to the apparent amusement of the legal adviser and solicitor, who exchanged smiles in reaction.

The implicit use of those terms highlights, and perhaps exacerbates, the paradox of summary justice in that it requires knowledge of legal provisions but denies access to that knowledge by the unstated and unexplained use of those provisions and principles. Carlen identified a similar issue in relation to the use of

---

[106] On this process of ritual individualisation in sentencing, see Tata (n 22). See also C Tata, *Sentencing: A Social Process* (Palgrave Macmillan, 2020).

[107] Campbell (n 53). See also R Nobles and D Schiff, 'Criminal Justice: Autopoietic Insights' in J Pribán and D. Nelken (eds), *Law's New Boundaries: The Consequences of Legal Autopoiesis* (Ashgate 2001).

jargon and signalling between advocates in magistrates' courts,[108] but increased reference to legal provisions via procedures introduced to encourage consistency and efficiency appear to have intensified this problem. Furthermore, the speed and informality of magistrates' court proceedings in particular (compared to Crown Courts) both operate to further obscure that paradox.

C. Case Management

A third type of hearing in which increased implicit reference to particular points of law appeared to be made was during the course of summary case management. Case management hearings have evolved from the suggestion that pre-trial review hearings may alleviate the volume of ineffective trial listings in magistrates' courts.[109] Subsequently, in his review of the criminal justice system, Auld LJ expressed concern about the number of pre-trial reviews and believed that the parties should take a more cooperative approach to case management.[110] Later, specific pre-trial review hearings were abandoned in favour of more proactive case management outside the court.[111] As the Cr.PR came into force, and Transforming Summary Justice was implemented (see chapter three), the magistrates' courts expected that all parties would be in a position to conduct case management at the first hearing.

Case management is completed by reference to a standardised form called a Preparation for Effective Trial form. Those forms have both administrative and legal roles in magistrates' court processes.[112] They require the parties to state the matters in dispute, the witness requirements (and reasons why witnesses are required), any further evidence to be served and any legal argument envisaged. As such, they require the parties to narrow the contested issues at trial so that court time can be used in the most efficient manner. The forms also aim to prevent the Crown from being 'ambushed' at trial by focusing the Crown prosecutor's time and resources only on disputed matters.[113]

While case management forms are part of the executive's desire to increase efficiency, they also require the parties to indicate how evidential burdens will be discharged and what factual and legal matters are in dispute. The wording of the form assumes that a defendant has received legal advice by repeatedly using

---

[108] Carlen (n 8).

[109] M Narey, 'Review of Delay in the Criminal Justice System' (Home Office, 1997).

[110] R Auld, 'Review of the Criminal Courts of England and Wales: Executive Summary' (The Stationery Office 2001).

[111] Office for Criminal Justice Reform, 'Delivering Simple Speedy Summary Justice. An Evaluation of Magistrates Court Tests' (London, 2007).

[112] Welsh and Howard (n 99).

[113] See comments made in *DPP v Chorley Justices and Andrew Forrest* [2006] EWHC 1795; *Malcolm v DPP* (2007) EWHC 363 (Admin). For discussion of how case management forms construct a particular type of justice, see Welsh and Howard (n 99).

terms such as 'Does the defendant understand that ...'. The form also requires a legal representative to indicate that a defendant has been advised that a trial can proceed in their absence if the defendant fails to attend court as directed,[114] which is also relevant to whether a charge of failing to attend in accordance with the Bail Act 1976 can be laid.

Additionally, the answers provided on case management forms about the issues in the case could be used as evidence during a trial as implied admissions to particular elements constituting an offence, such as presence at the scene.[115] The use of the form, therefore, becomes part of the process through which a problem is described and translated into particular legal categories.[116] About half of defence advocates and half of prosecutors interviewed felt that legal knowledge is necessary to complete a case management form appropriately. The majority of interviewees, particularly defence advocates, appeared to be acutely aware that what is recorded on the case management form could be referred to at subsequent hearings and indicated that this led them to consider completing the form very carefully.[117] The concerns of the lawyers I spoke to were borne out in the case of *Valiati v DPP; KM v DPP*,[118] which determined that information contained in a completed case management form can be used as evidence in a trial, as long as the party wishing to adduce the evidence successfully makes an appropriate application to put it before the court.[119] The case also went on the state that the parties are required to actively assist the court with identifying the issues, which is likely to be far easier for a lawyer to do than a non-legally trained participant.

The completion of case management forms represents an important convergence of law and bureaucratic measures designed to ensure consistency and efficiency. It provides an example of standardisation as questions are reduced to a series of tick-box answers with limited space to explain the issues.[120] This arguably represents one way in which legal practitioners execute their perceptions

---

[114] See *R (on the application of Drinkwater) v Solihull Magistrates' Court* [2012] EWHC 765 (Admin), *R v Jones* [2002] UKHL 5 for indications about when it would be appropriate to proceed in the absence of a defendant.

[115] While this practice was discouraged following the judgment given in *R v Newell* [2012] EWCA Crim 650, I have observed prosecutors putting the content of case management forms to defendants in cross examination.

[116] For discussion about the use of language to translate real-life problems into legal ones, see Smejkalová (n 51) and Jacobson (n 83)).

[117] Lawyers who spoke with Johnston (n 80) expressed similar concerns.

[118] *Valiati v DPP; KM v DPP* [2018] EWHC 2908 (Admin).

[119] In this case, there was no such application, so it was inappropriate for the court to have relied on information contained in the case management form. The possibility of information contained on the form being used as evidence does, however, remain per Sir Brian Leveson P's comments at paras 11 and 42.

[120] Examples include a yes/no answer as to whether the defendant has been advised about provisions that allow a reduction in sentence for entering an early guilty plea (incorporated in the Sentencing Act 2020).

about their responsibilities for keeping the court running smoothly[121] because completing the form enables cooperative case progression. However, Johnston noticed that some lawyers would use their expertise to adopt, during case management, 'a tactical or technical approach, which provided enough detail to the court but tactically, did not reveal their hand completely'.[122] In order to complete the form appropriately (be that tactically or completely openly), knowledge of both the nature of the charge and the evidential burdens which the Crown must satisfy to prove its case is required.[123] A specific section of the case management form asks whether the parties can agree on a basis of plea or plea to an alternative charge. As discussed in the previous chapter, the interview data indicated that both prosecutors and defence advocates view plea negotiations as useful, but they are again something that requires specialist knowledge. Thus defendants might be marginalised not only by the behaviours of the workgroup detailed in chapter three but also by the technical nature of the proceedings. These two features seem to go hand in hand to affect how effectively a defendant is able to participate in the process.

While aspects of the case management form serve to marginalise the ability of a defendant to participate effectively, others essentially force the defendant's hand – but in a way that fails to recognise they are not part of the court work-group. In *Valiati*, it was noted that where a defendant does not wish to do more than making the prosecutor prove their case at the case management stage, advancing a positive defence later in the trial could be a circumstance in which it would be appropriate for the Crown to apply for the case management form to be adduced as evidence.[124] Thus the defendant who refuses to cooperate places themselves in a precarious evidential position. This approach to case management reflects demands for efficiency but also builds the concept of obligatory participation into the defence. As Owusu-Bempah states,

> By interfering with the freedom to choose whether or not to actively participate in the criminal process, case management and sentencing practices are indicative of a system of obligatory participation. ... A system which can be characterised by the obligatory nature of defendant participation is difficult to reconcile with a process based on calling the state to account, as the purpose of requiring participation is to speed up the process and secure the defendant as an evidential resource.[125]

Securing defendants as evidential resources rather than autonomous partici-pants in the processes means that their needs and interests are marginalised in ways that may be both confusing and alienating.[126] Thus defendants can be

---

[121] These perceptions are discussed in Jacobson and Cooper (n 17).

[122] Johnston (n 80) 43.

[123] Form completion of this nature also appears to be problematic in areas of social welfare law. See J Robins and D Newman, *Justice in a Time of Austerity* (Bristol University Press, 2021).

[124] *Valiati v DPP; KM v DPP* [2018] EWHC 2908 (Admin).

[125] Owusu-Bempah (n 35) 45.

[126] Ibid; Owusu-Bempah, A, 'Understanding the Barriers to Defendant Participation in Criminal Proceedings in England and Wales' (2020) *Legal Studies* 1–21.

unable to participate through a lack of understanding brought about both by the use of law and how the workgroup operates, and forced to participate in ways contrary to their interest. Neither is conducive to avoiding processes that marginalise defendants.

Another example of forcing a defendant's hand during the course of case management appears in relation to the types of evidence that the prosecutor wishes to adduce during the trial. The version of the case management form in use in 2020 contained the following section:

The prosecution will rely on:	defendant's admissions in interview	▢
Tick / delete as appropriate	defendant's failure to mention facts in interview	▢
	[a summary] [a record] of the defendant's interview	▢
	[expert] [hearsay] [bad character] evidence	▢
	[CCTV] [electronically recorded] evidence	▢

Source: www.gov.uk/government/publications/preparation-for-trial-in-a-magistrates-court.

The types of evidence referred to in the above excerpt of the form are instances where the defendant is obliged to participate in the proceedings. That obligation arises either because there is a risk of adverse inferences being drawn against them in relation to a defendant's failure to mention facts in an interview[127] or because failure to serve and/or respond to the required application forms consistent with the obligations of the Cr.PR in relation to bad character[128] or hearsay evidence[129] can result in the admission of potentially highly prejudicial evidence or costs orders against the parties.[130] Despite these possible consequences, the language often used in court to discuss these provisions is rarely transparent when members of the court workgroup discuss the issues in a case. As Newman explains,

> even greater levels of detachment follow the appointment of a lawyer with these individuals [defendants], invariably, taking a back seat while the legal professionals go about their business with one another. In large part, this can be attributed to Magistrates' Courts' business becoming increasingly complicated over recent years, with regard to both legislation and bureaucratic procedure.[131]

---

[127] Sections 34–38 Criminal Justice and Public Order Act 1996. For a thorough analysis of the nature and detail of these obligatory forms of participation, see Owusu-Bempah (n 35).
[128] Part 11, Criminal Justice Act 2003 and Part 21, Cr.PR 2020.
[129] Chapter 2, Criminal Justice Act 2003 and Part 20, Cr.PR 2020.
[130] Owusu-Bempah (n 35).
[131] Newman (n 22) 9.

This serves several purposes, including the ability to process cases at speed and maintaining/reinforcing the status and hierarchy of the courtroom workgroup. But it comes at a significant cost to defendants. In some ways, the defendant is obliged to participate yet not afforded the tools to participate voluntarily. As such, their freedom of choice, and therefore, autonomy, in the process are undermined. At worst, 'legal procedure silences defendants who end up pleading guilty'.[132]

What we also see on the above section of the case management form is another example of specific references to legal provisions – such as character, hearsay and adverse inferences from silence[133] – without an explanation of what those provisions entail or where they can be found. For the unrepresented defendant, the legal advisers to the magistrates, or the DJ, ought to explain these provisions during a case management hearing, and many will do so. But the legal advisers and judges also form part of the magistrates' court workgroup and will likely employ the same language and modes of address as their peers. Alongside this, the complex rules of criminal procedure and evidence will always remain exclusionary without full, clear and time-consuming explanations offered to defendants. Several, albeit now quite old, studies have demonstrated that the legal adviser's main focus was enabling the court to operate within the procedural rules over ensuring effective or active participation, and that – as in any profession – there are varying standards of care exercised by court legal advisers towards unrepresented defendants.[134]

VI. COURT LEGAL ADVISERS AND DEFENDANTS

When asked about the behaviour of legal advisers towards unrepresented defendants, the defence lawyers and prosecutors that I interviewed reported a range of behavioural standards. Most interviewees felt that the way that an unrepresented defendant was treated varied from clerk to clerk,

> I've got one in mind who gives unrepresented defendants a rough time, a really really rough time and others that I can think of are straight down the line and completely straight, depends on the individual Court Clerk. (*Defence solicitor S*)

> Obviously you can get some clerks that are a lot more understanding and very softly softly with defendants and then you get other clerks that take advantage when a defendant's unrepresented and are almost sort of bullying towards them. (*Prosecutor N*)

---

[132] Campbell (n 53) 16.

[133] Section 34 Criminal Justice and Public Order Act 1986.

[134] See generally H Astor, 'The Unrepresented Defendant Revisited: A Consideration of the Role of the Clerk in Magistrates' Courts' (1986) 13(2) *Journal of Law and Society* 225–39; P Darbyshire, *The Magistrates' Clerk* (Barry Rose, 1984); A Mulcahy 'The Justifications of "Justice": Legal Practitioners' Accounts of Negotiated Case Settlements in Magistrates' Courts' (1994) 34(4) *British Journal of Criminology* 411.

I think there are some clerks who can rub defendants up the wrong way and there are others that almost charm them and make the process much much smoother. (*Prosecutor L*)

Some of them are extremely good and very patient and really help people. Some legal advisors I've seen are extremely short-tempered, extremely rude, you know, and just want to get the person out of their court. (*Defence solicitor E*)

Several others indicated that they felt that legal advisers try very hard to help unrepresented defendants,

I think they're a lot more patient and a lot more engaging with unrepresented defendants on the whole all of the legal advisors actually. I think they go out of their way to be I don't know what the word is, to help. (*Prosecutor P*)

I think the Court Legal Advisor, they're really, in the case of unrepresented defendants, really has to act as their friend and make sure that every point that could or ought to be raised is raised and considered and I think Court Advisors show infinite patience when dealing with unrepresented people and are at pains to impress on them how serious it is and make sure they understand what is happening. (*Defence solicitor K*)

I think the courts fall over themselves to be nice and helpful to unrepresented defendants. On the whole, I would say that the courts try to give a degree of help that they don't give to represented defendants, and I think understandably so because if a defendant's represented, you assume that the lawyer knows what he or she is doing. (*Defence solicitor B*)

This seems to tell us that court legal advisers often do their best to help unrepresented defendants through the process, but that standards are not necessarily consistent, and defendants are subject to a 'pot luck' of sorts, dependent on which adviser is in court on any given day. This is indicative of another potential paradox that exists in summary criminal justice. On the one hand, unrepresented defendants are unable to effectively participate partially because they do not have access to a representative with the necessary knowledge to run their case (ie they are less well equipped than represented defendants). On the other hand, the workgroups appear to make a greater effort to enable unrepresented defendants to understand whether or not that effort actually succeeds (ie there are more attempts by court staff to try and equip them with the necessary understanding). This paradox is illustrated by one observed example. A legal adviser conducting a case management hearing was concerned that an unrepresented defendant would not be able to conduct an effective case management, so was keen to adjourn to arrange representation. This is a good example of a legal adviser attempting to better equip the defendant to navigate through proceedings. However, the given reason for adjourning the case was 'it's going to be hard to agree s.9', with no further explanation about what that meant.[135] Thus the defendant may well have still

---

[135] This was a reference to provisions about agreeing with witness statements in accordance with s 9 Criminal Justice Act 1967.

lacked the knowledge about why this particular decision was made about the case.

It is important, however, to read those comments in light of three things. First, it did not necessarily match with my observations about the behaviour of court legal advisers. During those observations, I noted that the legal advisers routinely gave advice to magistrates outside of court and that when advisers were invited to speak with the magistrates in their retiring room, that process was only occasionally explained to defendants, regardless of the presence/absence of legal representation. In most cases, procedural or legal issues arose that were not explained to defendants, whether or not they were represented. Additionally, only a minority of unrepresented defendants were asked if they wanted to speak with a duty solicitor in open court, even though many were eligible to speak with a duty lawyer due to the nature of the case.

Second, the strength of the professional bond within the courtroom workgroup might cause the lawyers I interviewed to effectively see what their colleagues' behaviour in a more positive light. On this point, participants in another study also spoke favourably about how their courtroom peer group supported unrepresented defendants, though the extent of that support that related to understanding the nature and content of the proceedings was not clear.[136]

Third, as a defence practitioner myself, I had failed to notice these more exclusionary aspects of behaviour until I conducted the observations in this research. Ultimately, what the lawyers reported were perceptions about behaviour that do not neatly align with some of the observations of the same members of the workgroup, so the extent to which legal advisers explain legal provisions to unrepresented defendants is unclear. That said, another study reports that perceptions that the workgroup does its best to facilitate court user participation were borne out in observations, though the possibility of reactive effect was also noted.[137]

As the process of summary justice demands ever more efficiency, the policies and rules designed to achieve that efficiency – including case management – become part of the rules that need to be adhered to, and this might affect the way that all defendants experience the system as administered by court legal advisers. As has been noted elsewhere,

> In a system that demands efficiency, those rules become ingrained in standardised processes with little consideration given to what they mean for 'justice'. This means that the needs of vulnerable defendants, for example, are sometimes swept aside or lost in the system even when clerks and legal advisers want to assist.[138]

On this, even those interviewees who felt that court legal advisers did do a good job of trying to help unrepresented defendants noticed that the court advisers

---

[136] Kirby (n 6).
[137] Jacobson (n 83).
[138] Welsh et al (n 11) 403.

were being pulled further into demands that the court progresses its business as speedily as possible. This risks undermining the good work of those legal advisers who do take the time to assist unrepresented defendants in particular. Defence solicitor K, quoted above praising clerks for their behaviour towards unrepresented defendants, also said in relation to delays obtaining legal aid,

> Court clerks are just our bureaucrats to get through the list. It's also part of the overall demoralisation that they're not interested and why should they care when there is increased demands and pressure on them. They're not going to be accommodating of anything that makes their life more difficult.

There is no suggestion here that lawyers and court legal advisers are not ultimately doing their jobs properly, thoroughly and in a way that they consider appropriate to best meet their party's needs. It was noted above that lawyers regard explanations of the law to their clients as a very important part of the job, a view that I would also take as a practitioner. Those explanations will almost invariably take place outside of the courtroom itself, which may mitigate the defendant's confusion in the actual courtroom by attempting to enable effective participation through understanding. Indeed, in many cases observed, defendants (regardless of whether they were represented or not) appeared to be actively listening, nodding or – when represented – giving further instructions to their lawyer during proceedings. However, those explanations about the law and procedure do not assist a defendant to engage actively and meaningfully, through their own behaviour and voice, in the public arena that will ultimately determine their fate. The responses to defendants who attempted to speak during proceedings in response to prosecutors' comments varied between being told to be quiet and more active empathetic engagement by the workgroup. Even when the defendants did speak themselves, it was not clear that this amounted to effective participation, though it may have been active participation. For example, one very vocal defendant in a case that I observed left the magistrates concerned that proceedings 'had gone over their head' despite active engagement. Thus the distinction between active and effective participation becomes clear. The ability to participate in the actual courtroom voluntarily and effectively is ultimately undermined because the language and behaviour of the room itself take over. Newman argued that lawyers treated their clients disrespectfully while keeping them at a distance and 'leaving them in a continual state of ignorant dependence'.[139] The problem, as it seems to be here, is that these lawyers are time-poor in the context of their business needs, which encourages them to fall back on their professional status within the workgroup in a way that undermines the defendant's autonomy. Sadly, time poverty connected to funding cuts (chapter two), demands for efficiency, greater resort to legal provisions to govern procedure, and the professionalisation of the court workgroup has created a situation

---

[139] Newman (n 22) 98.

where the defendant is either obliged to participate or unable to make a truly voluntary decision to participate, thereby increasing their marginalisation as an outsider in the process.

VII. SUMMARY

The increased legalisation of summary justice appears to have occurred as a result of three things: the professionalisation of the process, more and more complex legislative control over court procedures and the admissibility of evidence, and demands for efficiency. Disentangling these three contributory factors is extremely difficult, if not impossible. To illustrate, demands for efficiency have taken form in regulatory practices designed to control the trial process through case management. This affects the behaviour of advocates, court staff and defendants. In this sense, the criminal justice system has become subject to greater regulation since the turn of the twenty-first century. Regulatory techniques are manifest in evidential and procedural rules via the Cr.PR, and in the use of forms that compel structured and standardised decision-making.

Another example of how efficiency has affected the legalisation of the court process arises through the use of diversion. Criminal justice services have become ever more anxious about meeting narrowly defined performance objectives,[140] which mean that the 'lowest hanging fruit' becomes an easy target to demonstrate effectiveness.[141] Diversion of offences and relaxation of evidential principles provide examples of legislation that encourage efficiency, target low hanging fruit and increase the legalisation of proceedings by encouraging only complex and/or contested cases to be put before the judicial Bench. Improving the efficiency of cases that reach court is assisted by the professionalisation of the magistrates' court and through measures contained in the Cr.PR that increase cooperation between advocates. All of these things have added to the legalisation of summary criminal proceedings while also increasing the marginalisation experienced by defendants. Furthermore, the processes of marginalisation in summary criminal justice are obscured as a result of the speed and informality with which proceedings operate in comparison to the Crown Court while remaining equally pervasive.

It seems that the frequency with which points of law arise in summary criminal proceedings has been either previously underestimated or that those references which did occur were limited, and there has been a change in the way magistrates court users refer to law. It appears most likely that increased levels

---

[140] E Bell *Criminal Justice and Neoliberalism* (Palgrave Macmillan 2011).
[141] A Sanders, 'Reconciling the Apparently Different Goals of Criminal Justice and Regulation: The "Freedom" Perspective' in G Smith, T Seddon and H Quirk (eds), *Regulation and Criminal Justice: Innovations in Policy and Research* (Cambridge University Press, 2010) 52.

of representation, alongside new legislation and procedural requirements, have increased references to points of law in summary criminal proceedings. Greater complexity in legal provisions and procedural and legal obligations to partici-pate add another dimension to the nature of marginalisation experienced by defendants because it becomes more difficult for defendants to participate in the proceedings in an autonomous way. Difficulties in participation are made worse by the way in which the workgroup translates those principles to manage workgroup cohesion while also meeting the goal of efficiency. It is, therefore, apparent that here, as in another study, translating cases into legal questions and answers is a process that marginalises defendants.[142]

Significantly, defendants may not understand the importance of particular issues that tend to be referred to in implicit ways because specialist use of language appears to prevent access to effective participation. This is most worrying in relation to those provisions that oblige defendants to participate in the process of prosecution. Levels of marginalisation do, however, poten-tially decrease when defendants are represented because lawyers indicate that they attempt to explain law and procedure to clients before entering the court-room. Such explanations also appear, given comments about unrepresented defendants, to enable cases to be processed more quickly. That is not to say that cooperation and language do not marginalise defendants from processes in the courtroom itself, particularly given the passivity of most defendants in court,[143] but rather that defence advocates do have an important role to play. For example, Kemp and Balmer's study records that represented defendants had a much greater understanding of what was happening in court than unrepre-sented defendants.[144] Being legally represented is undoubtedly a critical element of participation, and the courtroom workgroup recognises the importance of legal professionals in facilitating understanding. But representation alone is only one element of access to justice (chapter one) and is not sufficient to achieve defendants' voluntary and active participation when it also reinforces the use of law as part of a specialised performance where legal representatives are, physically and normatively, central to the proceedings.[145] Because it is clear

---

[142] P Cooper, 'Looking Ahead: Towards a Principled Approach to Supporting Participation' in J Jacobson and P Cooper (eds), *Participation in Courts and Tribunals* (Bristol University Press, 2020).

[143] C Tata et al, 'Does Mode of Delivery Make a Difference to Criminal Case Outcomes and Clients' Satisfaction? The Public Defence Solicitor Experiment' (2004) (Feb) *Criminal Law Review* 120.

[144] V Kemp and N Balmer, 'Criminal Defence Services: Users' Perspectives' (Legal Services Research Centre, 2008).

[145] A judge interviewed for another study acknowledged that when defendants are represented, the focus really lies with the representative rather than the defendant themselves (Jacobson and Cooper (n 17)). On courtroom layout, see especially L Mulcahy, 'Architects of Justice: The Politics of Courtroom Design' (2007) 16(3) *Social & Legal Studies* 383–403 and L Mulcahy and E Rowden, *The Democratic Courthouse: A Modern History of Design, Due Process and Dignity* (Routledge, 2019).

that 'the relationship between representation and participation is not entirely straightforward'[146] and the powerfully performative nature of words rests in a background of socially situated power relations,[147] much more can and should be done to improve the way that law is used to facilitate the ability of defendants to voluntarily participate in magistrates' court processes. To perpetuate a narrative that magistrates' courts are 'law-free' does a disservice to defendants by hiding from view the ways in which the use of law in summary proceedings marginalises these participants, and ignores the need for both descriptive (legal representation) and normative (understanding and participation) access to justice set out in chapter one.

---

[146] Kirby (n 6).
[147] Smejkalová (n 51).

5

Legal Aid Funding, Lawyers and Defendant Participation

I. INTRODUCTION

C HAPTER TWO EXAMINED the way in which political manoeuvres and policy-making has affected legal aid funding. It also provided an indication of how lawyers had – at a macro level – been affected by those manoeuvres. The impact can be seen through contractions in the legal aid market, meaning fewer lawyers are available to conduct publicly funded work for clients and increased bureaucracy and management risks for firms. In this chapter, I take those issues to a micro level to examine how the availability of and procedure for obtaining publicly funded representation in summary criminal proceedings affects relationships between defendants, their lawyers and the magistrates' courts. Consequently, this chapter focuses on the descriptive element of access to justice outlined in chapter one: the meaningful operation of the right to legal representation.

Between 1970 and 1990, England and Wales experienced an increase in magistrates' court legal aid expenditure, owing – in part – to an increasingly generous interpretation of the interests of justice (aka merits) test by magistrates' court clerks.[1] But, as highlighted in chapter two, there was a rise in the number of prosecutions during this period,[2] and the potential for miscarriages of justice to occur was in people's minds following the inquiry into the death of Maxwell Confait,[3] and the subsequent enactment of the Police and Criminal Evidence Act 1984, and Prosecution of Offences Act 1985, which bolstered demands for greater levels of defence representation. Despite that backdrop,

---

[1] C Tata, 'The Construction of "Comparison" in Legal Aid Spending: The Promise and Perils of a Jurisdiction-Centred Approach to (International) Legal Aid Research' in F Regan et al (eds), *The Transformation of Legal Aid: Comparative and Historical Studies* (Oxford University Press, 1999); R Young, 'Will Widgery do? Court Clerks, Discretion and the Determination of Legal Aid Applications' in R Young and D Wall (eds), *Access to Criminal Justice: Legal Aid, Lawyers and the Defence of Liberty* (Blackstone Press, 1996).

[2] Legal Action Group, *A Strategy for Justice: Publicly Funded Legal Services in the 1990s* (London, Legal Action Group, 1992).

[3] This case involved the wrongful conviction of three especially vulnerable young men who had made false confessions and were subsequently exonerated for the killing. See Home Office 'Report of an Inquiry into the Death of Maxwell Confait' (London: The Stationery Office, 1977).

Young noted that during the 1980s and 1990s, the government became 'determined to resist the arguments for any further colonisation of the magistrates' courts by publicly funded lawyers',[4] and set about changing legal aid application processes as described in chapter two. Professional/state interactions are inevitably influenced by the strategies adopted by both entities,[5] and Sommerlad argued that changes to the structure of legal aid provision in terms of rationalisation, increased competition and greater regulation have transformed the 'structure, culture and ethos of the profession'.[6] Furthermore, lawyers recently reported that it is not possible to run a profitable firm on the basis of magistrates' court work alone, so it is often subsidised by fees paid for Crown Court cases.[7]

The following examination explores the effects of those changes that appear to have had the greatest impact on criminal cases in magistrates' courts, according to the data obtained from observations and interviews with advocates. Those findings are situated within the context of other emerging data along the same themes. While the results of this work alone are not generalisable, when situated alongside other data, we can surmise the data paints a picture that is close to reality. The patterns that seem to emerge are significant in providing some explanation of the challenges faced by defence lawyers, which feed into the (in)ability of defendants to participate in summary criminal proceedings.

The themes arising during the research concerned solicitors' risk-taking behaviour related to obtaining funding, remuneration rates and methods affecting the services received by defendants, issues surrounding defendants' ability to engage in the process of actually applying for legally aided representation and delay caused by the reintroduction of means-testing. All these aspects of legal aid funding appear to affect the ability of lawyers to provide services to defendants to maximise their ability to effectively participate in the proceedings (as far as this is possible for defence lawyers alone). Furthermore, I suggest that, as lawyers become progressively more uncertain about legal aid payments, they increasingly struggle to manage their professional and ethical duties towards clients and are torn between giving effect to business needs or client needs. Services offered to defendants may suffer as lawyers' sense of professional identity is challenged by prevailing economic structures that undermine their understanding of the roles and rituals of legal practice. To demonstrate these

---

[4] Young (n 1) 140.

[5] K Macdonald, *The Sociology of the Professions* (Sage, 1995).

[6] H Sommerlad, 'Reflections on the Reconfiguration of Access to Justice' (2008) 15 *International Journal of the Legal Profession* 179; 182.

[7] House of Commons Justice Committee, *Oral evidence: (a) Court Capacity* (HC 2020-21 284); *(b) The Future of Legal Aid* (HC 2020–21 289). See also R Dehaghani and D Newman, 'The Crisis in Legally Aided Criminal Defence in Wales: Bringing Wales into Discussions of England and Wales' (2021) *Legal Studies* (online first) and J Thornton, 'The Way in Which Fee Reductions Influence Legal Aid Criminal Defence Lawyer Work: Insights from a Qualitative Study' (2019) *Journal of Law and Society* 46 (4) 559–85.

points, this chapter addresses issues of uncertainty about payment, concerns about the impact of fixed fee payment structures and the application process itself. It then examines how those issues can cause a delay in magistrates' court cases. Before concluding, the impact of two other publicly funded representation schemes, duty solicitor representation and court-appointed advocates are briefly discussed. First, to provide a setting for that discussion, I outline and contextualise the general pattern of representation identified.

II. LEVELS AND METHODS OF REPRESENTATION

Representation levels in summary criminal proceedings remain high, but there seems to be a consensus that the number of people appearing in magistrates' courts without legal representation has increased in recent years.[8] Of 183 cases observed during my fieldwork, 40 defendants appeared to be unrepresented, but 22 of those 40 people seemed to be eligible for representation through either the Duty Solicitor or a Representation Order.[9] Of the 143 defendants who were represented, the method under which representation was funded is as follows:

Method	Number of Cases
Representation Order (Legal Aid)	75
Pro Bono[10]	23
Duty Solicitor	23
Unclear	17
Privately fee paying	1
Costs reimbursed from central funds[11]	1
Court-appointed	3

In percentage terms, 22 per cent of cases I observed involved unrepresented defendants. These observations reflect similar findings to Kemp's 2010 study, in which 18 per cent of defendants were unrepresented. Kemp's study was

---

[8] P Gibbs, 'Justice Denied? The Experience of Unrepresented Defendants in the Criminal Courts.' (Transform Justice, 2016); E Duggan, 'This Man Had to Face Drugs Charges with No Lawyer Because He Couldn't Afford One' *Buzzfeed, (online*, 15 December 2017); P Gibbs and F Ratcliffe, 'Criminal Defence in an Age of Austerity: Zealous Advocate or Cog in a Machine?' (Transform Justice, 2019).

[9] I was unable to ascertain why those defendants did not take up that entitlement.

[10] Pro bono work includes, here, any and all unpaid work.

[11] A solicitor can claim for costs from central funds when a defendant is represented under a private fee-paying agreement, and the case is dismissed. In those circumstances, a solicitor can apply for the defendant's costs to be reimbursed by HMCTS. However, such claims will only be paid at legal aid rates, resulting in a shortfall referred to as the 'innocence tax' (See G Sturge and S Lipscombe, 'Is the Criminal Justice System Fit for Purpose?' (House of Commons Library, 2020) commonslibrary.parliament.uk/is-the-criminal-justice-system-fit-for-purpose/.

also conducted after the reintroduction of means-testing.[12] Other estimates suggest that the number of people appearing without representation is as high as 30 per cent.[13] All these figures suggest a gradual but steady increase in the number of defendants appearing in magistrates' courts without legal representation, from 18 per cent in 2010 to 22 per cent around 2014, 28 per cent in 2016/17[14] and around 30 per cent by 2017. The number of legal aid applications granted in magistrates' courts – especially in relation to summary only cases – have been on a downward trend for several years, up to and including during 2020.[15] When we consider the volume of business dealt with by the magistrates' court is in the region of 1.4m cases per year,[16] this means that more than 400,000 people appear there without legal representation. One magistrate, quoted by Gibbs, said:

> At the heart of the adversarial system is the concept of 'equality of arms', with both sides being equally able to present their case. This has been so seriously undermined by the lack of access to legal aid that it has become a regular and disquieting feature of the magistrates' court to find defendants attempting to respond to a charge they don't fully understand, with no experience of the law or of legal procedures, against qualified professionals with all the resources of the CPS behind them … They constitute a real threat to the long tradition of a fair trial for all who appear before us.[17]

Throughout my research, there was a general sense that more defendants appear in court without legal representation. Six interviewees (a mix of defence solicitors and prosecutors) specifically referred to a greater number of defendants appearing without legal assistance since the 2006 reintroduction of means-tested eligibility for representation (on means-testing, see chapter two). During the course of a conversation observed between a barrister and legal adviser at one magistrates' court, counsel observed that he thinks more people appear

---

[12] V Kemp, 'Transforming Legal Aid: Access to Criminal Defence Services' (Ministry of Justice, 2010).

[13] Duggan (n 8).

[14] J Campbell, *Entanglements of Life with the Law: Precarity and Justice in London's Magistrates Courts* (Cambridge Scholars Publishing, 2020).

[15] Ministry of Justice, 'Legal Aid Statistics England and Wales Bulletin Jul to Sep 2020' (Ministry of Justice, 2020) www.gov.uk/government/statistics/legal-aid-statistics-july-to-september-2020/legal-aid-statistics-england-and-wales-bulletin-jul-to-sep-2020#fn:2.

[16] It should be noted that a significant proportion of magistrates' court cases relate to minor motoring offences or train fare evasion, which arguably would never satisfy the interest of justice test required to obtain legal aid, even before funding was cut. From a crime control perspective, the relative level of punishment attached to these types of offences means that access to legal advice is not required. From a due process perspective, access to legal advice is necessary to check the propriety of the proceedings, protect against arbitrary state interference with civil liberties and protect defendants from the consequences of convictions for even minor offences, such as loss of driving licences, heavy financial penalties, creation of a criminal record, for example. It is up to the reader to decide which of these approaches they favour, though I tend towards the due process model.

[17] Gibbs (n 8) 1.

without representation since means-testing was reintroduced. The legal adviser agreed with that observation. We know, from chapter four, that unrepresented defendants are likely to be at a greater disadvantage navigating the court process than those who do have the benefit of legal assistance.

A distinction must be drawn according to the type of hearing to understand some of the nuances involved in assessing levels of unrepresented defendants. For instance, many summary motoring cases will involve unrepresented defendants who would never have qualified for publicly funded representation in any event. However, many of the hearings that I observed were first appearances for non-motoring offences at which defendants were expected to enter a plea. In 11 of 23 cases where I have recorded the representation type as pro bono, the defence advocate appeared to be making the application for legal aid at the first hearing, while in a further five cases, legal aid had been applied for but not yet granted.[18] Completing a legal aid application at the first hearing was a practice familiar to me as a practitioner. If legal aid was refused after the hearing, either the lawyer ends up unpaid for that work (if it was a case that concluded in a single hearing, as encouraged in recent years: chapter three), or the defendant appears unrepresented at subsequent hearings (unless they pay their own costs of representation), and the lawyer is unpaid for the first hearing. As discussed in chapter four, important case management decisions can be made at first hearings, which can affect the trajectory of the case as a whole. I commonly observed solicitors complaining about being required to conduct case management hearings when they were not in funds. Thornton similarly reported lawyers complaining about wasted time when legal aid was refused post hearing.[19] While a purely hypothetical exercise, if legal aid were refused in the above 11 cases, it would bring the number of unrepresented defendants in my sample up to 56 of 183 cases, or 30 per cent of cases observed. This scenario creates uncertainty for both defendants and defence lawyers, which can potentially impact the service received. It also means that defendants might be affected by decisions made at case management even though they do necessarily fully understand the implications of those decisions.[20]

III. UNCERTAINTY AND MANAGING RISK

As a result of changes surrounding the operation of legal aid followed up in interviews, it became apparent that solicitors were representing defendants at

---

[18] While the remaining seven cases involved pro bono representation, the reason for that was unclear.

[19] Thornton (n 7). See further L Welsh, '*The Effects of Changes to Legal Aid on Lawyers' Professional Identity and Behaviour in Summary Criminal Cases: A Case Study*' (2017) 44 (4) *Journal of Law and Society* 559–85.

[20] For similar observations, see Gibbs 'Justice Denied?' (n 8).

financial risk to their firm. During the course of observation, I was approached by one defence advocate who volunteered to me that his firm makes an application for legal aid in every case, even if they think it likely to be refused, in order to make a claim for pre-order cover (capped at £47.95), or under the early cover scheme (£68.44 plus VAT) and thereby receive some remuneration. An alternative claim of £22 for completing a means form with a client is also available.[21] This practice/viewpoint was not commonly held among solicitors that I spoke to, who tended – in line with my own experience – to think that the bureaucracy involved in completing these applications for 'fall back' cover outweighed the benefit of receiving it. In essence, the bureaucracy surrounding these procedures disincentivised time-poor defence lawyers from making these claims.[22] To contextualise the amounts that can be claimed, should be noted that a standard fee claim for an uncontested guilty plea hearing in the magistrates' court is £158.[23]

Interviewees commonly expressed uncertainty about remuneration, with one defence solicitor saying that work is conducted when remuneration is uncertain.

> All the time, all the time. I'd say if I was to go to court with six cases a day, roughly, for example, at least one of them would be a bit of a wing and a prayer job where you're hoping you would [be paid]. (*Defence solicitor S*)

Three prosecutors interviewed did not notice advocates working when they were unsure if they would be paid, but all of the other 19 interviewees (including the four remaining prosecutors) described this as a relatively common occurrence since the reintroduction of means-testing. While defence solicitors predictably had the strongest views about this issue (see below), prosecutors also commented that they sensed defence solicitors doing work when they were unsure about payment either a lot of the time or every time they had conduct of a magistrates' court case list.

Defence solicitors frequently spoke of conducting cases when they were unsure of payment. Four interviewees said that they worked in this way 'all the time', while four more described this way of working as a daily occurrence.

---

[21] The terms under which these claims can be made are found in Annex A of the Legal Aid Manual (Legal Aid Agency 'Criminal Legal Aid Manual Applying for Legal Aid in Criminal Cases in the Magistrates' and Crown Court' (Ministry of Justice, 2020). Since this research, an Evidence Provision Assistance fee has been introduced but, for reasons that are unclear, this only applies in Crown Court cases.

[22] Similar issues were raised by lawyers in R Dehaghani and D Newman, 'Criminal Legal Aid and Access to Justice: An Empirical Account of a Reduction in Resilience' (2021) *International Journal of the Legal Profession* (online first); D Newman and L Welsh, 'The Practices of Modern Criminal Defence Lawyers: Alienation and its Implications for Access to Justice' (2019) 48(1–2) *Common Law World Review* 64–89; J Thornton, 'Is Publicly Funded Criminal Defence Sustainable? Legal Aid Cuts, Morale, Retention and Recruitment in the English Criminal Law Professions' (2020) 40(2) *Legal Studies* 230–51.

[23] The Criminal Legal Aid (Remuneration) (Amendment) Regulations 2016.

Four defence solicitors talked about attempting to secure payment via legal aid in terms of 'taking a risk' or 'a gamble'. One defence lawyer explained these issues in the following way:

> These cases end up being dealt with pro bono by solicitors who, you know, have an ongoing, or have had an ongoing, relationship with the client and don't want to see people stuck high and dry. I don't think it happens for trials but I'm pretty sure it happens quite a lot for guilty pleas. ... You complete the legal aid application form. You then have to send him [the client] off to get his copies of his wage slips. What are you going to do if he doesn't send them back? Sue him? You're not because you know he's got no money and so you've done that case for free ... You've no idea where he is ... you have done 200 quid's worth of work for absolutely nothing at all ... cases where you are taking that risk happen every day. (*Defence solicitor F*)

Conducting unpaid work seemed to be a common occurrence among criminal defence service providers, despite the acknowledged financial strains already faced by their businesses.[24] This places defence lawyers in a precarious employment and business position themselves.[25] The above comment suggests that lawyers seek to mitigate defendants' marginalisation (by providing free representation) as a result of pre-existing relationships. The nature and extent of that mitigation may, however, be limited by uncertainty about payment and low remuneration levels, as is discussed below. Potentially, in the future, when such relationships have not been established, more and more defendants will appear in court without representation. Furthermore, it is likely that the goodwill that encourages lawyers to provide representation of this nature decreases as funding stagnates further.[26]

It must also be recognised that there may be other reasons why solicitors represent defendants on a pro bono basis, including maintaining good working relationships with the court and prosecutors. As discussed in chapter three, a high degree of cooperation exists between court personnel, and that cooperation seems to be crucial to the smooth running of busy courts. Acting in a cooperative way also enables defence solicitors to maintain credibility and, therefore, remain a member of the exclusive group of personnel who work in summary criminal courts. Furthermore, defence solicitors may be of the view that, by conducting a degree of pro bono work, they will maintain a good reputation with (potential) clients, and this might allow for a small morale boost in the context of feeling undervalued and unappreciated for the work they do perform.[27] Alternatively, by continuing to act in such circumstances, lawyers

---

[24] A Clarke and L Welsh, 'Criminal Cases Review Commission: Legal Aid and Legal Representatives Stage 4 Interviews – Report' (Brighton, University of Sussex, 2020); Dehaghani and Newman, *The Crisis* (n 7); Welsh (n 19).

[25] See generally E Cooke, 'The Changing Occupational Terrain of the Legal Aid Lawyer in Times of Precariousness' (Doctor of Philosophy (PhD) thesis, University of Kent, 2019).

[26] On this, see Thornton (n 7); Newman and Welsh (n 22).

[27] See also Newman and Welsh (n 22); Dehaghani and Newman, *The Crisis* (n 7); Thornton (n 22).

may be performing a type of 'defiant resilience'[28] in which they try to act in accordance with their understanding of the defence lawyer role by emphasising the service-oriented nature of their work.[29] This could be a coping mechanism that allows lawyers to protect their professional identity in the face of change. As Newman found, lawyers can simultaneously hold both negative and positive attitudes towards their work without necessarily being conscious of the inherent contradictions in these attitudes.[30]

However, interviewed defence advocates recognised that, by taking risks in relation to the likelihood of payment, they are playing into the hands of a system that considers efficiency to be of extreme importance. This highlighted the disparate and contradictory needs of defence practice in the magistrates' courts, which could feed into the cognitive dissonance experienced in relation to their role. For example, one interviewee said

> Magistrates were trained and said absence of legal aid is no reason to adjourn and again solicitors were not, I think a) because we are professional and care about our clients but b) because we're terrified someone else will come along and look after them and we'll lose our market share, solicitors have facilitated the courts. ... we've allowed it to happen and we shouldn't have done. (*Defence solicitor K*)

Defence solicitor G felt that the magistrates' courts were aware of the willingness of advocates to take that risk and take advantage of that behaviour. Thus, by failing to resist the difficulties they encounter, solicitors become complicit in their own subordination,[31] which can develop into, or exacerbate, a sense of powerlessness.[32] That sense of powerlessness can lead to low morale, with consequent effects for market sustainability, market contraction and decreasing availability and quality of service for defendants.

Uncertainty about payment appeared to arise as a result of bureaucracy surrounding the legal aid application process (discussed below) and because lawyers had concerns about how the Legal Aid Agency (LAA) would process the application forms and administer the test. In chapter two, we saw that lawyers had described a culture of refusal at the LAA. While the solicitors that I spoke to did not express their concerns in the same way and were not prompted about their views on the LAA, it was clear that they were anxious about the way the

---

[28] L. Burke et al, 'Probation Migration(s): Examining Occupational Culture in a Turbulent Field' (2017) 17 *Criminology and Criminal Justice* 192; 201.

[29] See also Cooke (n 25), who discussed legal aid lawyers' reliance on the altruistic nature of their work as a form of resilience against the increasingly precarious nature of their work.

[30] D Newman, 'Are Lawyers Neurotic?' (2017) 25 (1) *International Journal of the Legal Profession* 3–29.

[31] Newman took the view that criminal defence solicitors do regard themselves as subordinate to other members of the legal profession and they attempt to justify the poor service that they provide as a result of the attack on their egos (Newman D, *Legal Aid, Lawyers and the Quest for Justice* (Hart Publishing 2013)). Solicitors may be more tempted to provide a limited service if they are uncertain about receiving payment.

[32] Newman and Welsh (n 22).

LAA processed applications for legal aid. Defence solicitor B described legal aid application forms being returned for 'quite petty reasons', while several other defence solicitors spoke of forms being returned because a particular box had not been ticked. Defence solicitor F explained:

> ... even for fairly basic things like you send the form off and you tick the box that the client is single and then it gets sent back to you because you haven't ticked the next box which is to indicate whether he is single, widowed, divorced ...

Similar issues were reported by Defence solicitor I, who said

> if there is one box that isn't ticked correctly or even though you've described the reasons why you think they're eligible, someone won't read the form properly and rather than actually dealing with that case then it's much easier just to send it back and hopefully someone else will have to deal with it.

Several other defence solicitors described the way that the LAA processed applications as 'cumbersome' (Defence solicitor G) or 'bureaucratic' (Defence solicitors C and O). These comments suggested a breakdown in trust and communication between the LAA and defence solicitors, leading to a loss of faith in fair and reasonable treatment. This is not the only study that suggests relationships between the LAA and defence lawyers are poor. Lawyers conducting appellate work at the other end of the criminal justice system expressed opinions that indicated distrust between solicitors and the LAA that flows both ways.[33] These issues increase the bureaucratic burdens faced by time-poor defence lawyers, feed into poor morale[34] and ultimately into the service that a defendant receives in several ways: because the defendant cannot get funding in good time for case preparation; because lawyers have less time to prepare the case; because there is low morale among defence lawyers; or because these issues feed into the overall market contraction observed in recent years. In the end, it is suspects and defendants who will suffer and who are potentially at greater risk of becoming victims to a miscarriage of justice.

Even when publicly funded representation is in place, the way that fees are paid has the potential to affect the way that defendants experience the magistrates' court process. When legal aid is in place, most summary criminal cases are paid by a fixed fee. The method and rate of payment may both explain solicitors' willingness to take risks about payment[35] and affect the level of service received by defendants.

---

[33] R Vogler et al, 'Criminal Cases Review Commission: Legal Aid and Legal Representatives. Final Report' (Brighton, University of Sussex, 2020).

[34] Weber had earlier noted that greater levels of bureaucracy could result in professionals becoming less emotionally attached to their work (see generally M Weber, 'Legitimate Authority and Bureaucracy' in L Boone and D Bowen (eds), *The Great Writings in Management and Organizational Behavior* (Irwin, 1987).

[35] As long as legal aid is eventually granted, payment at the same rate would be received as if legal aid had been in place at the outset, and so little is actually lost.

IV. THE EFFECT OF FIXED (OR STANDARD) FEES

As discussed in chapter two, standard fee payments were reintroduced in the mid-1990s over concerns about the rising cost of criminal legal aid.[36] While there is a body of literature that discusses legal aid funding – especially cuts and/ or undercutting brought about by inflation – and defence lawyering, there exists 'relatively little published direct empirical examination of the effects of standard fees for summary work'.[37] The views expressed by solicitors I spoke with about the effect of working under a standard fee scheme were surprisingly candid and supported by subsequent research.[38]

Seven of the 12 defence solicitors interviewed expressed an opinion about the level of payment received under the fixed fee scheme. Prosecutors made no similar comments but largely confessed to knowing little about the way that defence advocates are paid (even the two who had formerly been defence solicitors). One prosecutor erroneously believed that defence solicitors are paid for every hearing, and lawyers would, therefore, be pleased when cases are adjourned.

Most of the defence lawyers interviewed felt that a standardised fee payment scheme was in principle acceptable. One defence solicitor summarised the situation as follows:

> I understand entirely the logic behind standard fees and I think that it's swings and roundabouts and, in any standard fee situation, there are going to be cases where you lose and there will be cases where you win. It's not ideal, obviously I'd prefer to be paid for everything I do, but that would also mean that there would be some cases where I would be putting in a bill for less than £50. So, on a swings and roundabouts basis I think that fixed fees are fine. I think that it is a very good thing when you go outside standard fees you are paid for what you do and that that is looked at by the Legal Aid Agency and they will tax it down if they think you're billing stuff that you shouldn't be billing for because that incentivises two things. First of all, it incentivises hard work on the client's behalf and secondly, it means that you don't do unnecessary things. I think it's a perfectly sensible way of dealing with criminal legal aid funding. So, I don't have very much complaint or really any complaints about the magistrates' court fee structure as I think that it's fine – certainly in the provinces. (*Defence solicitor F*)

In contrast, Defence solicitor B said, 'I think it's terrible. I cannot think of another profession that would allow itself to be paid in the way that we are; on the basis of not in proportion to the work that you've actually done'. Another two defence solicitors described the profession as 'on its knees' due to the fact

---

[36] R Young and D Wall, 'Criminal Justice, Legal Aid and the Defence of Liberty' in R Young and D Wall (eds), *Access to Criminal Justice: Legal Aid, Lawyers and the Defence of Liberty* (Blackstone Press 1996).

[37] C Tata and F Stephen, 'Swings and Roundabouts: Do Changes to the Structure of Legal Aid Remuneration Make a Real Difference to Criminal Case Management and Case Outcomes?' (2006) 8 *Criminal Law Review* 722–41; 722.

[38] Dehaghani and Newman, *The Crisis* (n 7); Thornton (n 22).

that there has been no rise in the fees paid since the late 1990s and payment rates are too low. Consequently, it seems necessary to make a distinction between payment by way of standard fee in principle and standard fee in practice. There is an ever-growing consensus that the rates at which payments are made are more problematic than the payment regime in itself. When first introduced, lower crime legal aid payment rates – including for magistrates' court proceedings – initially were only 'a little bit below the rate paid for private work',[39] but there has been no rise in payment in line with inflation, amounting to significant undercutting of fees, alongside an 8.75 per cent fee cut in 2014.[40] Kemp found that solicitors asserted that they 'were not adequately paid for the services they provided and they felt this would have a detrimental impact on the quality of service'.[41] One defence solicitor was similarly disparaging in saying:

> I mean one talks about the swings and roundabouts of legal aid but in my view it's neither fun nor fair so this analogy should be dropped [...] Fixed fees in the magistrates' and Crown Court act, can act as a disincentive to do work thoroughly and properly and then there's the whole question of the rates of remuneration that have not increased for I forget however many years. The cuts that have been sustained, [...] numerous things have ceased to be an item for payment or rolled into the standard fees and so I think the whole system is underfunded and does not act as an incentive to more or less provide quality and good service. Whereas I was brought up for most of my career to say to clients 'if you pay me privately you'll get no better service than if you've got legal aid', that parted some time ago. (*Defence solicitor K*)

This solicitor was clearly of the view that the level of remuneration received under legal aid affects the service that defendants receive. Most of the defence solicitors interviewed generally acknowledged that payment via the standard fee system provides an incentive to work less thoroughly on cases than if payment were made by the hour, including Defence solicitor F, who agreed with the system in principle. Interviewee I gave an example of a firm drawing up case plans which incorporated how much a case was worth and only working to that value, which seems to be a manifestation of lawyer-centred (rather than client-centred) approaches to casework discussed by Newman.[42] These findings also resonate with Sommerlad's argument that economic controls on lawyers' publicly funded work create 'an irresistible pressure towards routinised justice and the positioning of legal aid clients'.[43]

Of those defence solicitors who did acknowledge that payment via standard fee could mean that less time would be spent on case preparation than if paid by hourly rate, three were keen to say that the system did not affect the way that

---

[39] Justice Committee, *Criminal Legal Aid Twelfth Report of Session* (HC 2017–19 1069).
[40] The Criminal Legal Aid (Remuneration) (Amendment) Regulations 2014.
[41] Kemp (n 12) 107.
[42] Newman (n 31).
[43] Sommerlad (n 6) 183. See also on these points, forthcoming work by D Newman and R Dehaghani, *Experiences of Criminal Justice* (Bristol University Press, 2021).

they personally work, while also acknowledging that their resources are somewhat stretched. The remaining defence solicitors tended to acknowledge that standard fees provide a disincentive to put in extra work on a case, but in general terms – such as by saying 'it's human nature, you try and do as little as you can get away with and I think that's the big fault of the fixed fee system' (Defence solicitor B) – rather than indicating that it affected their behaviour personally. One defence solicitor who noted that initial client contact is focused on how to get paid and that this taints the relationship went on to say:

> You're inclined to get through things as quickly as possible. You're torn between doing something properly which is what you want to do and ... Working for minimum wage. You think, what is the point in going through this in any detail when odds on it won't pan out that way, whereas before you would be able to fine tooth comb as one ought to and that's the thing that I find most difficult just from what I do with files ... It's not that people suddenly don't want to do their jobs properly, it's just that you can't and it's incremental and we probably don't even notice that sort of jaded approach is creeping in. (*Defence solicitor A*)

Another defence solicitor (who also spoke of the fee system being acceptable in principle, above) told of the struggle between the professional obligations of the job as against trying to run a profitable business:

> When you've got fixed fees there is always going to be a time at which you start looking at your watch and you start thinking how much are we actually being paid to do this ... And that mental calculation has got to be done by anybody who is running a business. And there comes a point where on a fixed fee structure you say 'sorry, enough's enough'. Well, you don't say 'sorry enough's enough' but you are thinking enough's enough and you have to start looking at, you know, exactly what level of service you are providing ... Yes, we're professionals and, yes, we are supposed to be providing a professional service, but that doesn't mean that we aren't also having to run, try and run a profitable business and it's very difficult to do that if you don't have an eye on costs and the amount of time you are spending doing work for which you can't be paid. (*Defence solicitor F*)

A third defence solicitor, Defence solicitor D, similarly commented that less staff have to do more work to balance the books, which places additional pressure on case preparation. These comments resonate with the comments of lawyers in other studies across the UK. In one study, a lawyer said, 'I struggle with balancing giving a service and meeting business demand ...',[44] and in another study, another lawyer said

> You have to think to yourself, 'what's most cost effective?' To make sure that I am doing what I'm required to do in providing an appropriate level of service to the client, but not bankrupting the firm while I'm doing it ....[45]

---

[44] Dehaghani and Newman, *Criminal Legal Aid* (n 22); 12. See also Dehaghani and Newman, *The Crisis* (n 7).
[45] Thornton (n 7) 579.

We can, therefore, surmise that these lawyers experienced role conflict (their role as defence lawyers against their role as firm managers) and that the struggle lawyers felt to maintain their practices in the face of cuts and stagnation is a national issue. Furthermore, it seems to be an issue that affects the ability of defence lawyers to provide the level of service that would match the traditional ideal of civic morality that lawyers hold dear in principle.[46] Sommerlad demonstrated that lawyers felt reforms had reduced their professional autonomy (a key feature of professional identity[47]), and they were increasingly being made subject to intrusive surveillance by the administrative body for legal aid as firms 'are propelled into ever greater cost consciousness'.[48] Of course, the person who ultimately loses out in all of this is the defendant, although these practices also increase the risk that victims and witnesses will suffer the consequences of flawed case outcomes.

The behaviours which appear to be reflected in my data suggest that changes to legal aid have transformed 'traditional value rationality into an instrumental calculative rationality'[49] where '[t]here is virtually no time for a human dimension or real diagnosis'.[50] Such activities could also reflect a shift away from ethical rationalities (based on normative beliefs that behaviour is morally good) towards means-end rationalities, which are oriented further towards self-interest within prescribed regulatory boundaries.[51] The concerns expressed by these lawyers provide some evidence of conflict between ethically motivated rationalities and environmental moulding through funder and, separately, courtroom expectations. Funder expectations are significant in light of the contracting arrangements discussed in chapter two. As Defence solicitor K indicated above, being paid through a third-party funder rather than by clients directly might also influence the way in which cases are managed.[52]

However, advocates did express some discomfort with that position, suggesting that they would prefer to take a political stance (which involves a more robust, resistant approach to bureaucratic procedures in favour of

---

[46] H Sommerlad '"I've lost the Plot": An Everyday Story of Legal Aid Lawyers' (2002) 28 (3) *Journal of Law and Society* 335–60. See also Newman (n 30); Dehaghani and Newman, *The Crisis* (n 7); Cooke (n 25).

[47] J Evetts, 'The Construction of Professionalism in New and Existing Occupational Contexts: Promoting and Facilitating Occupational Change' (2003) 23(4/5) *International Journal of Sociology and Social Policy* 22.

[48] H Sommerlad, 'The Implementation of Quality Initiatives and the New Public Management in the Legal Aid Sector in England and Wales: Bureaucratisation, Stratification and Surveillance' (1999) 6 *International Journal of the Legal Profession* 311.

[49] Sommerlad (n 6) 187.

[50] Ibid, 186.

[51] S Kalberg, 'Max Weber's Types of Rationality: Cornerstones for the Analysis of Rationalization Processes in History' (1980) 85 *American Journal of Sociology* 1145.

[52] For an indication that direct/indirect funding can affect partisanship in cases in another jurisdiction, see H Saito, 'The Impact of Lawyer Fees on Lawyer Partisanship: The Reciprocity Norm May Matter' (2020) *International Journal of the Legal Profession* (online first).

client-centred approaches)[53] if the pressure of running a business were not present. This builds on Newman's findings.[54] He believed that lawyers expressed a client-centred approach but acted in a way that was dismissive of clients' needs.[55] My findings may provide some explanation for Newman's result, although it seems that my interviewees openly recognised the difficulties in representing clients in this way. Newman was of the view that lawyers actively embraced the working patterns encouraged by fixed fees, demonstrated by a 'clear disregard for their clients'.[56] In contrast, the lawyers I spoke to were keenly aware of how standard fees pitted their business needs against the needs of clients and the harm that this could cause. Defence advocates that I interviewed appeared to recognise that payment by standard fee incentivises volume processing of cases over spending a significant degree of time examining the fine details of any given case.[57] The implications of this are obvious: relevant evidential or legal points may not be identified and exploited, client care might worsen and details missed as cases are processed in routinised ways.

The data also supports Newman's finding that lawyers were concerned to process cases as quickly as possible[58] because, in order 'to sustain themselves, many lawyers insisted that they were forced to compromise their behaviour; discontinuous representation was a necessity to survive'.[59] My interviewees described themselves as 'torn' between their duties to the client and business needs. They expressed insight into the difficulties this can cause defendants in that they described a temptation to 'cut corners' or perform as little work as possible in order to maximise profit.[60] That the fee system incentivises such practices is further reinforced by recent research conducted by Dehaghani and Newman in Wales. Lawyers they spoke with discussed 'cutting corners' or 'doing less' and stripping back services so that case files, while still audit quality compliant, are less comprehensive than previously.[61] These concerns were also expressed to Thornton by lawyers who said, '[t]he tighter you cut the funding, the more pressure there is on everyone to cut corners and put your own interests first …'.[62] As with the issue of role conflict, these findings, taken alongside my own, lend support to the idea that funding cuts and stagnation under the standard fee regime have led to reductions in the quality of work that lawyers feel able to perform.

---

[53] M McConville et al, *Standing Accused. The Organisation and Practices of Criminal Defence Lawyers in Britain* (Oxford University Press, 1994).

[54] Newman (n 31).

[55] Ibid.

[56] Ibid, 87.

[57] Lawyers interviewed by Thornton (n 22) expressed similar sentiments, describing 'bare minimum preparation' practices.

[58] Newman (n 30) 78.

[59] Ibid, 86.

[60] In fact, Newman's own participants did express similar concerns that 'the client loses out in the need to get through the list' (Newman (n 31) 96).

[61] Dehaghani and Newman, *Criminal Legal Aid* (n 22). See also Newman and Welsh (n 22).

[62] Thornton (n 7) 581. See further Thornton (n 22).

These comments appear to specifically undermine the once politically popular theory that lawyers provide services that are unnecessary in order to maximise income by claiming higher fees.[63] Sommerlad suggested that lawyers were demoralised by this theory, as they felt it reflected a lack of governmental understanding about the nature of publicly funded work.[64] Indeed, the theory remains unproven. Instead, and in line with managerial demands for efficiency, lawyers seem to work to volume generally.[65] McConville and Marsh also argued that 'criminal lawyers increasingly find themselves unable to do justice to a single case for fear of losing out on the volume of business ultimately needed to keep their firms or chambers afloat'.[66] Defence advocates seemed keen to conduct cases with maximum efficiency (or minimum effort) even at potential harm to the client, though they appeared to recognise the risks that this entailed and seemed to find those practices demoralising. This finding tended to confirm that defence solicitors were inclined to reduce the amount of time spent on cases that would clearly not break out of the lower standard fee category.[67] The comments made by these interviewees support Stephen, Fazio and Tata's findings that the introduction of fixed fees in Scotland meant that solicitors put less effort into conducting cases and reduced 'expenditure on those activities which are incorporated in the core payment of the standard fee'.[68] It was apparent that advocates felt constrained by the business circumstances in which they found themselves, and this caused some conflict with what they considered to be their professional duties towards their clients. Conflict may result from struggles over jurisdiction,[69] arising from the unique public/private position of legal aid lawyers:[70] that is, the question of whether the legal profession or the state is best placed to determine the operation of legal aid.

Young and Wall had earlier noted that the contracting scheme under which standard fees were introduced was likely to lead to conveyor-belt type case processing as firms struggled to remain profitable.[71] The contractual terms of

---

[63] Young and Wall (n 36).

[64] Sommerlad (n 6).

[65] Newman and Welsh (n 22); this pattern of working/ need to work at volume appears to be replicated in police station work: Dehaghani and Newman, *Criminal Legal Aid* (n 22). See also Dehaghani and Newman, *The Crisis* (n 7).

[66] M McConville and L Marsh, 'Factory Farming and State-Induced Pleas' in J Hunter et al (eds), *The Integrity of Criminal Process. From Theory into Practice* (Hart Publishing, 2016) 100.

[67] A Gray, P Fenn and N Rickman, 'Controlling Lawyer's Costs through Standard Fees: An Economic Analysis' in R Young and D Wall (eds), *Access to Criminal Justice. Legal Aid, Lawyers and the Defence of Liberty* (Blackstone Press, 1996).

[68] F Stephen, G Fazio and C Tata, 'Incentives, Criminal Defence Lawyers and Plea Bargaining' (2008) 28(3) *International Review of Law and Economics* 212; 213. In their study, Stephen et al found that how solicitors conducted plea bargaining practices discussed in ch 3 was influenced by the reintroduction of a fixed fee system.

[69] Macdonald (n 5).

[70] T Halliday, *Beyond Monopoly: Lawyers, State Crises, and Professional Empowerment* (University of Chicago Press, 1987).

[71] Young and Wall (n 36).

the legal aid franchising system (chapter 2) appear to place limits on lawyers' ability to make flexible, autonomous decisions[72] because 'the development of a direct relationship with the state raised the possibility of managerial control over the legal aid sector'.[73] It seems that Young and Wall were correct to predict that 'if the only way of making a profit under legal aid is to offer hurried, standardised services, then access to justice must suffer'[74] as lawyers are pressurised into dealing with cases (rather than clients) in standardised ways.[75] Standardisation is the antithesis of individualised service provision,[76] the latter of which would arguably cater better to the needs of each defendant's ability to actively participate in the proceedings.

The above data confirms that the legal aid system 'is characterised by the competing rationalities that arise from the conflicting professional agendas of the groups involved in the process'.[77] The conflicts seen in this research exist between the court's demands for efficiency and compliance with bureaucratic procedures (see chapter three), the advocate's duties to clients, and the advocate's need to maintain a business. In response, and in line with Newman's findings, lawyers demonstrated a tendency to adopt a managerial stance involving volume processing.[78] As a result, the standard fee payment structure clearly has the potential to place defendants at significant risk of inadequate access to justice in the proceedings as zealous defence advocacy[79] becomes an increasingly unattainable standard in an era of increasingly squeezed financial positions. However, the complexities of the legal aid system do not just affect the way that lawyers approach cases. As well as the possibility of defendants' exclusion from active participation in the process via absent or poor service, the application process exacerbates the defendant's exclusion at an early stage in the proceedings. There appeared to be a tendency for interviewees to attribute the uncertainties involved in applying for legal aid to what is perceived as burdensome bureaucratic requirements (such as the need for self-employed applicants to provide business paperwork[80] or problems with the correct

---

[72] H Sommerlad, 'Criminal Legal Aid Reforms and the Restructuring of Legal Professionalism' in R Young and D Wall (eds), *Access to Criminal Legal Aid: Legal Aid, Lawyers and the Defence of Liberty* (Blackstone Press, 1996).

[73] Ibid, 297.

[74] Young and Wall (n 36) 12.

[75] Ibid.

[76] C Tata, '"Ritual Individualisation": Creative Genius at Sentencing, Mitigation and Conviction' (2019) 46 (1) *Journal of Law and Society* 112–40.

[77] D Wall, 'Keyholders to Criminal Justice? Solicitors and Applications for Criminal Legal Aid' in R Young and D Wall (eds), *Access to Criminal Justice: Legal Aid, Lawyers and the Defence of Liberty* (Oxford, Blackstone Press, 1996) 115.

[78] McConville et al (n 54); Newman (n 31).

[79] T Smith, 'The "Quiet Revolution" in Criminal Defence: How the Zealous Advocate Slipped into the Shadow' (2013) 20:1 *International Journal of the Legal Profession* 111–37.

[80] Kemp also found defence solicitors expressing concern about the administrative burdens placed on self-employed defendants who attempt to apply for legal aid (Kemp (n 12)). Thornton noted that because of the struggle to obtain legal aid for self-employed people, this type of client was regarded as 'undesirable' by lawyers he spoke with (Thornton (n 7)).

information being held by the Department of Work and Pensions).[81] Given that many defendants have somewhat chaotic lifestyles, interviewees felt they struggle to comply with administrative demands placed upon them as part of the legal aid application process.

V. DEFENDANTS, LAWYERS AND THE LEGAL AID APPLICATION PROCESS

Most interviewees felt that specialist legal knowledge is necessary in order to complete an application for legal aid appropriately. This results from the need to understand whether or not a case will meet the interests of justice test.[82] The interests of justice test is a legal test,[83] and one which Defence solicitor A described as 'really long winded'. The test requires applicants to consider whether a case meets the custody threshold in sentencing, what evidential issues are likely to arise and the conduct of cross examination, in addition to more client-specific features that can denote particular defendant vulnerability. To satisfy this test, it follows that legal knowledge is at least advantageous, if not vital.[84] Kemp also noted that the discretionary nature of the interests of justice test alongside the administrative requirements of the means-test 'have the potential to create obstacles to legal representation, particularly for vulnerable defendants'.[85] Even for experienced solicitors, the process of applying for legal aid is time-consuming: 'it's a good, I reckon, 25–30 minutes spent filling in a form like that and that's for a qualified, experienced solicitor' (Defence solicitor F). That solicitors complete legal aid applications on behalf of their clients is mutually beneficial. As Wall says:

> First, the legal aid certificate is an important source of income to the legal practitioner ... Secondly, clients are not always aware of the importance of the application form and, in the solicitor's experience, tend to leave the application to the last minute or to forget about it altogether. Thirdly, the clients prefer to leave the application

---

[81] Defence Solicitor O highlighted this as a particular issue. When defendants receive Job Seeker's Allowance, Employment Support Allowance or Income Support, they should be automatically entitled to legal aid, subject to the interests of justice test. Whether or not that entitlement exists is checked via records held by the Department of Work and Pensions. Interviewees in Kemp's study reported similar problems in accessing information held by the Department of Work and Pensions (Kemp (n 12)).

[82] Both the interests of justice test and the means-test must be passed to secure legally aided representation. The interests of justice test allow the court to test whether the case is one in which a defendant requires specialist (ie legal) assistance to advance their case properly. The criteria are set out in ch 2.

[83] See s17 Legal Aid, Sentencing and Punishment of Offenders Act 2012.

[84] All merits tests applied by the LAA require specialist legal knowledge. In another study, lawyers highlighted the difficulties surrounding the nebulousness of the Sufficient Benefit Test, which requires legal advisers to consider the likelihood of certain legal criteria being satisfied (Clarke and Welsh (n 24)).

[85] Kemp (n 12) 66.

to the solicitor because of the complex legal knowledge and expertise required to complete it. Fourthly defendants are encouraged by the information pamphlets ... to apply through a solicitor.[86]

Six of the 12 defence solicitors and two of the seven prosecution advocates interviewed also felt that defendants struggle with the additional information required to satisfy the means-test and the interests of justice test. Defence solicitors generally spoke in disparaging terms about the legal aid application process, but one prosecutor also noted that there seemed to be problems sorting out legal aid promptly (which sits in contrast to demands for cases to be processed quickly), and the whole system seemed unnecessarily complex. Defence lawyers' views about the process are illustrated by the following quotes about the legal aid application:

> [the application is] virtually designed to irritate and be as difficult as possible to complete ... Even intelligent, articulate people who have to fill in this form get it wrong. (*Defence solicitor F*)

> ... you've now got increasingly complicated forms. When I very first qualified legal aid forms were very very simple, very straightforward. The court also had the power to grant legal aid so you could fill in a legal aid form, you could go to court, the Court Clerk could look at it and could grant you legal aid straightaway based on a very simple form, and again, the forms that you completed at the end of the case were relatively straightforward. I could literally go to court, fill in my legal aid form on the way there, do a case, get legal aid, finish it, fill in the form on the way back to the office and have my claim off literally almost on the same day. Now forms are much more complex, they want far more from you. (*Defence solicitor B*)

> If you're representing four or five clients as you will frequently do with legal aid you spend half the time that you are physically in court filling in legal aid forms when that time could be more profitably put to actually sitting down and advising the clients with regards to the case. (*Defence solicitor D*)

> I would say you can spend nearly as much time as you can preparing a trial than you can trying to get legal aid on a case ... I think the whole admin system and the way Legal Aid is granted could be much more streamlined and much more effective than it actually is. (*Defence solicitor I*)

As well as concerns about bureaucracy surrounding the procedure, defence solicitors felt that they had been misled about the degree to which they would need to assist in resolving problems with legal aid. They stated that when means-testing was initially reintroduced, defence lawyers were told that any problems that arose would be resolved between the court and the applicant. Despite this, advocates felt that they are expected to liaise between the court and the applicant in order to assist the legal aid application process, which eats into fee-earning time. This finding is supported by Kemp's conclusion that lawyers

---

[86] Wall (n 77) 117.

felt the means-test had added to the administrative burdens placed on them.[87] Lawyer-led campaign groups felt that defence lawyers 'were expected to bear the cost of administering the [means-testing] scheme' by assisting applicants to complete the forms, gathering evidence of means, and liaising between the legal aid body and the client.[88] This further illustrates that lawyers' professional duties towards their clients are compromised, as time spent organising legal aid may reduce time spent dealing with clients' concerns, and this was certainly a view expressed during interviews, as the above quotes about the application process illustrate. Hynes and Robins also noted that defence solicitors had been expected to assist defendants in completing forms, gathering evidence for the means-test and liaising between the legal aid provider and the client.[89] The transfer of day-to-day administrative costs (in terms of time and uncertainty) to lawyers is not a new phenomenon,[90] but as the system becomes both more complex and remote, the associated costs to lawyers increase but without recognition that claimable fees have stagnated.

In terms of defendant impact, solicitors tended to believe that the complexity of the legal aid application process delayed case progression. They generally appeared to be of the view that magistrates are unsympathetic to those problems and that the court process forces them into action – partly because magistrates are aware that advocates are prepared to take the risk of non-payment in a proportion of cases. For example, defence solicitor F expressed concern that 'there is sometimes a lack of understanding on the Bench, particularly the lay Bench, as to just how difficult it can be to get a client legal aid' as a result of the bureaucracy surrounding the form. These views were, to some extent, supported by prosecutors:

> Unfortunately, the current Criminal Procedure Rules have made the Court be less sympathetic [to issues surrounding legal aid] because the encouragement now is for Courts to make progress and therefore despite them possibly being sympathetic, they feel compelled to make progress and therefore require defence to press on. (*Prosecutor H*)

> In the early days, they would be more willing to grant adjournments for lengthy periods of time if there were problems with payslips and the like but I think nowadays they're not as patient as they used to be and they're more pushing towards progressing case management even when legal aid is not in place. (*Prosecutor N*)

The data further demonstrated that advocates believed that the reintroduction of means-testing had a negative effect on defendants. While only two prosecutors stated that defendants find it difficult to comply with the conditions

---

[87] Kemp (n 12).

[88] S Hynes and J Robins, *The Justice Gap. Whatever Happened to Legal Aid?* (Legal Action Group, 2009) 118.

[89] Ibid.

[90] For example, solicitors were expected to complete the administration of the earlier 'green form' scheme referred to in ch 2.

required to obtain legally aided representation, four of the seven believed that defendants tend to have vulnerabilities affecting their ability to participate effectively in the legal aid application process or that their motivation is not sufficient to enable effective participation.[91] One prosecutor described many defendants as not having 'a great education', while another stated that the majority of defendants either have learning difficulties or literacy problems. Prosecutor J similarly expressed the opinion that a defendant might be able to complete a legal aid application 'providing they can read and write in the first place of course … let's face it, a lot of them can't. I've looked at the form once and it didn't seem that easy to understand'.[92] While prosecutors highlighted literacy or educational difficulties as a hindrance to defendants successfully applying for legal aid, defence solicitors noted additional factors that they felt had an impact on defendants' ability to participate effectively in the legal aid application process. By way of example, defence solicitor C said, 'I understand that the clients make no effort whatsoever to get legal aid sorted but then my clients are drug addicts and vulnerable people so, you know, they don't live by normal everyday rules'. Newman took the view that such opinions demonstrated an unhealthy lawyer/client relationship on the basis that it was part of the lawyer's desire to distinguish the client as belonging to 'a different breed',[93] a bad category of citizen. Given the strength of the courtroom workgroup, and its habitus in terms of the way language is used, dress and courtroom layout (chapter three), there is likely some truth to that reasoning, though most lawyers probably do not consciously recognise it. It should, however, also be acknowledged that the private views expressed by defence solicitors about their clients may not reflect the way that they actually act in court. The criminal courtroom has long been recognised as a place of performance,[94] something Newman also alludes to in his use of the phrase 'pyrotechnics' to explain what lawyers did in the courtroom itself.[95] While performance acts as a barrier to effective participation as many defendants fail to understand the 'stage directions' involved, it – of itself – does not necessarily equate with legally incorrect decisions being made or outcomes produced. Comments of the above nature about clients could also reflect a form of 'canteen culture',[96] a desire/need to

---

[91] On suspect vulnerability, see generally R Dehaghani, 'Interrogating Vulnerability: Reframing the Vulnerable Suspect in Police Custody' (2021) 30(2) *Social & Legal Studies* 251–71.

[92] On vulnerable defendants, see generally J Jacobson and J Talbot *Vulnerable Defendants in the Criminal Courts: A Review of Provision for Adults and Children* (London, Prison Reform Trust, 2009).

[93] Newman (n 31); 46; J Katz, *Poor People's Lawyers in Transition* (Rutgers University Press, 1982).

[94] J Rowbotham and K Stevenson, 'For Today in this Arena …' Legal Performativity and Dramatic Convention in the Victorian Criminal Justice System (2007) 14 (2) *Journal of Criminal Justice and Popular Culture* 113–41; K Leader, 'Trials, Truth-telling and the Performing Body' (Doctoral Thesis (PhD), University of Sydney, 2010).

[95] Newman (n 31) 133.

[96] See, eg P Waddington, 'Police (Canteen) Sub-culture. An Appreciation' (1999) 39(2) *British Journal of Criminology* 287–309; M van Hulst, 'Storytelling at the Police Station: The Canteen Culture Revisited' (2013) 53(4) *The British Journal of Criminology* 624–42.

let off steam in what is emotionally and mentally demanding work,[97] a statement of fact that many defendants suffer from complex vulnerabilities[98] or
some form of cognitive dissonance employed by lawyers to counter low levels
of morale caused – at least partially – by the legal aid landscape.[99]

Interviewees involved in Kemp's study made similar comments to the
lawyers that I spoke with, which led her to conclude that 'solicitors were also
concerned that the bureaucratic requirements of the means-test were too onerous when they were dealing with people who lead chaotic lifestyles, have severe
mental illness, or have little or no English'.[100] An acute example of these issues
was provided via observation at one court hearing. A defendant appeared before
the weekend sitting of the magistrates' court after breaching his bail conditions
imposed at the Crown Court. He was represented by the on-duty solicitor, who
explained that the defendant was not legally represented in the proceedings
because he had failed the means-test. He had failed the means-test because he
had been hospitalised numerous times as a result of mental health problems and
could not, therefore, provide the necessary income information to the LAA. The
Crown Court judge was reportedly extremely concerned that the defendant was
not legally represented and had adjourned the case a number of times to try
and resolve the problems, but the defendant remained without publicly funded
representation, even though he would have passed both the means and merits
test if he had been able to provide the evidence in support of the claim. This case
illustrated how a defendant's inability to engage with the application process
might cause a delay in the proceedings and risk inadequate access to justice
through inability to participate.[101] While this is an extreme example, observations provided numerous examples of situations in which a defendant's case had
been hindered because legal aid was not in place. The example also highlights
the role of the defendant as outside the process and the vicious cycle that this
can create for some people: the defendant needed legal assistance to get legal
aid. This seems to highlight the defendant's status as an outsider from the very
outset of proceedings, as a message is conveyed that arranging representation is

---

[97] See generally L Flower, 'Emotional Labour, Cooling the Client Out and Lawyer Face' in
J Phillips et al (eds), *Emotional Labour in Criminology and Criminal Justice* (Routledge, 2020);
Cooke (n 25).

[98] See generally R Helm, 'Conviction by Consent? Vulnerability, Autonomy and Conviction
by Guilty Plea' (2019) 83(2) *The Journal of Criminal Law* 161–72; S Fairclough 'It doesn't
Happen … and I've Never Thought it was Necessary for It to Happen': Barriers to Vulnerable
Defendants Giving Evidence by Live link in Crown Court Trials' (2017) 21(3) *The International
Journal of Evidence & Proof* 209–29; Campbell (n 14).

[99] See generally Dehaghani and Newman, *The Crisis* (n 7); Thornton (n 22); Newman and Welsh
(n 22); See also evidence given to the Justice Committee (n 7).

[100] Kemp (n 12) 71.

[101] While this is perhaps an extreme example, it does not appear to be an isolated one. Baksi noted
in 2011 that the then Legal Services Commission received criticism for delays in processing legal aid
applications and leaving people without representation in serious cases (C Baksi, 'Djanogly Urged
to Ease Legal Aid Backlog' *Law Society Gazette* (London, 23 June 2011).

a matter best left to lawyers, the LAA and the court, that is, the insiders. The digitalisation of the legal aid application process itself (chapter two) reinforces that message, especially as a not insignificant proportion of the population (11 million people) lack basic digital skills.[102] At a more obvious level, these issues also appeared to result in a delay in the proceedings, also commented upon during the interviews.

VI. DELAY

As noted above, the administrative requirements of the legal aid application procedure, coupled with personal difficulties faced by many defendants, mean that it is difficult to know if or when legal aid will be granted. Defence solicitors above complained that it might take as long to try and resolve issues with legal aid as it would actually to prepare the case. Seventy-five per cent of defence solicitors and 71 per cent of prosecutors interviewed felt that problems with obtaining legal aid caused a delay in summary criminal proceedings.

Defence advocates raised concerns that delay in obtaining legal aid not only means that they cannot start preparing cases as early as they would wish, but also that the inability to prepare properly meant that defendants were sometimes forced into situations that were not necessarily beneficial to them. For example, one solicitor expressed concern that it was difficult to know how far to take instructions unless or until legal aid is in place, while defence solicitor E noted that forcing defendants to enter a plea before the advocate is prepared forces solicitors to advise defendants to enter a not guilty plea because the burden of proving the case remains with the prosecution (chapter three). While another study recorded similar practices,[103] it must be noted that other studies suggest that funding issues (may) feed into decisions to advise a guilty plea prematurely, and practices appear to be variable in this regard.[104] The upshot, however, is that defendants may not be receiving as full advice about a plea as they might legitimately expect to obtain.

---

[102] JUSTICE (2018) Preventing Digital Exclusion from Online Justice https://justice.org.uk/wp-content/uploads/2018/06/Preventing-Digital-Exclusion-from-Online-Justice.pdf. Furthermore, approximately a quarter of Law Centre clients in Merseyside had access to neither a smartphone nor a computer (J Robins and D Newman, *Justice in a Time of Austerity* (Bristol University Press, 2021)).

[103] A Herbert, 'Mode of Trial and Magistrates Sentencing Powers: Will Increased Powers Inevitably Lead to a Reduction in Committal Rate?' (2003) *Criminal Law Review* 314.

[104] See, eg, Thornton (n 7) and R Helm, 'Constrained Waiver of Trial Rights? Incentives to Plead Guilty and the Right to a Fair Trial' (2019) 46 *Journal of Law and Society* 423–47. For discussion on balancing interests, see C Tata, 'In the Interests of Clients or Commerce? Legal Aid, Supply, Demand, and "Ethical Indeterminacy" in Criminal Defence Work' (2007) 34 *Journal of Law & Society* 489.

One prosecutor noted that demanding efficiency when legal aid is not in place causes delay at later stages:

> We are told that we should object to an adjournment just so that the defence can get legal aid but it got very difficult for people to sort out their legal aid … forcing a plea always forced a not guilty at an early stage which would have an impact on the case management hearings. (*Prosecutor M*)

Prosecutor H similarly commented that the reintroduction of means-testing 'delays the start of legal aid and therefore delays defence solicitors from taking proper instructions', while defence solicitor C commented that the courts require decisions to be made about the conduct of cases at a time when advocates 'don't necessarily have the opportunity to go through the papers as much as we would wish and subsequently, you know, we might get cross examined upon it'. Another interviewee – Defence solicitor K – expressed some criticism of this behaviour, as noted above, in stating 'means testing delays the grant of legal aid and so solicitors continue to facilitate the system to run at speed by allowing cases to be progressed, representing people when they don't have legal aid'. The fact that prosecutors and defence advocates alike note this issue suggests that it is not simply defence solicitors 'talking the talk'[105] in relation to due process. As is discussed in chapter three, forcing pleas at too early a stage in the proceedings is detrimental for all participants. The difficulty appears to result from a combination of delay in obtaining legal aid, the court's desire to improve efficiency in the proceedings (which means that applications for adjournments are less likely to be tolerated by the judicial Bench) and advocates' desire to conform to usual cooperative workgroup behaviour.

Ultimately, both defending and prosecuting interviewees stated that by refusing to adjourn cases when legal aid is not in place, cases ultimately take longer to conclude. This is because pleas are entered prematurely and cases involving unrepresented defendants take longer to be processed. One way, however, of mitigating some of the issues of delay and entering pleas is through the duty solicitor scheme.

VII. DUTY SOLICITORS AT COURT

As discussed in chapter two, the Duty Solicitor scheme is available to people who have been charged with an imprisonable offence or appear before the court in custody. The services of the Duty Solicitor are available on one occasion during the course of any given case. The LAA creates a rota of suitably qualified Duty Solicitors according to information provided by firms local to each magistrates' court area. The Duty Solicitor on the rota will be available

---

[105] Newman (n 31).

at court to provide full representation services (on that occasion) to those who qualify for representation under the scheme. The Duty Solicitor can then claim payment for being on the duty rota from the LAA.

When the Law Society expanded the Duty Solicitor scheme in the 1970s and early 1980s, Ashworth described it as considerably improving the provision of legal aid.[106] About a third of my interviewees (both prosecutors and defenders) felt that the Duty Solicitor scheme generally provides a good service in ensuring that defendants receive some advice before entering the courtroom. One defence solicitor said that the scheme is useful because a Duty Solicitor can help people to make a sensible decision about a plea:

> A lot of people don't seek legal advice before going to court, a lot of people are disorganised … All the more so given the problems in getting funding for that legal advice in advance of the court. So, I think the duty solicitor scheme plays a vital role in ensuring that people who turn up to court without a lawyer make sensible decisions about what, what's going to happen to them. There have been many occasions where people have walked in saying 'I'm coming in, I'm pleading guilty' and you sit down with them and you actually work out 'actually no you're not'. (*Defence solicitor D*)

However, several other interviewees believed that the scheme does not operate well. Both prosecution and defence advocates stated that the Duty Solicitor is often over-burdened, especially since the reinstatement of means-testing for legal aid. This results in delay in the proceedings as courts wait for the Duty Solicitor to be ready to deal with cases and could have a detrimental effect on the service received by defendants. Robins and Newman found that Duty Solicitors who represented clients in housing cases before magistrates' courts reported similar difficulties since funding for legal aid in civil cases was drastically cut as part of the Legal Aid, Sentencing and Punishment of Offenders Act 2012.[107]

Problems faced by Duty Solicitors at court provide a further example of the conflict between a desire for efficiency and a requirement to act in the client's best interests (which may require a degree of delay because the solicitor needs to review the evidence and take instructions). However, when the Duty Solicitor is over-burdened with cases, they may be unable to provide as thorough advice and assistance as a solicitor instructed via a full legal aid Representation Order. The Duty Solicitor in these circumstances becomes somewhat of a triage service, only capable of providing limited, 'emergency' assistance rather than full access to justice or fully empowering defendants themselves to participate in proceedings. In his recent study of magistrates' courts, Campbell felt that Duty Solicitors provided only a minimal service that was of questionable quality.[108] That said, courtroom observations did not reveal any discernible difference in the way that

---

[106] A Ashworth, 'Legal Aid, Human Rights and Criminal Justice' in R Young and D Wall (eds), *Access to Criminal Justice: Legal Aid, Lawyers and the Defence of Liberty* (Blackstone Press, 1996) 64.

[107] Robins and Newman (n 102).

[108] Campbell (n 14).

Duty Solicitors made representations to the court compared to advocates who were funded either privately or via a Representation Order.

VIII. COURT-APPOINTED ADVOCATES

Section 38, Youth Justice and Criminal Evidence Act 1999 (YJCEA) allows the court to appoint a solicitor to cross-examine certain witnesses if the court feels it is in the interests of justice to do so – that is because it would be inappropriate for the defendant to cross-examine the witness directly (under the provisions in sections 34–36 YJCEA). Strictly speaking, the role of court-appointed advocates is limited to preparing cross-examination points for trial, taking the defendant's instructions and performing the cross-examination of particular witnesses during the course of the trial.[109] Such advocates are not, therefore, obliged to attend preliminary administrative hearings (and are not allowed to claim payment for doing so). Nevertheless, there may be tactical advantages in attending preliminary hearings because the advocate will then be aware of any issues that have arisen, will be able to negotiate with the prosecutor, and will be able to gain the confidence of the defendant. In line with my own practitioner experience, Campbell often observed solicitors appointed by the magistrates' court representing clients beyond the remit of the section 38 appointment.[110]

In 2017, the Bar Council (which represents barristers' interests) said of court appointment '[i]n practice, the appointment of counsel by the court to act as a legal representative is not likely to be a frequent occurrence.'[111] However, in the magistrates' courts that I observed, the frequency with which appointed advocates appear in court seems to have increased since the means-test for legal aid was reintroduced, and bureaucracy around legal aid funding increased. While only three cases obviously involved a court-appointed solicitor, those who were refused legal aid after the initial hearing might have ultimately been represented by a court-appointed lawyer during the trial. Given the limited role that court-appointed advocates are supposed to play in court proceedings, it is a difficult category to analyse purely on the basis of observational data.

Consequently, I followed up this issue with interviewees, who clearly pointed towards an increase in the number of advocates appointed by the courts since the reintroduction of means-testing. It should be noted that, in my two or three

---

[109] The role of court-appointed advocates in the UK differs significantly from other jurisdictions where courts are empowered to appoint lawyers for especially vulnerable or indigent defendants, including the USA, Japan, China, Australia and Germany. In those jurisdictions, the focus seems to be on ensuring the defendant is represented, whereas the purpose of court appointments in England and Wales is to protect particularly vulnerable witnesses.

[110] Campbell (n 14).

[111] The Bar Council Court, 'Appointed Legal Representatives' (Bar Council for England and Wales, 2017) www.barcouncilethics.co.uk/wp-content/uploads/2017/10/Court-appointed-legal-representatives-1.pdf.

years as a practitioner prior to the reintroduction of means-testing, I had never heard of an advocate being appointed by the court. One prosecutor told me that, similarly, 'I don't think I'd ever heard of it, s.36 directions, until it [means-testing] changed' (prosecutor J). By the time I raised this issue with interviewees, there was a near-unanimous agreement that the number of advocates appointed by the court had increased. Only one prosecutor had not noticed an increase in the number of advocates who were appointed by the court, though the interviewee also said that they probably saw a court-appointed advocate appear about once per week. Not only was there near-universal agreement about an increase in the number of appointments, but most interviewees took the view that it was a significant increase. Interviewees described the change by saying 'we've got a lot more of those' (defence solicitor G), there has been a 'vast increase' (prosecutor H), that court appointment 'certainly happens far more often nowadays than it ever used to' (defence solicitor K) and by explaining the change as being 'huge' (defence solicitor R). The types of cases concerned often involved especially vulnerable or intimidated prosecution witnesses, so it was undoubtedly in the overall interests of justice that a lawyer was appointed for cross-examination purposes.

While costs for court-appointed advocates are still administered by the LAA through their Criminal Cases Unit, suggested payment rates (costs are audited and taxed on a case-by-case basis) are more generous than the fees claimable under a Representation Order.[112] This was a live issue in this study, with prosecutors recognising that the system of court appointments 'is more expensive than it would be if they actually granted legal aid' (prosecutor M) because 'the fee structure is far better for doing that kind of thing' (prosecutor H). Defence lawyers were aware that they would probably be paid more for preparing and attending only part of a hearing than they would if they had dealt with the entire case under a Representation Order. Participants in this study described this situation as 'crazy' (prosecutor N), 'ludicrous' (defence solicitor R) and as a 'faux economy' (defence solicitor K). Being alive to these issues did lead a minority of defence solicitors to admit that they would ask to be appointed in a relevant case where legal aid is refused. Prosecutors had noted a similar pattern, with one saying that occasionally defence lawyers 'with less scruples might actually angle more for the court-appointed because of the fees payable' (prosecutor H).

As the role of a solicitor appointed to conduct cross-examination is limited in scope, there was variation about what participants felt should be the appropriate role for a court-appointed advocate. One prosecutor pointed to a lack of clarity about the level of appropriate disclosure of evidence and information to court-appointed lawyers, while defence solicitor G felt that the limited role of a

[112] See guidance on www.gov.uk/guidance/claim-back-costs-from-cases-in-the-criminal-courts and www.gov.uk/guidance/solicitors-guideline-hourly-rates.

court-appointed lawyer meant that the details of a case could not be analysed because the defence has a less proactive role. This creates a paradox whereby the defence lawyer is paid more handsomely to perform a more limited role, while defendant participation is limited – obviously – by the restriction placed on cross-examination and – less obviously – by then being left to deal with the rest of the case as an unrepresented defendant. These provisions are primarily designed to protect prosecution witnesses. While vulnerable and intimidated witnesses are deserving of that protection, the defendant is left in a halfway house of very likely being unable to manage the case by themselves but only receiving very particular and limited assistance unlikely to facilitate meaningful defendant participation. Defendant experiences of court-appointed advocates do not yet appear to have been examined, but it seems likely to be a confusing experience because their active, and sometimes obligatory, participation in person is required, while at other times, the defendant is prevented from participation in person.

It is not generally the interests of justice test that is the issue preventing a grant of legal aid in these cases, but the means-test. It is not possible to say here whether the money saved by refusing legal aid is outweighed by the cost of greater levels of court-appointed solicitors, but it does tell us that this system does not function in a coherent manner. It would seem to be better in the interests of all parties to simply grant legal aid in such cases, as this would result in greater clarity about access to materials in the case, would enable the defence to prepare more thoroughly and protect the witness concerned.

IX. SUMMARY

Lawyers are obliged to act in their clients' best interests while also acting as officers of the court. The contracts under which legal aid is paid also dictate the conditions of defence lawyers' working practices. Lawyers conveyed that they feel their duties towards clients are compromised by the legal aid payment regime. Changes to legal aid appear to have affected how lawyers manage summary criminal cases in several different ways. The remuneration regime causes concern about the quality of legally aided criminal defence services, but this concern seems to arise mainly due to the payment rates rather than the existence of a standard fee system alone. That said, this, and other data, has indicated that a standard fee system creates a risk that lawyers are increasingly tempted to cut corners when conducting casework. It is a matter of common sense that the more finances are squeezed, the greater the temptation to cut corners, no matter how demoralising and upsetting lawyers might find that situation. In a system where there is a strong workgroup culture that works in a system designed to increase efficiency (chapter three) and increasingly complex legal issues are obscured by the habitus of that workgroup (chapter four), there is a very real danger that defendants are simply swept along in the process in such a way that there is no time to pause and allow for increased levels of defendant participation.

While lawyers cannot alone solve all the issues that prevent defendants from being able to properly participate in the proceedings, and in some ways, they perpetuate those issues, chapters four and four have shown us that they are still important facilitators of access to justice for defendants. However, what this and other data shows is that although '[t]he lawyer is an important resilience mechanism for their clients, [...] the resilience of lawyers has been diminished by the manner in which their work has been devalued and the ways in which they have had to respond to fee cuts and stagnation'.[113]

Additionally, the reintroduction of means-testing appears to have placed further burdens on the dynamics of the relationships between lawyers, their clients and the courts. Interviewees appeared to believe that the legal aid application process is too onerous on defendants, many of whom have significant socio-economic problems. Defence solicitors and prosecutors alike regard the legal aid application process as unnecessarily complex and bureaucratic. These difficulties appear to result in a delay when trying to obtain publicly funded representation (if it is obtained at all) and uncertainty for lawyers in securing remuneration. Such delay and uncertainty affect the lawyer/client relationship in that it limits the ability of a solicitor to provide full advice at early stages in the proceedings and potentially intensifies a 'need' to cut corners as described above. Although defence solicitors may try to alleviate some of these problems by acting even when payment is uncertain, they also acknowledge that the level of service provided in those circumstances is limited. This may be exacerbated by the apparent feeling that defence lawyers have been over-burdened in the requirement to assist during the application procedure itself. That lawyers are expected to complete the application process for their clients already positions the defendant as marginal in the process.

Further, although the Duty Solicitor scheme may alleviate some of the above issues, many interviewees also felt that this system was overly burdensome on defence advocates and caused delays in court. Overwhelming on-duty defence solicitors with cases may also encourage limited advice given in haste, which further undermines the ability of a defendant to participate in the proceedings. This is especially concerning in the case of defendants who plead not guilty when represented by a Duty Solicitor but then must manage the rest of the case alone where they are not eligible for or have problems obtaining legally aided representation. Furthermore, in those cases where a defendant might be 'represented' by a court-appointed advocate, that representation is not designed to increase the ability of a defendant to understand and participate in the proceedings; it is designed to protect prosecution witnesses.

---

[113] Dehaghani and Newman, *Criminal Legal Aid* (n 22) 15.

Therefore, it seems that publicly funded representation is a facility that, despite existing as a way to minimise defendants being treated only as dummy players,[114] has faced challenges in remaining easily accessible and enabling lawyers to provide a high-quality service. Increased uncertainty about payment has led lawyers to conduct more unremunerated work at the early stages of a case but be less inclined to invest time to provide more than a basic level of service at that point. As other studies have shown, client care is likely to suffer under that system,[115] leaving defendants less likely to be able to participate effectively. Indeed, defendants cannot properly participate in the legal aid application process, which conveys, at an early stage in proceedings, a message that such matters are best left to lawyers and/or the court.

Ultimately, the existence of *effective* defence representation is crucial to minimise the risk of defendants' rights being undermined. However, the ability of defence solicitors to provide effective services may be compromised not only by both bureaucratic and professional pressures but also by low levels of remuneration via legal aid. Lawyers recognise that the payment regime incentivises standardised case progression but added that uncertainty about whether or not they will be paid, alongside demands that they conduct case management regardless of funding, means that they may make decisions that are not necessarily in the client's best long-term interests. It seems that lawyers conduct cases when they are uncertain about payment out of a sense of professional obligation to both their clients and the courts, but lawyers also recognise that the payment regime does not incentivise them to provide a high-quality service. It seems clear that lawyers feel the administrative obligations placed on them by the funding regime compromise their autonomous decision-making abilities while the payment regime itself disincentivises meticulous case management. This undermines lawyers' ability to individualise cases in a way that would provide an ethical status to their work[116] and appears to be demoralising to the profession. This further means that defendants are less likely to be treated as autonomous individuals, and their ability to participate in proceedings as such a person is further compromised by the funding regime. Consequently, funding problems that prevent meaningful operation of the right to legal representation worsen problems associated with facilitating meaningful defendant participation to increase overall access to justice.

---

[114] Newman (n 31).

[115] Tata and Stephen (n 37); Vogler et al (n 33).

[116] C Tata, 'Displaying Justice. What, if Anything, Does "Ritual individualisation" at conviction and sentencing Achieve?' (2017) Socio-Legal Studies Association Annual Conference, Newcastle University, 6 April 2017. See further Tata (n 76).

6

Conclusion: The Defendant's Role in Summary Criminal Justice

I T IS CLEAR that defendants have always experienced marginalisation as dummy players in the process of summary criminal prosecution. This marginalisation results from the specialised nature of the process, lack of adequate access to properly funded and effective legal advice, court personnel behaviour, and the court's desire to process cases at speed. There is thus a complex set of practices at work in which a number of competing interests jostle for priority. While the organisational culture attributed to magistrates' courts has always seemed to limit the ability of defendants to play an effective role in proceedings, the structure of the workgroup and demands placed upon it have changed in light of demands for efficiency and austerity measures, including legal aid cuts. As the workgroup continues to operate in such a way that the defendant is obliged to submit to its technical professional knowledge, the inability of defendants to participate and play an effective role in summary criminal justice has increased.

I. REFLECTIONS ON POLITICS, THE MAGISTRATES' COURT WORKGROUP AND ACCESS TO JUSTICE

As illustrated in chapters two to five, the relationship between political ideology and access to justice is well-demonstrated by examining the availability of effective representation funded through legal aid. Public funding is affected by a political ideology that reflects neoliberal policies that valorise marketised managerial strategies in publicly funded institutions and through austerity, resulting in significant cuts in criminal justice funding. As adherents to neoliberalism have tweaked markets through re-regulation, privatisation and adoption of managerial strategies, its ideological premises have been able to adapt to challenges faced by governments so that neoliberalism remains an influential ideology in policy design (chapter one).

Proponents of neoliberalism viewed those services that remained under state control as inefficient and wasteful, intensifying the demand for magistrates' courts to deal with cases quickly (chapter two). Governments not only viewed public services as inefficient but also began viewing the activities of public service professionals with suspicion. Those views led to the introduction of legislation and initiatives designed to encourage more efficient working practices in publicly funded institutions. Furthermore, by introducing a franchising scheme for legal aid funding, the government – through aggressive re-regulation (chapter two) – created a new type of legal professional who was pushed further away from altruistic service provision towards more self-interested behaviour via managerialist imperatives.

Governmental distrust of criminal defence lawyers justified not only greater intrusion in the system of publicly funded representation via the creation of first the Legal Services Commission and then the Legal Aid Agency (LAA) but also further market re-regulation through the reintroduction of fixed standard fees for legally aided representation. Lawyers have been encouraged to accommodate re-regulation of their work because they depend on the government for funding, and various governments have paid insufficient attention to lawyers' ability to improve access to justice. As austerity measures took greater hold, governments continued to restrict the scope of legal aid eligibility (chapter two), and have – more recently – reduced the payment rates available to lawyers conducting publicly funded work.[1] This restricted the ability of lawyers to give cases and clients as much time as they might like (chapter five). Data in this book and elsewhere[2] increasingly indicates that fee cuts have resulted in lawyers reducing the level of service provided to their clients. While chapter four indicates that members of the workgroup (such as court legal advisers) make some effort to try and facilitate participation by all defendants, all defendants remain marginalised by the complexity, shared habitual understanding and speedy progression of their cases through the magistrates' courts.

Even though the evidence presented throughout this book suggests that lawyers, through their position within the professional court workgroup, assist the efficient running of magistrates' court business, policymakers have resisted the expansion of legal aid provision because of governmental concerns that increasing levels of legal representation would lead to more cases being contested. While remaining apprehensive about the cost of legally aided representation, governments also needed to allow access to publicly funded lawyers to give the appearance of legitimacy in summary criminal proceedings. Legal representation goes some way to assist defendants as it at least enables

---

[1] The report of the Independent Criminal Legal Aid Review is eagerly awaited by defence practitioners. See www.gov.uk/government/groups/independent-review-of-criminal-legal-aid.

[2] V Kemp, *Transforming Legal Aid: Access to Criminal Defence Services* www.justice.gov.uk/downloads/publications/research-and   analysis/lsrc/TransformingCrimDefenceServices_29092010. pdf (Legal Services Commission, 2010); F Stephen, G Fazio and C Tata, 'Incentives, Criminal Defence Lawyers and Plea Bargaining' (2008) 28(3) *International Review of Law and Economics* 212; D Newman and R Dehaghani, *Experiences of Criminal Justice* (Bristol University Press, forthcoming 2021); J Thornton, 'The Way in Which Fee Reductions Influence Legal Aid Criminal Defence Lawyer Work: Insights from a Qualitative Study' (2019) 46 (4) *Journal of Law and Society* 559–85.

participation by proxy[3] (below). However, governmental preferences for private-sector style managerial techniques resulted in increasingly intrusive forms of regulation of the criminal justice process via efficiency drives and legal aid contracting schemes, and these encouraged defence advocates to act in increasingly standardised and more cooperative ways (chapter three). These processes have manifested to the detriment of adversarial principles, and limit defendants' ability to exercise their voice in the process.

At the same time, neoliberal approaches to government legitimised the view that defendants are responsible for their own fate by encouraging individualism and consumerism, thereby removing any ideological need to provide more than minimal levels of state-funded assistance (chapter one). Authors such as Wacquant,[4] Bell[5] and Squires and Lea[6] have alerted us to neoliberalism's tendency to produce precarious, demonised and criminalised groups through greater recourse to penal measures in the prison estate and the use of civil preventative measures such as non-conviction Restraining Orders and the Antisocial Behaviour Injunction.[7] This work further demonstrates that the same processes of marginalisation can be seen within the actual processual elements of summary criminal prosecution. Demands for efficiency and alterations to funding, which effectively oblige lawyers to work to volume in order for their firms to remain viable, have exacerbated defendants' inability to play an effective role in the proceedings because cases have to be processed quickly and in standardised ways. This inability to participate effectively emphasised defendants' status as (generally) precariat members of society.

Defence solicitors adapted to and incorporated policy initiatives based in neoliberal-style ideology rather than resisting them. Several factors explain this: maintaining good working relationships (chapter three), maintaining reputation, seen as useful for negotiating power (chapter three) and assisting business needs (chapter five). This supports Young's view of workgroup behaviour,[8] Carlen's research[9] and Bourdieu's understanding of a 'field' as a site where professionals will develop tools to manage and adapt to external intervention.[10] All of the above reasons that explain lawyers' willingness to adapt to politically

---

[3] A Owusu-Bempah, 'The Interpretation and Application of the Right to Effective Participation' (2018) 22 (4) *International Journal of Evidence and Proof* 321–41.

[4] L Wacquant, *Punishing the Poor. The Neoliberal Government of Social Insecurity* (Duke University Press, 2009).

[5] E Bell, *Criminal Justice and Neoliberalism* (Palgrave Macmillan, 2011).

[6] P Squires and J Lea, 'Introduction: Reading Loic Wacquant – Opening Questions and Overview' in P Squires and J Lea (eds), *Criminalisation and Advanced Marginality. Critically Exploring the Work of Loic Wacquant* (The Policy Press, 2012).

[7] Anti-Social Behaviour, Crime and Policing Act 2014.

[8] R Young, 'Exploring the Boundaries of Criminal Courtroom Workgroup' (2013) 42 *Common Law World Review* 203.

[9] P Carlen, *Magistrates' Justice* (Martin Robertson 1976).

[10] P Bourdieu, *The Logic of Practice* (Stanford University Press 1990).

motivated intervention in summary criminal justice can also be seen as beneficial to clients, who will presumably want their advocates to be able to wield some power and have a good reputation in court. Solicitors also view some of these goals as beneficial to clients even though they also acknowledge that demands for efficiency and difficulties in obtaining sufficient funding can counter defendants' interests and encourage solicitors to make case management decisions prematurely (see chapter five). Consequently, by absorbing rather than opposing initiatives designed to improve efficiency, defence advocates (inadvertently) bolstered the professional network responsible for case progression. The result was increased defendant marginalisation, limiting their ability to deviate from the norms performed by members of the workgroup to meet the courts' expectations.

The evidence presented in this book also indicates that lawyers will take risks with funding to suit the needs of the court even though they recognise that uncertainty about and reductions in rates of pay can increase the temptation to cut cuts and/or provide a less comprehensive service to clients than one might expect (chapter five). This was exemplified by the frequency with which lawyers represented defendants at first hearings despite lack of clarity about whether funding was, or ever would be, in place. By representing clients when they were unsure whether they would be paid to do so, lawyers tended to accommodate court demands even when concerns about funding meant that they might not provide a comprehensive service to clients. Accommodating court demands over clients' best interests can strengthen the professional network while also further reducing the ability of defendants to participate in the process of summary prosecution effectively. Defendant ability to participate is undermined because – in the circumstances just described – they appear to receive a limited service, the boundaries of that service appear to be unclear, and the case is being processed for the sake of expediency over due process principles.

This premise is further supported by evidence surrounding the legal provisions that standardise proceedings and manage uncertainty and risk (chapter four). The workgroup culture absorbed those provisions and used them in implicit terms that accommodate the workgroup's needs. This further increases the defendant's inability to participate in the proceedings because the language used and complexity of provisions mean that they remain incomprehensible to the untrained or unindoctrinated ear. As noted throughout this book, understanding of the process is necessary to enable fully informed and voluntary participation and is recognised as an important element of due process in criminal cases (chapter one).

It is clear that defence advocates feel that they are operating as best they can in an increasingly challenging environment. Solicitors interviewed expressed both regret about and insight into the processes which mean they are required to expedite cases and acknowledged that workgroup demands mean that clients' needs sometimes suffer. Solicitors tended to blame externally introduced policy for that suffering but also acknowledged that they have not strenuously resisted changing demands concerning fees and case management because of the need to maintain a business and professional reputation. Ultimately, however, the more that defence lawyers cannot exercise their professional autonomy in the proceedings, the more defendants also lose their ability to act as autonomous individuals in cases. Disempowering lawyers seems to disempower their clients further.

Given their expressed regrets about the problems faced by defendants in magistrates' courts, it does not appear that lawyers, by their very nature, exacerbate defendant marginalisation, but that the political and cultural environment in which they operate encourages behaviours that worsen marginalisation. Lawyers have multiple identities, and governments have, in recent decades, seen lawyers as potential drivers of efficiency rather than as champions of access to justice.[11] This view undermines the importance of lawyers' roles and means that policy design neglects principles that encourage access to justice. This approach to policy design has meant that the initiatives developed in summary criminal proceedings, by which lawyers must abide to remain financially successful, pay insufficient regard to defendants' interests. As advocates who rely on government resources, defence solicitors are, through those initiatives, discouraged from practising in such a way that prioritises defendant needs and participatory practices.

II. REFLECTIONS ON DEFENDANTS IN MAGISTRATES' COURTS

As is seen in chapter two, it was not until the beginning of the twentieth century that governments recognised that unrepresented defendants might be at a disadvantage in criminal proceedings and that this might be politically problematic. Once the executive identified that unrepresented defendants might need assistance to navigate the criminal process, liberal approaches to government recognised that allowing access to justice through participation (by proxy) should improve the legitimacy of the criminal process.

Legal representation does undoubtedly assist defendants who would, without representation, suffer even greater marginalisation through a general inability to at least follow the jargon and signalling used by court personnel. Representation does not, however, as Carlen[12] and McBarnet[13] predicted, operate to completely rectify the defendant's exclusion from the process because the way in which laws and procedures designed to encourage efficiency became absorbed in workgroup culture. These procedures appear to have reinforced the

---

[11] See further L Welsh, 'The Effects of Changes to Legal Aid on Lawyers' Professional Identity and Behaviour in Summary Criminal Cases: A Case Study' (2017) 44(4) *Journal of Law and Society* 559–85 and Thornton (n 2).

[12] Carlen (n 9).

[13] D McBarnet, 'Two Tiers of Justice' in Lacey, N (ed), *A Reader on Criminal Justice* (Oxford, Oxford University Press, 1994).

professional networks operating in the courtroom via greater recourse to, for example, the completion of standard case management forms (chapter four) and the use of plea negotiations as a method of case resolution (chapter three). These developments intensified the marginalisation of defendants, who are unlikely to be able to understand the increased implicit reference to legal provisions. The use of such implicit references and demands to work at greater speed also strengthens the professional networks in the workgroup, who share the common goals of working at speed and maintaining their professional reputation. As a result, defendants suffer further exclusion as non-members of that professional network. Implicit references to provisions such as Criminal Justice: Simple, Speedy, Summary (chapter three) and the Criminal Justice Act 2003 (chapter four) not only mean that technical points are reduced to mundane yet largely inaccessible professional practices, but also that the use of jargon increases.

Thus the culture of magistrates' courts intensifies the marginalisation of defendants, who are – as Carlen[14] noted – unable to fully engage in the proceedings as a result of a number of factors, including courtroom layout and jargon (through implicit reference to legal provisions and procedures) and signalling between court personnel alongside bureaucratic requirements to process cases at speed. As identified in chapter four, interpersonal signalling is exacerbated by the ways in which law is used within the workgroup. As workgroup behaviour obscures references to legal provisions, defendants are less likely to be afforded the opportunity to understand and engage with the cases against them.

III. REFLECTIONS ON WHAT DEFENDANT PARTICIPATION MEANS FOR ACCESS TO JUSTICE

Before turning to ways of addressing problems related to defendant participation, let us return to the story introduced at the beginning of this book, of the defence solicitor leaning on the dock with their back to their client sitting passively behind the Plexiglass. This scenario humanises several of the issues raised throughout the discussion in this book.

First, the position of the defendant in a dock. The defendant was physically segregated from the courtroom workgroup to the side of the court in a small see-through box room on their own. This immediately physically places the defendant as outside the business of the court, which takes place in the main body of the courtroom itself. This defendant was fortunate to be legally represented, in the sense that at least one person within the main area of the courtroom was present to monitor, with expertise, what was being said and done. However, that same representative used the dock as a leaning post while

---

[14] Carlen (n 9).

speaking with the prosecutor, placing a further physical barrier between the defendant and the main courtroom. It is likely that the lawyer completed the legal aid application on behalf of this client, already indicating to the defendant that the legal process and form completion are both best left to professionals with minimal defendant engagement.

Second, the interaction between the prosecutor and the defence solicitor served to reinforce the relationship between those professional practitioners as members of a collegial workgroup described in chapter three. In this instance, the solicitor (likely subconsciously) chose to reinforce their relationship with a colleague over their relationship with the client. This indicates how the dynamics of a strongly cooperative and collegiate, yet formally adversarial, organisational culture can further alienate an 'outsider' to the pre-existing group.

Third, no one explained the nature and purpose of the magistrates' retirement to the defendant at that moment, nor did any member of the workgroup check that the defendant understood what was going on at that time. I can only surmise and hope that, as I was both told and in my own experience, the solicitor explained these processes outside the courtroom. That does, of course, mitigate concerns about lack of understanding to an extent, but – as mentioned in chapters four and five – this does not assist a defendant in the courtroom and only serves to reinforce the notion that the defendant does not speak unless spoken to within the courtroom. In the context of specialised language and procedures used in magistrates' courts highlighted in chapter four, this serves to strengthen workgroup cohesion at the expense of individual defendants and leaves defendants vulnerable to misunderstandings that they are likely unable to identify and correct.

We can only hypothesise about what might have happened if the defendant had not been legally represented, but the findings detailed in this book suggest that not much would have been different in the courtroom itself. The defendant would likely still have been asked to sit in the dock. The demands for efficiency described in chapter two would still have meant that the professional members of the court workgroup needed to conduct the case at speed. The magistrates would likely still have retired, and the findings in chapter four indicate that there is no guarantee that any of these processes would have been explained to the defendant by other members of the workgroup. However, without the benefit of a lawyer, there is even less chance that the defendant would have been told what was happening/had happened and even less chance that any errors or problems could have been identified and rectified.

I appreciate that some of the participants in my research may not be pleased with this analysis, particularly in relation to the prioritisation of court needs over defendants' interests. I have suffered a degree of 'standpoint crisis'[15] in

---

[15] S Wakeman, 'Fieldwork, Biography and Emotion. Doing Criminological Autoethnography' (2014) 54(5) *British Journal of Criminology* 705.

relation to my role as a practitioner, have felt discomfort at reporting some of my findings, and have been forced to reflect on my own behaviour as a defence advocate. I hope, however, that the participants in my research will see that, by their own acknowledgement, there has been little resistance to the processes described above, which have further marginalised defendants. I further appreciate (and indeed understand) that solicitors operate in a very difficult and complex area in which there is a constant struggle to balance competing interests even though they are acutely aware that their professional roles have been devalued. I hope that defence advocates can accept my view that processes of neoliberalisation have effectively forced them into situations where, not only does the government view their role with scepticism but also further undermines their ability to act as altruistic public servants via demands for efficiency. I am keenly aware that the criminal justice system is in a particularly volatile state of change as I write, especially in light of the ongoing Independent Criminal Legal Aid Review,[16] and hope that the current crisis will result in an effective dialogue between the agencies of criminal procedure to improve access to justice for all concerned.

IV. IMPROVING ACCESS TO JUSTICE THROUGH THE LENS OF PARTICIPATION

The task of improving access to justice through defendant participation is clearly an extremely difficult one in light of the complex political and cultural factors that have exacerbated defendant marginalisation in summary criminal justice over several decades. It is, of course, unlikely that any of those factors operate in isolation, but the 'trickle down' effect of a change to some structural factors might, alongside some awareness training, gradually alter some cultural practices of the workgroup and create more space for defendants to participate in the process of summary criminal justice meaningfully. I preface what follows with the recognition that unless funding across the criminal process is increased, sustainable change will be extremely hard to achieve. Clearly, the rates at which lawyers are paid for providing legally aided services should rise at least in line with inflation, and a regular mechanism for review of payment rates should be developed.

However, lawyers are neither the beginning nor the end of the story of defendants' (in)ability to participate in magistrates' court proceedings meaningfully and effectively, and their role in relation to defendant participation is complex. As members of the professional workgroup, defence lawyers become imbued in a culture of courtroom processes that encourage efficiency through standardised practices surrounding law and criminal procedure. In this way, the process becomes more opaque to transient members of the group, that is, defendants.

[16] See https://www.gov.uk/government/groups/independent-review-of-criminal-legal-aid.

Nonetheless, it also seems clear that lawyers do go some way to mitigate the problems associated with defendant participation by engaging with their clients outside the courtroom itself. While the inner sanctum of the court might remain a place of mystery and subservience, engagement with a lawyer outside the courtroom appears to be crucial to defendant understanding, and understanding is a necessary prerequisite to effective and meaningful participation. While this book has focused on the details of procedural justice (fair process) rather than the details of substantive justice (fair outcome), lawyer's contributions to substantive justice ought not to be overlooked. Furthermore, substantive and procedural justice are intertwined, just as procedural and substantive elements of access to justice (see chapter one) can be difficult to decisively separate from each other. Advocates of due process would argue that an unfair process can never produce a fair outcome, though adherents of crime control might be slightly more willing to sacrifice fair procedures for an outcome that the parties regard as just overall.

Additionally, the legalisation of proceedings discussed in chapter four means that defence lawyers undoubtedly have an important role in ensuring substantive justice through the appropriate application of doctrinal legal provisions, even where procedural justice could be improved. Thus, while accessing a lawyer is not the crux of the problem of access to justice through participation in magistrates' courts, being represented does mitigate some of the effects of barriers to defendant participation. Consequently, the operation of the means test for legal aid applicants needs to be revised so that the majority of applicants are not financially excluded from obtaining state-funded legal assistance.

Relatedly, governments need to alter their approach to policy design by challenging the notion of the 'fat cat' legal aid lawyer and recognising that lawyers are able to improve the legitimacy of criminal proceedings and courtroom efficiency. Criminal defence firms have evolved in such a way that defence advocates operate in a competitive market to retain the goodwill of clients and the court. However, governments' distrust of professionals working in public services led to greater bureaucratic intrusion, leaving lawyers feeling undermined and unable to properly exercise professional judgment. That intrusion has also increased their workload by requiring that particular forms be completed and procedures are followed. Many lawyers are clear that the LAA adopts complex procedures and aggressively audits practitioners in a way that is detrimental to the services that they can provide to clients. At the same time, income has been reduced via the reintroduction of fixed fees, fee cuts and stagnation. In short, government distrust of professional behaviour has increased demands on lawyers who are increasingly expected to perform more work for less money. As such, reducing bureaucracy in summary criminal proceedings – both in the court itself and in terms of what the LAA requires of lawyers and legal aid applicants – has the potential to produce several positive outcomes. One positive outcome would be the promotion of mutual trust between the government and the workgroup, thereby encouraging the possibility of meaningful debate about the meaning of access to justice and defendant participation. If the LAA were to become more accessible to legal aid applicants and their lawyers,[17] defendants would – hopefully – feel more empowered at the initial stages of a case, thereby promoting greater involvement in case progression overall.

While governments could be concerned that returning greater levels of autonomy to defence lawyers could encourage inefficiency, it seems that this would, in fact, allow resources to be directed to the most appropriate services and the competitive nature of the criminal defence service 'market' would regulate behaviour. This manifested through the finding described in chapter five that lawyers were keen to retain their clients. Reducing bureaucratic procedures would ease defence advocates' workload, meaning that there would be more time within the fixed fee system – which advocates did not in principle disagree with – to devote to client needs. Increasing fixed fee payments in line with inflation would retain an incentive to work efficiently while allowing lawyers more flexibility in the way they work and greater control over their resources because profit margins would not be so strained. This might also rebalance professional relationships so that lawyers feel less compromised between business and client needs. Reducing bureaucracy would mean that defence solicitors would have more time to take defendant needs into account, which could, albeit slowly, start to shift professional culture so that greater priority is given to protecting defendant needs. Relieving defence lawyers of their bureaucratic workload, and the financial uncertainty associated with undertaking publicly funded magistrates' court work, would create greater space for improved client care, which could improve client understanding and confidence to enable the development of more effective and meaningful participation in the process of summary justice.

A further way of encouraging professionals to engage more with defendant interests in preference to workgroup interests would be by training. Advocates seemed to be aware of some ways that their behaviour might marginalise defendants but tended not to consider the extent to which courtroom layout and intra-personnel jargon (such as implicit references to legal provisions) could do so. Jargon should be removed from standardised forms, and explanatory notes should be provided to empower defendants to meaningfully participate in document completion themselves.[18] In an ideal world, both public legal education would improve, and the use of jargon on forms used by the public and the courtroom itself would decrease. Removing jargon from these processes should go some way to improving defendants' ability to understand the process and give voice to their needs, but it is not an alternative to allowing access to properly

---

[17] The Fabian Society recommended that the Legal Aid Agency be replaced by a Justice Commission, but that recommendation has not found favour with the government. See The Fabian Society 'The Right to Justice: The Final Report of the Bach Commission' (Fabian Society, 2017).

[18] Robins and Newman make the same recommendation in relation to cases involving areas of social welfare law that have suffered significant funding cuts (J Robins and D Newman, *Justice in a Time of Austerity* (Bristol University Press, 2021)).

funded legal representation. As well as increasing public legal education more generally,[19] it would be appropriate for all members of the courtroom work-group and policymakers to be made aware of these issues through training and development. In the European Union, participants in several member states successfully implemented a training scheme that encourages defence lawyers to effectively and actively realise clients' rights and identify their needs in the police station through a client-centred approach to defence practice which encouraged lawyers to focus on effective communication skills, experiential learning and the development of reflective skills.[20] A similar scheme in relation to court processes and procedures could prove useful in this jurisdiction.

Another quick and easy partial remedy to defendant marginalisation would be to avoid using the dock in all cases unless there is a clear risk – supported by reliable evidence – of escape and/or of violence from the defendant. Courtroom layout has long been recognised as a barrier to participation (chapter three) and seemed to be a prominent feature of the observed example described above and in chapter one. Though the notion that magistrates' courts deal with trivial cases is contested here, they do deal largely with less serious cases than Crown Courts' caseloads, so routine use of the dock should be challenged.[21] Where a defendant poses minimal risk of causing a disturbance in court, it is not at all clear why a defendant should not be viewed as a party to the proceedings in the main body of the court, as opposed to sectioned off in a sub-room to the side.

Essentially, defendant marginalisation appears to be exacerbated as a result of the competing rationales between the executive and the workgroup and among members of the workgroup itself. Courtroom layout exacerbates processes that indicate to the defendant that they are only peripheral to the process. Many of these problems seem to exist because governments have compromised principles of adversarial justice with ever greater demands for efficiency. Governments have focused on lawyers' ability to increase efficiency and undermined their ability to improve access to justice through facilitating meaningful engagement with the criminal process. In consequence of concerns about cost and efficiency, governments have paid insufficient attention to the procedural elements of access to justice, including the ability of defendants to participate effectively and meaningfully.

---

[19] Furthering public legal education is also advocated for by the Fabian Society (n 17) and Robins and Newman (n 18).

[20] A Pivaty et al, 'Contemporary Criminal Defence Practice: Importance of Active Involvement at the Investigative Stage and Related Training Requirements' (2020) 27(1) *International Journal of the Legal Profession* 25–34. See further https://www.netpralat.eu/.

[21] Mulcahy and Campbell have each separately made the same point elsewhere: L Mulcahy, 'Putting the Defendant in Their Place: Why Do We Still Use the Dock in Criminal Proceedings?' (2013) 53(6) *British Journal of Criminology* 1139–56; J Campbell, *Entanglements of Life with the Law: Precarity and Justice in London's Magistrates Courts* (Cambridge Scholars Publishing, 2020).

In short, several changes are necessary to improve the ability of defendants to participate in summary justice meaningfully and effectively. First, greater access to legal representation would help to mitigate some of the barriers to participation associated with the specialised nature of the proceedings. Second, all members of the magistrates' court workgroup need to better understand the ways in which procedural fairness is undermined by courtroom layout, intra-personnel signalling and jargon. Third, legal representatives need to be better paid in order to have space for client care activities that facilitate participation through understanding. Fourth, there needs to be a shift away from focusing on the speed at which cases progress towards focusing on ensuring sufficient time is given to a case to allow all parties to fully understand and be given the opportunity to participate in proceedings meaningfully. Fifth, greater attention should be paid to the courtroom layout. Thus, as explained in chapter one, if access to summary justice is to be improved, attention must be paid not only to the vital descriptive element of access to justice (meaningful access to legal advice) but also to the equally important normative elements of access to justice (recognising the defendant's right, as an autonomous individual, to participate in the criminal justice process meaningfully and effectively).

In an immediately post-pandemic society, there might be little motivation to address these more qualitative aspects of procedurally fair justice over substantive justice, especially in the context of criminal case backlogs exacerbated by the socio-economic effects of Covid-19.[22] However, we must remember that one aspect of procedural fairness lies in recognising that defendants in criminal cases are directly and fundamentally valuable for the dialogue they can bring to proceedings.[23] Unless criminal justice processes are substantively *and* procedurally fair, they are vulnerable to illegitimacy and injustice.

---

[22] H Siddique, 'Crown Court Backlog has Reached "Crisis Levels", report warns' *The Guardian* 30 March 2021.

[23] A Owusu-Bempah, 'Understanding the Barriers to Defendant Participation in Criminal Proceedings in England and Wales' (2020) 40(4) *Legal Studies* 609–29.

Bibliography

Adams, T, Ellis, C and Holman Jones, S, 'Autoethnography' in J Matthes, C Davis and R Potter (eds), *The International Encyclopaedia of Communication Research Methods* (Hoboken, John Wiley and Sons, 2017).

Adams-Prassl, J and Adams-Prassl, J, 'Systemic Unfairness, Access to Justice and Futility: A Framework' (2020) 40(3) *Oxford Journal of Legal Studies* 561–90.

Adler, P and Adler, P, *Membership Roles in Field Research* (Thousand Oaks CA, Sage, 1987).

Albertson, K, Corcoran, M and Phillips, J (eds), *Marketisation and Privatisation in Criminal Justice* (Bristol, Policy Press, 2020).

Aliber, R and Zoega, G (eds), *The 2008 Global Financial Crisis in Retrospect* (Cham, Palgrave Macmillan, 2019).

Allen, D and Blackham, A, 'Using Empirical Research to Advance Workplace Equality Law Scholarship: Benefits, Pitfalls and Challenges' (2018) 27:3 *Griffith Law Review* 337–65.

Ames, J, 'Tony Blair was Wrong to Brand Lawyers Fat Cats, says Ally' The Times (London, 3 June 2019).

Ashworth, A, 'Magistrates and the Right to a Fair Trial' in D Faulkner (ed), *The Magistracy at the Crossroads* (Hook, Waterside Press, 2012).

Ashworth, A and Redmayne, M, *The Criminal Process* 3rd edn (Oxford, Oxford University Press, 2005).

Ashworth, A and Zedner, L, 'Defending the Criminal Law: Reflections on the Changing Character of Crime, Procedure and Sanctions' (2008) (2) *Criminal Law and Philosophy* 21.

Ashworth, A, 'Legal Aid, Human Rights and Criminal Justice' in R Young and D Wall (eds), *Access to Criminal Justice: Legal Aid, Lawyers and the Defence of Liberty* (Oxford, Blackstone Press, 1996).

Astor, H, 'The Unrepresented Defendant Revisited: A Consideration of the Role of the Clerk in Magistrates' Courts' (1986) 13(2) *Journal of Law and Society* 225–39.

Atiyah, P, *Law and Modern Society* (Oxford, Oxford University Press, 1995).

Atkinson, R, 'The New Legal Aid Settlement is an Insult' *The Times* (London, 5 March 2020).

Auld, R, 'Review of the Criminal Courts of England and Wales: Executive Summary' (London, The Stationery Office 2001).

Baksi, C, 'Djanogly Urged to Ease Legal Aid backlog' *Law Society Gazette* (London, 23 June 2011).

Baksi, C, 'Lawyers Must Embrace IT, Says Minister' *Law Society Gazette* (London, 25 February 2013).

Baksi, C, 'No Extra Pay for "Speedy" Justice' *Law Society Gazette* (London, 19 July 2012).

Baksi, C, 'Speeding Up Cases "Risks Miscarriages"' *Law Society Gazette* (London, 29 November 2012).

Baldwin, J and McConville, M, *Negotiated Justice: Pressures on Defendants to Plead Guilty* (London, Martin Robertson, 1977).

Baldwin, J, 'Research on the Criminal Courts' in R King and E Wincup (eds), *Doing Research on Crime and Justice* (Oxford, Oxford University Press, 2000).

Bano, S, 'Standpoint, Difference and Feminist Research' in R Banakar and M Travers (ed), *Theory and Method in Socio-Legal Research* (Oxford, Hart Publishing, 2005).

Barry, N, 'Conservative Thought and the Welfare State' (1997) 45 *Political Studies* 331–45.

Bell, B and Dadomo, C, 'Magistrates' Courts and the 2003 Reforms of the Criminal Justice System' (2006) 14(4) *European Journal of Crime, Criminal Law and Criminal Justice* 339.

Bell, E, *Criminal Justice and Neoliberalism* (London, Palgrave Macmillan, 2011).

Bibas, S, *The Machinery of Criminal Justice* (Oxford, Oxford University Press, 2012).

Bizimungu, C, 'An Examination of the Impacts of Rape Myths and Gender Bias on the Legal Process for Rape in Rwanda' (Doctoral thesis (PhD), University of Sussex, 2019).

Bottoms, A and McClean, J, *Defendants in the Criminal Process* (Abingdon, Routledge, 1976).

Bourdieu, P, 'The Force of Law: Toward a Sociology of the Juridical Field' (1987) 38 (July) *The Hastings Law Journal* 805.

Bourdieu, P, *The Logic of Practice* (California, Stanford University Press, 1990).

Bowcott, O, 'High Court Upholds Plan to Slash On-call Legal Aid Solicitors' *The Guardian* (London, 18 February 2015).

Bowcott, O, 'Jump in Unrepresented Defendants as Legal Aid Cuts Continue to Bite' *The Guardian* (London, 24 November 2019).

Bowcott, O, 'Legal Aid Cuts: Lawyers to Begin Boycott that Could See Courts Grind to a Halt' *The Guardian* (London, 30 June 2015).

Brannick, T and Coghlan, D, 'In Defense of Being "Native": The Case for Insider Academic Research' (2007) 10(1) *Organizational Research Methods* 59–74.

Brenneis, D, 'Reforming Promise' in A Riles (ed), *Documents. Artefacts of Modern Knowledge* (Ann Arbor, University of Michigan Press, 2006).

Bridges, L, 'The Reform of Criminal Legal Aid' in R Young and D Wall (eds), *Access to Criminal Justice: Legal Aid, Lawyers and the Defence of Liberty* (Oxford, Blackstone Press, 1996).

Brown, W, *Undoing the Demos: Neoliberalism's Stealth Revolution* (Cambridge MA, MIT Press, 2015).

Bryman, A, *Social Research Methods* (Oxford, Oxford University Press, 2012).

Burke, L, Millings, M and Robinson, G, 'Probation Migration(s): Examining Occupational Culture in a Turbulent Field' (2017) 17 *Criminology and Criminal Justice* 192.

Cameron, L, 'Do our Buildings Make Us? Covid-19 and the Courts Reforms' *Counsel Magazine* (London, May 2020).

Campbell, E, '"Apparently Being a Self-Obsessed C**t Is Now Academically Lauded": Experiencing Twitter Trolling of Autoethnographers' (2017) 18(3) *Qualitative Social Research* 16.

Campbell, J, *Entanglements of Life with the Law: Precarity and Justice in London's Magistrates Courts* (High Wycombe, Cambridge Scholars Publishing, 2020).

Cape, E, 'Rebalancing the Criminal Justice Process: Ethical Challenges for Criminal Defence Lawyers' (2006) 9(1) *Legal Ethics* 56.

Cape, E and Moorhead, R, 'Demand Induced Supply? Identifying Cost Drivers in Criminal Defence Work' (Legal Services Research Centre, 2005).

Cappelletti, M, Garth, B and Trocker, N, 'Access to Justice: Comparative General Report.' (1976) 40(3/4) *The Rabel Journal of Comparative and International Private Law* 669–717.

Carlen, P, 'Struggling for Justice' (2018) 27(2) *Griffith Law Review* 176–81.

Carlen, P and França, L, (eds), *Justice Alternatives* (Abingdon, Routledge, 2019).

Carlen, P, *Magistrates' Justice* (London, Martin Robertson, 1976).

Carlen, P, 'The Staging of Magistrates' Justice' (1976) 16(1) *British Journal of Criminology* 48.

Castellano, U, 'Beyond the Courtroom Workgroup: Caseworkers as the New Satellite of Social Control' (2009) 31(4) *Law and Policy* 429.

Cattan, S, Conti, G, Farquharson, C and Ginja, R, 'The Health Effects of Sure Start' (London, Institute for Fiscal Studies, 2019).

Chalmers, J, 'Frenzied Law Making': Overcriminalization by Numbers. (2014) 67(1) *Current Legal Problems* 483–502.

Chalmers, J and Leverick, F, 'Tracking the Creation of Criminal Offences' (2013) *Criminal Law Review* 543–60.

Chalmers, J and Leverick, F, 'Quantifying Criminalisation' in R A Duff et al (eds), *Criminalization: The Aims and Limits of the Criminal Law* (Oxford, Oxford University Press, 2014) 54–79.

Chalmers, J, Leverick, F and Shaw, A, 'Is Formal Criminalisation Really on the Rise? Evidence from the 1950s' (2015) 3 *Criminal Law Review* 177–91.

Clarke, A and Welsh, L, 'Criminal Cases Review Commission: Legal Aid and Legal Representatives Stage 4 Interviews – Report' (Brighton, University of Sussex, 2020).

Clarke, S, *Social Work and Community Development* (London, Ashgate, 2017).

Clements, L, 'Little Justice – Judicial Reform and the Magistrates' in Thomas, P (ed), *Discriminating Lawyers* (London, Cavendish, 2000).

Cooke, E, 'The Changing Occupational Terrain of the Legal Aid Lawyer in Times of Precariousness' (Doctor of Philosophy (PhD) thesis, University of Kent, 2019).

Cooper, P, 'Looking Ahead: Towards a Principled Approach to Supporting Participation' in J Jacobson and P Cooper (eds), *Participation in Courts and Tribunals* (Bristol, Bristol University Press, 2020).

Cornford, T, 'The Meaning of Access to Justice' in E Palmer, T Cornford, A Guinchard and Y Marique (eds), *Access to Justice: Beyond the Policies and Politics of Austerity* (Oxford, Hart Publishing, 2016).

Darbyshire, P, *The Magistrates' Clerk* (Chichester, Barry Rose, 1984).

Darbyshire, P, 'An Essay on the Importance and Neglect of the Magistracy' (1997) (September) *Criminal Law Review* 627.

Darbyshire, P, 'Strengthening the Argument in Favour of the Defendant's Right to Elect' (1997) (December) *Criminal Law Review* 911.

Darbyshire P 'For the New Lord Chancellor – Some Causes for Concern About Magistrates' (1997) (December) *Criminal Law Review* 861.

Darbyshire, P, 'A Comment on the Powers of Magistrates' Clerks' (1999) (May) *Criminal Law Review* 377.

Darbyshire, P, *Sitting in Judgment: The Working Lives of Judges* (Oxford, Hart Publishing, 2011).

Davies, M, 'A New Training Initiative for the Lay Magistracy in England and Wales – A Further Step Towards Professionalisation?' (2005) 12(1) *International Journal of the Legal Profession* 93.

Dean, J, *Democracy and Other Neoliberal Fantasies* (Durham, Duke University Press, 2009).

Dehaghani, R, 'Interrogating Vulnerability: Reframing the Vulnerable Suspect in Police Custody' (2021) 30(2) *Social & Legal Studies* 251–71.

Dehaghani, R and Newman, D, 'We're Vulnerable Too': An (alternative) Analysis of Vulnerability within English Criminal Legal Aid and Police Custody. (2017) 7(6) *Oñati Socio-Legal Series* 1199–228.

Dehaghani, R and Newman, D, 'Criminal Legal Aid and Access to Justice: An Empirical Account of a Reduction in Resilience' (2021) *International Journal of the Legal Profession* (online first).

Dehaghani, R and Newman, D, 'The Crisis in Legally Aided Criminal Defence in Wales: Bringing Wales into Discussions of England and Wales' (2021) *Legal Studies* (online first).

Demetriou, S, 'From the ASBO to the Injunction: A Qualitative Review of the Anti-Social Behaviour Legislation Post-2014' (2019) (April) *Public Law* 343–61.

Dennis, I, 'Judging Magistrates' (2001)(February) *Criminal Law Review* 71.

Department for Constitutional Affairs, *A Fairer Deal for Legal Aid* (Cm 6591, 2005).

Department for Constitutional Affairs, *Supporting Magistrates' Courts to Provide Justice* (Cm 6681, 2005).

Department for Constitutional Affairs, 'Procurement of Criminal Defence Services: Market-Based Reform' (London, DCA, 2006).

Dingwall, G and Hillier, T, *Blamestorming, Blamemongers and Scapegoats: Allocating Blame in the Criminal Justice Process* (Bristol, Policy Press, 2015).

Donoghue, J, 'Reforming the Role of Magistrates' (2014) 77 *Modern Law Review* 928–63.

Donzelot, J, 'Pleasure in Work' in G Burchell, C Gordon and P Miller (eds), *The Foucault Effect: Studies in Governmentality* (London, Harvester Wheatsheaf, 1991).

Drakeford, M, 'Private Welfare' in Powell M (ed), *Understanding the Mixed Economy of Welfare* (Bristol, Policy Press, 2007).

Driver, S and Martell, L, 'Left, Right and the Third Way' (2000) 28(2) *Policy & Politics* 147–61.

Eisenstein, J and Jacob, H, *Felony Justice: An Organisational Analysis of Criminal Courts* (London, Little Brown, 1977).

Equality and Human Rights Commission, 'Inclusive Justice: A System Designed for All' (Equality and Human Rights Commission, 2020).

Evetts, J, 'The Construction of Professionalism in New and Existing Occupational Contexts: Promoting and Facilitating Occupational Change' (2003) 23(4/5) *International Journal of Sociology and Social Policy* 22.

Fairclough, S, 'It Doesn't Happen … And I've Never Thought It was Necessary for It to Happen': Barriers to Vulnerable Defendants Giving Evidence by Live Link in Crown Court Trials' (2017) 21(3) *International Journal of Evidence & Proof* 209–29.

Fairclough, S, 'Speaking up for Injustice: Reconsidering the Provision of Special Measures Through the Lens of Equality' (2018) *Criminal Law Review* 4–19.

Fairclough, S, 'The Consequences of Unenthusiastic Criminal Justice Reform: A Special Measures Case Study' (2021) 21(2) *Criminology & Criminal Justice* 151–68.

Falconer, C, 'Labour Helped these Devastating Legal Aid Cuts Along. Now It's Time to Fix It' *The Guardian* (London, 31 Dec 2018).

Faulkner, D, 'Policy and Practice in Modern Britain: Influences, Outcomes and Civil Society' in P Green and A Rutherford (eds), *Criminal Policy in Transition* (Oxford, Hart Publishing, 2000).

Fielding, N, Braun, S and Hieke, G, 'Video Enabled Justice Evaluation' (Guildford, University of Surrey 2020).

Finkel, N, 'Commonsense Justice, Culpability, and Punishment' (2000) 28(3) *Hofstra Law Review* 4.

Flint, J and Hunter, C, 'Governing by Civil Order: Towards New Frameworks of Support, Coercion and Sanction?' in H Quirk, T Seddon and G Smith (eds), *Regulation and Criminal Justice* (Cambridge, Cambridge University Press, 2011).

Flood, J, 'Socio-Legal Ethnography' in R Banakar and M Travers (eds), *Theory and Method in Socio-Legal Research* (Oxford, Hart Publishing, 2005).

Flower, L, 'Emotional Labour, Cooling the Client Out and Lawyer Face' in J Phillips, J Waters, C Westaby and A Fowler A (eds), *Emotional Labour in Criminology and Criminal Justice* (Abingdon, Routledge, 2020).

Fouzder, M, 'Falconer: My "Regret" Over Labour's Effort to Curb Legal Aid Budget' *Law Society Gazette* (London, 31 May 2019).

Fouzder, M, 'CPS Embarks on Hiring Spree' *Law Society Gazette* (London, 13 January 2020).

Fouzder, M, 'Legal Aid Fees: MoJ Offer to Receive Resounding "No"' *Law Society Gazette* (London, 20 March 2020).

Fouzder, M, 'Magistrate Numbers Worse Than Thought Due to HR Error' *Law Society Gazette* (London, 18 September 2020).

Fouzder, M, 'Landmark Report Paints Bleak Picture of Criminal Legal Aid' *Law Society Gazette* (London, 12 February 2021).

Friedland, S, 'On Common Sense and the Evaluation of Witness Credibility' (1989) 40 *Case Western Reserve Law Review* 165.

Frost, T, 'A Simple Solution' *Law Society Gazette* (London, 7 September 2007).

Galligan, D, 'Regulating Pre-Trial Decisions' in N Lacey (ed), *A Reader on Criminal Justice* (Oxford, Oxford University Press, 1994).

Garland, D, *The Culture of Control: Crime and Social Order in Contemporary Society* (Chicago, University of Chicago Press, 2002).

Garside, R, Ford, M, Mills, H and Roberts, R, 'UK Justice Policy Review. Volume 6' (London, Centre for Crime and Justice Studies, 2017).

Garside, R, Grimshaw, R, Ford, M and Mills, H, 'UK Justice Policy Review. Volume 8' (London, Centre for Crime and Justice Studies 2019).

Gibbs, P, 'Defendants on Video – Conveyor Belt Justice or a Revolution in Access?' (London, Transform Justice, 2017).

Gibbs, P, 'Justice Denied? The Experience of Unrepresented Defendants in the Criminal Courts' (London, Transform Justice, 2016).

Gibbs, P and Kirby, A, 'Judged by Peers? The Diversity of Lay Magistrates in England and Wales' (Howard League for Penal Reform, What is Justice? Working Papers 6/2014, 2014).

Gibbs, P and Ratcliffe, F, 'Criminal Defence in an Age of Austerity: Zealous Advocate or Cog in a Machine?' (London, Transform Justice, 2019).

Goriely, T, 'The Development of Criminal Legal aid in England and Wales' in R Young and D Wall (eds), *Access to Criminal Justice: Legal Aid, Lawyers and the Defence of Liberty* (Oxford, Blackstone Press, 1996).

Gray, A, Fenn, P and Rickman, N, 'Controlling Lawyer's Costs through Standard Fees: An Economic Analysis' in R Young and D Wall (eds), *Access to Criminal Justice. Legal Aid, Lawyers and the Defence of Liberty* (Oxford, Blackstone Press, 1996).

Gregory, A, '"British Justice is in Jeopardy": Legal Aid System is Doomed Without More Criminal Defence Lawyers, Solicitors Warn' *The Independent* (London, 28 February 2020).

Grindley, P, 'Legal aid Reforms Proposed by the Carter Report – Analysis and Commentary' (LECG Corporation, 2006).

Grove, T, *The Magistrate's Tale* (London, Bloomsbury Publishing, 2003).

Halliday, T, *Beyond Monopoly: Lawyers, State Crises, and Professional Empowerment* (Chicago, University of Chicago Press, 1987).

Harvey, D, *A Brief History of Neoliberalism* (Oxford, Oxford University Press, 2005).

Helm, R, 'Constrained Waiver of Trial Rights? Incentives to Plead Guilty and the Right to a Fair Trial' (2019) 46 *Journal of Law and Society* 423–47.

Helm, R, 'Conviction by Consent? Vulnerability, Autonomy and Conviction by Guilty Plea' (2019) 83(2) *The Journal of Criminal Law* 161–72.

Her Majesty's Court Service, 'CJ: SSS Project Defence Questions' (London, 2008).

Herbert, A, 'Mode of Trial and Magistrates Sentencing Powers: Will Increased Powers Inevitably Lead to a Reduction in Committal Rate?' (2003) *Criminal Law Review* 314.

Hirsch, D, 'Report on the Affordability of Legal Proceedings for Those who are Excluded from Eligibility for Criminal Legal Aid under the Means Regulations, and for Those Required to Pay a Contribution Towards their Legal Costs' (Loughborough, Loughborough University, 2018).

HM Crown Prosecution Service Inspectorate, 'Area Assurance Inspection of CPS Cymru-Wales. CP001:1261' (London, HMCPSI 2019).

HM Crown Prosecution Service Inspectorate, 'Business as Usual? A Follow-up Review of the Effectiveness of the Crown Prosecution Service Contribution to the Transforming Summary Justice Initiative' (London, HMCPSI, 2017).

HM Crown Prosecution Service Inspectorate, 'Disclosure of Unused Material in the Crown Court' CP001:1267 (London, HMCPSI, 2020).

HM Treasury, 'The Green Book' (London, 2020).

Hodgson, J, 'The Challenge of Universal Norms: Securing Effective Defence Rights Across Different Jurisdictions and Legal Cultures' (2019) 46 *Journal of Law and Society* 95–114.

Hodgson, J, *The Metamorphosis of Criminal Justice: A Comparative Account* (Oxford, Oxford University Press, 2020).

Home Office, 'Report of an Inquiry into the Death of Maxwell Confait' (London, The Stationery Office, 1977).

Home Office, *Report of the Departmental Committee on Legal Aid in Criminal Proceedings* (Cmnd 2934, 1966).

Hood, C, 'A Public Management for all Seasons?' (1991) 69 (1) *Public Administration* 3–19.

Hosticka, C, 'We Don't Care About What Happened, We Only Care About What is Going to Happen: Lawyer-Client Negotiations of Reality' (1979) 26(5) *Social Problems* 599.

House of Commons Justice, 'Committee Criminal Legal Aid. Twelfth Report of Session 2017–2019' (HC 1069, 2019).

House of Commons Justice Committee, 'Disclosure of Evidence in Criminal Cases Eleventh Report of Session 2017–19' (HC 859, 2018).

House of Commons Justice Committee, 'Impact of Changes to Civil Legal Aid under Part 1 of the Legal Aid, Sentencing and Punishment of Offenders Act 2012' (HC 311, 2015).

House of Commons Justice Committee, 'The Role of the Magistracy. Sixth Report of Session 2016–17' (HC 165, 2016).

Howard, G and Freilich, J, 'Durkheim's Comparative Model and Criminal Justice Theory' in D Duffee and E Maguire (eds), *Criminal Justice Theory: Explaining the Nature and Behaviour of Criminal Justice* (Abingdon, Routledge, 2007).

Howard, H, 'Effective Participation of Mentally Vulnerable Defendants in the Magistrates' Courts in England and Wales – The 'Front Line' from a Legal Perspective' (2021) 85(1) *The Journal of Criminal Law* 3–16.

Hughes, G, McLaughlin, E and Muncie, J, *Crime Prevention and Community Safety. New Directions* (London, Sage, 2002).

Hunter, G, 'Policy and Practice Supporting Lay Participation' in J Jacobson and P Cooper (eds), *Participation in Courts and Tribunals* (Bristol, Bristol University Press, 2020).

Hunter, R, Roach Anleu, S and Mack, K, 'Judging in lower courts: Conventional, procedural, therapeutic and feminist approaches' (2016) 12(3) *International Journal of Law in Context* 337–360.

Hynes, S and Robins, J, *The Justice Gap. Whatever Happened to Legal Aid?* (London, Legal Action Group, 2009).

Hynes, S, *Austerity Justice* (London, Legal Action Group, 2012).

Jacobson, J, 'Introduction' in J Jacobson and P Cooper (eds), *Participation in Courts and Tribunals* (Bristol, Bristol University Press, 2020).

Jacobson, J, 'Observed Realities of Participation' in J Jacobson and P Cooper (eds) *Participation in Courts and Tribunals* (Bristol, Bristol University Press, 2020).

Jacobson, J and Cooper, P (eds.) *Participation in Courts and Tribunals: Concepts, Realities and Aspirations* (Bristol, Bristol University Press 2020).

Jacobson, J and Talbot, J, 'Vulnerable Defendants in the Criminal Courts: A Review of Provision for Adults and Children' (London, Prison Reform Trust, 2009).

Jacobson, J, Hunter, G and Kirby, A, *Inside Crown Court* (Bristol, Policy Press, 2016).

James, A and Raine, J, *The New Politics of Criminal Justice* (London, Longmans, 1998).

Jessop, B, *The Future of the Capitalist State* (Hoboken, Wiley, 2002).

Jessop, B, *The State: Past, Present, Future* (Cambridge, Polity, 2015).

Johnson, M (ed), *Precariat: Labour, Work and Politics* (Abingdon, Routledge, 2016).

Johnston, E, 'The Adversarial Defence Lawyer: Myths, Disclosure and Efficiency – A Contemporary Analysis of the Role in the Era of the Criminal Procedure Rules' (2020) 24(1) *International Journal of Evidence & Proof* 35–58.

Jones, C, 'Auditing Criminal Justice' (1993) 33 *British Journal of Criminology* 187.

Judicial College, 'Good Practice for Remote Hearings' (Judicial College ETBB Committee, 2020).

JUSTICE, 'Preventing Digital Exclusion from Online' (London, Justice Working Party, 2018).

Kalberg, S, 'Max Weber's Types of Rationality: Cornerstones for the Analysis of Rationalization Processes in History' (1980) 85 *American Journal of Sociology* 1145.

Katz, J, *Poor People's Lawyers in Transition* (New Brunswick, Rutgers University Press, 1982).

Kemp, V, 'Transforming Legal Aid: Access to Criminal Defence Services' (Legal Services Research Centre, 2010).

Kemp, V and Balmer, N, 'Criminal Defence Services: Users' Perspectives' (Legal Services Research Centre, 2008).

King, M, *The Framework of Criminal Justice* (London, Croom Helm, 1981).

Kirby, A, 'Conceptualising Participation' in J Jacobson and P Cooper (eds), *Participation in Courts and Tribunals* (Bristol, Bristol University Press, 2020).

Kirby, A, 'Effectively Engaging Victims, Witnesses and Defendants in the Criminal Courts: A Question of "court culture"?' (2017) 12 *Criminal Law Review* 949–68.

KPMG LLP, *Ministry of Justice Procurement of Criminal Legal Aid Services: Financial Modelling* (London, 2014).

Lacey, N, *In Search of Criminal Responsibility* (Oxford, Oxford University Press, 2016).

Langbein, J, *The Origins of Adversary Criminal Trial* (Oxford, Oxford University Press, 2005).

Lange, B, 'Researching Discourse and Behaviour as Elements of Law in Action' in R Banakar and M Travers (eds), *Theory and Method in Socio-Legal Research* (Oxford, Hart Publishing, 2005).

Law Commission, *The Sentencing Code: A Report. Summary* (Law Com No 382 (Summary), 2018).

Law Society Gazette, 'Unrepresented Defendants Crowd Criminal Courts' *Law Society Gazette* (London, 2 May 2016).

Le Grand, J, 'Knights, Knaves or Pawns? Human Behaviour and Social Policy' (1997) 26(2) *Journal of Social Policy* 149.

Lea, J and Hallsworth, S, 'Bringing the State Back In: Understanding Neoliberal Security' in P Squires and J Lea (eds), *Criminalisation and Advanced Marginality. Critically Exploring the Work of Loïc Wacquant* (Bristol, Policy Press, 2012).

Leader, K, 'From Bear Gardens to the County Court: Creating the Litigant in Person' (2020) 79(2) *Cambridge Law Journal* 260–87.

Leader, K, 'Trials, Truth-telling and the Performing Body' (Doctoral Thesis (PhD), University of Sydney 2010).

Legal Action Group, 'A Strategy for Justice: Publicly Funded Legal Services in the 1990s' (London, Legal Action Group, 1992).

Legal Aid Agency, 'Criminal Legal Aid Manual. Applying for Legal Aid in Criminal Cases in the Magistrates' and Crown Court' (London, Ministry of Justice, 2020).

Leverick, F and Chalmers, J, 'Criminal Law in the Shadows: Creating Offences in Delegated Legislation' (2018) 38(2) *Legal Studies* 221–41.

Leverick, F and Duff, P, 'Court Culture and Adjournments in Criminal Cases: A Tale of Four Courts' (2002) 39 *Criminal Law Review* 44.

Lister, M, 'Citizens, Doing It for Themselves? The Big Society and Government through Community' (2014) *Parliamentary Affairs* 1–19.

Long, V, 'Online Courts: Re-assessing Inequality in the "Remote" Courtroom' (2021) 11(1) *Excursions* 77–102.

Loveday, B, 'Tough on Crime or Tough on the Causes of Crime? An Evaluation of Labour's Crime and Disorder Legislation' (1999) 1(2) *Crime Prevention and Community Safety* 7–24.

Lowe, R, *The Welfare State in Britain Since 1945* (Basingstoke, Macmillan, 1999).

Macdonald, K, *The Sociology of the Professions* (London, Sage, 1995).

Mack, K and Anleu SR, 'Getting Through the List': Judgecraft and Legitimacy in the Lower Courts.' (2007) 16(3) *Social & Legal Studies* 341–361.

Marshall, T, *Social Policy in the Twentieth Century* (London, Hutchinson and Co, 1975).

McBarnet, D, 'Magistrates' Courts and the Ideology of Justice' (1981) 8(2) *British Journal of Law and Society* 181–97.

McBarnet, D, *Conviction: Law, the State and the Construction of Justice* (Basingstoke, Macmillan, 1981).

McBarnet, D, 'Two Tiers of Justice' in N Lacey (ed), *A Reader on Criminal Justice* (Oxford, Oxford University Press, 1994).

McConville, M and Marsh, L, 'Adversarialism goes West: Case Management in Criminal Courts' (2015) 19(3) *The International Journal of Evidence & Proof* 172–89.

McConville, M and Marsh, L, 'Factory Farming and State-Induced Pleas' in J Hunter, P Roberts, S Young and D Dixon (eds), *The Integrity of Criminal Process. From Theory into Practice* (Oxford, Hart Publishing, 2016).

McConville, M, Hodgson, J, Bridges, L and Pavlovic, A, *Standing Accused. The Organization and Practices of Criminal Defence Lawyers in Britain* (Oxford, Oxford University Press, 1994).

McConville, M, Sanders, A and Leng, R, *The Case for the Prosecution* (Abingdon, Routledge, 1991).

Mckee, G and Franey, R, *Time Bomb: The Guildford Four* (London, Bloomsbury, 1988).

Ministry of Justice, 'Criminal Legal Aid Review: An Accelerated Package of Measures Amending the Criminal Legal Aid Fee Schemes' (London, Ministry of Justice, 2020).

Ministry of Justice, 'Legal Aid Statistics England and Wales Bulletin Jul to Sep 2020' (London, Ministry of Justice, 2020).

Ministry of Justice, 'Restructuring the Delivery of Criminal Defence Services' (London, Ministry 2010).

Ministry of Justice, 'The Strengths and Skills of the Judiciary in the Magistrates' Courts (London, Ministry of Justice, 2011).

Ministry of Justice, *Swift and Sure Justice: The Government's Plans for Reform of the Criminal Justice System* (Cm 8388, 2012).

Ministry of Justice, *Transforming Legal aid: Delivering a More Credible and Efficient System* (CP14/2013, 2013).

Mirowski, P, 'Postface: Defining Neoliberalism' in P Mirowski and D Plehwe (eds), *The Road from Mont Pèlerin* (Cambridge MA, Harvard University Press, 2015).

Morgan, K, 'Britain in the Seventies – Our Unfinest Hour?' (2017) *Revue Française de Civilisation Britannique* XXII- Hors Série.

Morgan, R, 'Austerity, Subsidiarity and Parsimony: Offending Behaviour and Criminalisation' in A Silvestri (ed), *Lessons for the Coalition: An End of Term Report on New Labour and Criminal Justice* (London, Centre for Crime and Justice Studies 2010).

Morgan, R and Russell, N, 'The Judiciary in the Magistrates' Courts' (London, Home Office 2000).

Morgan, R, 'Magistrates: The Future According to Auld' (2002) 29(2) *Journal of Law and Society* 308.

Mulcahy, A, 'The Justifications of "Justice": Legal Practitioners' Accounts of Negotiated Case Settlements in Magistrates' Courts' (1994) 34(4) *British Journal of Criminology* 411.

Mulcahy, L, 'Architects of Justice: The Politics of Courtroom Design' (2007) 16(3) *Social & Legal Studies* 383–403.

Mulcahy, L, 'Putting the Defendant in Their Place: Why Do We Still Use the Dock in Criminal Proceedings?' (2013) 53 (6) *The British Journal of Criminology* 1139–56.

Mulcahy, L and Rowden, E, *The Democratic Courthouse: A Modern History of Design, Due Process and Dignity* (Abingdon, Routledge, 2019).

Mulcahy, L, *Legal Architecture: Justice, Due Process and the Place of Law* (Abingdon, Routledge, 2011).

Mullin, C, *Error of Judgement* (Dublin, Poolbeg, 1990).

Narey, M, 'Review of Delay in the Criminal Justice System' (Home Office, 1997).

National Audit Office, 'Effective Use of Magistrates' Court Hearings' (London, The Stationery Office, 2006).

Newman, D, 'Are Lawyers Alienated Workers?' (2016) 22(3) *European Journal of Current Legal Issues*.

Newman, D, 'Are Lawyers Neurotic?' (2017) 25 (1) *International Journal of the Legal Profession* 3–29.

Newman, D and Dehaghani, R, *Experiences of Criminal Justice* (Bristol, Bristol University Press, forthcoming 2021).

Newman, D and Welsh, L, 'The Practice of Modern Defence Lawyers: Alienation and Its Implications for Access to Justice' (2019) 48(1–2) *Common Law World Review* 64–89.

Newman, D, *Legal Aid, Lawyers and the Quest for Justice* (Oxford, Hart Publishing, 2013).

Nobles, R and Schiff, D, 'Criminal Justice Unhinged: The Challenge of Guilty Pleas' (2018) 39 *Oxford Journal of Legal Studies* 100.

Nobles, R and Schiff, D, 'Criminal Justice: Autopoietic Insights' in J Pribán and D Nelken (eds), *Law's New Boundaries: The Consequences of Legal Autopoiesis* (London, Ashgate, 2001).

O'Barr, W and Conley, J, 'Litigant Satisfaction Versus Legal Adequacy in Small Claims Court Narratives' (1985) 19(4) *Law and Society Review* 661.

Office for Criminal Justice Reform, 'Delivering Simple Speedy Summary Justice. An Evaluation of Magistrates Court Tests' (London, 2007).

Oksala, J, *Foucault, Politics and Violence* (Evanston, Northwestern University Press, 2012).

Owusu-Bempah, A, 'The Interpretation and Application of the Right to Effective Participation' (2018) 22(4) *International Journal of Evidence & Proof* 321–41.

Owusu-Bempah, A, *Defendant Participation in the Criminal Process* (Abingdon, Routledge, 2017).

Owusu-Bempah, A, 'Understanding the Barriers to Defendant Participation in Criminal Proceedings in England and Wales' (2020) *Legal Studies* 1–21.

Packer, H, *The Limits of Criminal Sanction* (California, Stanford University Press, 1968).

Paz-Fuchs, A, Kinghan, J and Yeatman, L, *Clinical Legal Education: Theory and Practice* (Oxford, Oxford University Press, forthcoming).

Peay, J and Player, E, 'Pleading Guilty: Why Vulnerability Matters' (2018) 81 *Modern Law Review* 929.

Peck, J, 'Zombie Neoliberalism and the Ambidextrous State' (2010) 14 *Theoretical Criminology* 104.

Peck, J, *Constructions of Neoliberal Reason* (Oxford, Oxford University Press, 2010).

Pivaty, A, *Criminal Defence at Police Stations: A Comparative and Empirical Study* (Abingdon, Routledge, 2019).

Pivaty, A, Vanderhallen, M, Daly, Y and Conway, V, 'Contemporary Criminal Defence Practice: Importance of Active Involvement at the Investigative Stage and Related Training Requirements' (2020) 27(1) *International Journal of the Legal Profession* 25–44.

Pollitt, C and Bouckaert, G, *Public Management Reform: A Comparative Analysis* (Oxford, Oxford University Press, 2000).

Porter, A, 'Prosecuting Domestic Abuse in England and Wales: Crown Prosecution Service "Working Practice" and New Public Managerialism' (2019) *Social & Legal Studies* 493–516.

Porter, A, *Prosecuting Domestic Abuse in Neoliberal Times* (London, Palgrave Macmillan, 2020).

Posner, R, *The Problematics of Moral and Legal Theory* (Cambridge MA, Harvard University Press,1999).

Quirk, H, *The Rise and Fall of the Right to Silence* (Abingdon, Routledge, 2016).

Regan, F, 'Criminal Legal Aid: Does Defending Liberty Undermine Citizenship?' in R Young and D Wall (eds) *Access to Criminal Justice: Legal Aid, Lawyers and the Defence of Liberty* (Oxford, Blackstone Press, 1996).

Renwick Riddell, W, 'Common Law and Common Sense' (1918) 27(8) *The Yale Law Journal* 993–1007.

Riddle, H, 'Advancing the Case for Swift Action' *Law Society Gazette* (London, 18 October 2012) 32.

Riles, A (ed), *Documents. Artifacts of Modern Knowledge* (Ann Arbor, University of Michigan Press, 2006).

Roach, K, 'Four Models of the Criminal Process' (1999) 89 *Journal of Criminal Law and Criminology* 671.

Roach Anleu, S and Mack K, 'Intersections Between In-Court Procedures and the Production of Guilty Pleas' (2009) 42(1) *Australian & New Zealand Journal of Criminology* 1–23.

Roberts, R and Garside, R, 'Punishment Before Justice? Understanding Penalty Notices for Disorder' (London, Centre for Crime and Justice Studies, 2005).

Robin-D'Cruz, C and Whitehead, S, 'Pre-court Diversion for Adults: An Evidence Briefing' (London, Centre for Justice Innovation, 2019).

Robins, J and Newman, D, *Justice in a Time of Austerity* (Bristol, Bristol University Press, 2021).

Rose, N, 'Governing 'Advanced' Liberal Democracies' in A Barry, T Osborne and N Rose (eds), *Foucault and Political Reason. Liberalism, Neo-liberalism and Rationalities of Government* (London, UCL Press, 1996).

Ross, L, 'An Account from the Inside: Examining the Emotional Impact of Qualitative Research Through the Lens of "Insider" Research' (2017) 4(3) *Qualitative Psychology* 326–37.

Rowbotham, J and Stevenson, K, 'For Today in this Arena ...' Legal Performativity and Dramatic Convention in the Victorian Criminal Justice System. (2007) 14 (2) *Journal of Criminal Justice and Popular Culture* 113–41.

Rowden, E, 'Virtual Courts and Putting "Summary" Back into "Summary Justice": Merely Brief, or Unjust?' in J Simon, N Temple and R Tobe (eds). *Architecture and Justice: Judicial Matters in the Public Realm* (Farnham, Ashgate, 2013).

Rutherford, A, *Transforming Criminal Policy* (Hook, Waterside Press, 1996).

Saito, H, 'The Impact of Lawyer Fees on Lawyer Partisanship: The Reciprocity Norm may Matter' (2020) *International Journal of the Legal Profession* (online first).

Samuels, A, 'The Unrepresented Defendant in Magistrates' Courts' (London, JUSTICE 1971).

Sanders, A, 'Core Values, the Magistracy, and the Auld Report' (2002) 29(2) *Journal of Law and Society* 324.

Sanders, A, *Community Justice. Modernising the Magistracy in England and Wales* (London, Institute of Public Policy Research, 2000).

Sanders, A, 'Reconciling the Apparently Different Goals of Criminal Justice and Regulation: The 'Freedom' Perspective' in G Smith, T Seddon, and H Quirk (eds), *Regulation and Criminal Justice: Innovations in Policy and Research* (Cambridge, Cambridge University Press 2010).

Sanders, A, 'What was New Labour Thinking? New Labour's Approach to Criminal Justice' in A Silvestri (ed), *Lessons for the Coalition: An End of Term Report on New Labour and Criminal Justice* (London, Centre for Crime and Justice Studies, 2010).

Siddique, H, 'Crown Court Backlog has Reached "Crisis levels", Report Warns' *The Guardian* (London, 30 March 2021).

Skinns, L, Sorsby, A and Rice, L '"Treat Them as a Human Being": Dignity in Police Detention and Its Implications for "Good" Police Custody' (2020) 60(6) *British Journal of Criminology* 1667–88.

Skinns, L, Sprawson, A, Sorsby, A, Smith, R and Wooff, A, 'Police Custody Delivery in the Twenty-first Century in England and Wales: Current Arrangements and their Implications for Patterns of Policing' (2017) 4(3) *European Journal of Policing Studies* 325–48.

Slack, J and Doyle, J, 'Legal Aid Payouts to Fat Cat Lawyers will be Slashed by a Third, says Justice Secretary' *The Daily Mail* (London, 10 April 2013).

Smejkalová, T, 'Legal Performance: Translating into Law and Subjectivity in Law' (2017) 22 *Tilburg Law Review* 62.

Smith, R, 'Proposals for the Reform of Legal Aid in England and Wales. Response' (London, JUSTICE, February 2011).

Smith, T, 'The "Quiet Revolution" in Criminal Defence: How the Zealous Advocate Slipped into the Shadow' (2013) 20:1 *International Journal of the Legal Profession* 111–37.

Smith, T and Cape, E, 'The Rise and Decline of Criminal Legal Aid in England and Wales' in A Flynn and J Hodgson (eds), *Access to Justice and Legal aid: Comparative Perspectives on Unmet Legal Need* (Oxford, Hart Publishing, 2017).

Smith, T and Johnston, E, 'Marketisation and Competition in Criminal Legal Aid: Implications for Access to Justice' in K Albertson, M Corcoran and J Phillips (eds), *Marketisation and Privatisation in Criminal Justice* (Bristol, Policy Press, 2020).

Snipes, J and Maguire, E, *Foundations of Criminal Justice Theory* (Abingdon, Routledge, 2007).

Sommerlad, H, 'Criminal Legal Aid Reforms and the Restructuring of Legal Professionalism' in R Young and D Wall (eds), *Access to Criminal Legal Aid: Legal Aid, Lawyers and the Defence of Liberty* (Oxford, Blackstone Press, 1996).

Sommerlad, H, 'The Implementation of Quality Initiatives and the New Public Management in the Legal Aid Sector in England and Wales: Bureaucratisation, Stratification and Surveillance' (1999) 6 *International Journal of the Legal Profession* 311.

Sommerlad, H, '"I've Lost the plot": An Everyday Story of Legal Aid Lawyers' (2002) 28 (3) *Journal of Law and Society* 335–60.

Sommerlad, H, 'Some Reflections on the Relationship between Citizenship, Access to Justice, and the Reform of Legal Aid' (2004) 31(3) *Journal of Law and Society* 345.

Sommerlad, H, 'Reflections on the Reconfiguration of Access to Justice' (2008) 15:3 *International Journal of the Legal Profession* 179–93.

Soubise, L, 'Prosecuting in the Magistrates' Courts in a Time of Austerity' (2017) 11 *Criminal Law Review* 847–59.

Soubise, L, 'Prosecutorial Discretion and Accountability: A Comparative Study of France and England and Wales' (Doctoral thesis (PhD), University of Warwick, 2015).

Sprack, J and Sprack, M, *A Practical Approach to Criminal Procedure* (Oxford, Oxford University Press, 2019).

Squires, P and Lea, J, 'Introduction: Reading Loïc Wacquant – Opening Questions and Overview' in P Squires and J Lea (eds), *Criminalisation and Advanced Marginality. Critically Exploring the Work of Loïc Wacquant* (Bristol, The Policy Press, 2012).

Standing, G, *The Precariat: The New Dangerous Class* (London, Bloomsbury, 2011).

Stenson, K and Edwards, A, 'Policy Transfer in Local Crime Control: Beyond Naïve Emulation' in T Newburn and R Sparks (eds), *Criminal Justice and Political Cultures* (Cullompton, Willan Publishing, 2004).

Stephen, F, Fazio, G and Tata, C, 'Incentives, Criminal Defence Lawyers and Plea Bargaining' (2008) 28(3) *International Review of Law and Economics* 212.

Stewart, H, 'Theresa May Pledges End to Austerity in Tory Conference Speech' *The Guardian* (London, 3 October 2018).

Stewart, J, 'The Mixed Economy of Welfare in Historical Context' in M Powell (ed), *Understanding the Mixed Economy of Welfare* (Bristol, Policy Press, 2007).

Storer, C, 'Legal Aid Practitioners Group Response to the Ministry of Justice Consultation: Proposals for the Reform of Legal Aid in England and Wales' (Legal Aid Practitioners Group 2013).

Sturge, G, 'Court Statistics for England and Wales Briefing Paper Number CBP 8372' (London, House of Commons Library, 2019).

Sturge, G and Lipscombe, S, 'Is the Criminal Justice System Fit for Purpose?' (London, House of Commons Library, 2020).

Sudnow, D, 'Normal Crimes: Sociological Features of the Penal Code in a Public Defender Office' (1965) 12(3) *Social Problems* 255.

Susskind, R, 'Covid-19 Shutdown Shows Virtual Courts Work Better' *Financial Times* (London, 7 May 2020).

Susskind, R, *Online Courts and the Future of Justice* (Oxford, Oxford University Press, 2019).

Tata, C, 'In the Interests of Clients or Commerce? Legal Aid, Supply, Demand, and 'Ethical Indeterminacy' in Criminal Defence Work' (2007) 34(4) *Journal of Law and Society* 489.

Tata, C, 'The Construction of 'Comparison' in Legal Aid Spending: The Promise and Perils of a Jurisdiction-Centred Approach to (International) Legal Aid Research' in F Regan, A Paterson, D Fleming, and T Goriely (eds), *The Transformation of Legal Aid: Comparative and Historical Studies* (Oxford, Oxford University Press, 1999).

Tata, C and Stephen, F, 'Swings and Roundabouts: Do Changes to the Structure of Legal Aid Remuneration Make a Real Difference to Criminal Case Management and Case Outcomes?' (2006) 8 *Criminal Law Review* 722–41.

Tata, C, 'Ritual Individualisation': Creative Genius at Sentencing, Mitigation, and Conviction.' (2019) 46 (1) *Journal of Law and Society* 112–40.

Tata, C, *Sentencing: A Social Process* (London, Palgrave Macmillan, 2020).

Tata, C, Goriely, T, Duff, P, Henry, A and Sherr, A, 'Does Mode of Delivery Make a Difference to Criminal Case Outcomes and Clients' Satisfaction? The Public Defence Solicitor Experiment' (2004) (Feb) *Criminal Law Review* 120.

Tepperman, L, 'The Effect of Court Size on Organisation and Procedure' (1973) 10(4) *The Canadian Review of Sociology and Anthropology* 346.

Terpstra, J and Fyfe, N, 'Mind the Implementation Gap? Police Reform and Local Policing in the Netherlands and Scotland' (2015) 15(5) *Criminology & Criminal Justice* 527–44.

The Bar Council Court, 'Appointed Legal Representatives' (Bar Council for England and Wales, 2017).

The Fabian Society, 'The Right to Justice: The Final Report of the Bach Commission' (London, Fabian Society, 2017).

The Justice Gap, *Whatever Happened to Legal Aid?* (London, Legal Action Group, 2009).

The Law Society, 'Response of the Law Society of England and Wales to Swift and Sure Justice: The Government's Plans for Reform of the Criminal Justice System' (London, The Law Society, 2012).

The Secret Barrister, *Stories of the Law and How It's Broken* (Basingstoke, Macmillan, 2018).

Thomson, J and Becker, J, 'Unrepresented Defendants: Perceived Effects on the Crown Court in England and Wales – Practitioners' Perspectives' (London, Ministry of Justice, 2019).

Thornton, J, 'Is Publicly Funded Criminal Defence Sustainable? Legal Aid Cuts, Morale, Retention and Recruitment in the English Criminal Law Professions' (2020) 40(2) *Legal Studies* 230–51.

Thornton, J, 'The Way in Which Fee Reductions Influence Legal Aid Criminal Defence Lawyer Work: Insights from a Qualitative Study' (2019) 46 (4) *Journal of Law and Society* 559–85.

Tooze, A, *Crashed. How a Decade of Financial Crises Changed the World* (London, Penguin Books, 2018).

Tyler, T, 'Procedural Justice, Legitimacy, and the Effective Rule of Law' (2003) 30 *Crime and Justice* 283–357.

Tyler, T, 'What is Procedural Justice? Criteria Used by Citizens to Assess the Fairness of Legal Procedures' (1988) 22(1) *Law and Society Review* 103.

Van Der Luit-Drummond, J, 'Further Criminal Legal Aid Cuts Untenable and Short-Sighted' *Solicitors' Journal* (London, 23 March 2017).

Van Hulst, M, 'Storytelling at the Police Station: The Canteen Culture Revisited' (2013) 53(4) *The British Journal of Criminology* 624–42.

Vogler, R, *Reading the Riot Act: The Magistracy, the Police and the Army in Civil Disorder* (Milton Keynes, Open University Press, 1991).

Vogler, R, Welsh, L, Clarke, A, Wiedlitzka, S and McDonnell, L, 'Criminal Cases Review Commission: Legal Aid and Legal Representatives. Final Report' (Brighton, University of Sussex, 2021).

Wacquant, L, *Punishing the Poor. The Neoliberal Government of Social Insecurity* (Durham, Duke University Press, 2009).

Waddington, B, 'Is Stop Delaying Justice! working?' *Law Society Gazette* (London, 2012).

Waddington, B, 'Rules of Engagement. Stop Delaying Justice!' *Law Society Gazette* (London, 29 November 2012).

Waddington, P, 'Police (Canteen) Sub-culture. An Appreciation' (1999) 39(2) *British Journal of Criminology* 287–309.

Wakeman, S, 'Fieldwork, Biography and Emotion. Doing Criminological Autoethnography' (2014) 54(5) *British Journal of Criminology* 705.

Walker, C and Starmer, K, *Miscarriages of Justice: A Review of Justice in Error* (Oxford, Oxford University Press, 1999).

Wall, D, 'Keyholders to Criminal Justice? Solicitors and Applications for Criminal Legal Aid' in R Young and D Wall (eds) *Access to Criminal Justice: Legal Aid, Lawyers and the Defence of Liberty* (Oxford, Blackstone Press, 1996).

Walters, M, Wiedlitzka, S and Owusu-Bempah, A, 'Hate Crime and the Legal Process: Options for Law Reform. Project Report' (Brighton, University of Sussex, 2017).

Ward, J, 'Transforming "Summary Justice" Through Police-led Prosecution and "Virtual Courts"' (2015) 55 *British Journal of Criminology* 341.

Ward, J, *Transforming Summary Justice* (Abingdon, Routledge, 2017).

Weber, M, 'Legitimate Authority and Bureaucracy' in L Boone and D Bowen (eds), *The Great Writings in Management and Organizational Behavior* (Boston, Irwin, 1987).

Welsh, L, 'Are Magistrates' Courts Really a "Law Free Zone"? Participant Observation and Specialist Use of Language' (2013) 13 *Papers from the British Criminology Conference* 3–16.

Welsh, L, 'The Effects of Changes to Legal Aid on Lawyers' Professional Identity and behaviour in Summary Criminal Cases: A Case Study' (2017) 44(4) *Journal of Law and Society* 559–85.

Welsh, L and Howard, M, 'Standardization and the Production of Justice in Summary Criminal Courts: A Post-Human Analysis' (2019) 28(6) *Social and Legal Studies* 774–93.

Welsh, L, Skinns, L and Sanders, A, *Sanders and Young's Criminal Justice* 5th edn (Oxford, Oxford University Press, 2021).

White, A, 'What is the Privatization of Policing?' (2020) 14(3) *Policing: A Journal of Policy and Practice* 766–77.

Whittington, V, 'The Role of the Common Law Jury as Direct Deliberative Mechanism for the Democratic Self-Legitimation of Law' (2015) 24 *Studies in Social and Political Thought* 15–40.

Whitworth, A, 'Neoliberal Paternalism and Paradoxical Subjects: Confusion and Contradiction in UK Activation Policy' (2016) 36(3) *Critical Social Policy* 412–31.

Wilcox, A and Young, R, 'Understanding the Interests of Justice: A Study of Discretion in the Determination of Applications for Representation Orders in Magistrates' Courts' (Legal Services Commission, 2006).

Wilding, J, *The Legal Aid Market: Challenges for Publicly Funded Immigration and Asylum Legal Representation* (Bristol, Policy Press, 2021).

Woodcock, A, 'Coronavirus: Boris Johnson Promises Pandemic will not Lead to Return of Austerity' *The Independent* (London, 27 June 2020).

Wooding, D, 'Fat-cat Lawyers Raking in £3 Million per Trial for Defending Suspects in Rape, Terror Murder and Fraud Cases' *The Sun* (London, 1 January 2017).

Young, R and Wall, D, 'Criminal Justice, Legal Aid and the Defence of Liberty' in R Young and D Wall (eds), *Access to Criminal Justice: Legal Aid, Lawyers and the Defence of Liberty* (Oxford, Blackstone Press, 1996).

Young, R, 'Exploring the Boundaries of Criminal Courtroom Workgroup' (2013) 42 *Common Law World Review* 203.

Young R, 'Managing the List in the Lower Criminal Courts: Judgecraft or Crafty Judges? (2012) 41(1) *Common Law World Review* 29–58.

Young, R, 'Will Widgery do? Court Clerks, Discretion and the Determination of Legal Aid Applications' in R Young and D Wall (eds), *Access to Criminal Justice: Legal Aid, Lawyers and the Defence of Liberty* (Oxford, Blackstone Press, 1996).

Zander, M, 'Departmental Committee Report: Legal Aid in Criminal Proceedings' (1966) 29(6) *Modern Law Review* 639.

Zander, M, *Cases and Materials on the English Legal System* (Oxford, Oxford University Press, 2007).

Index

Ingram Content Group UK Ltd.
Milton Keynes UK
UKHW021846140323
418574UK00001B/7